Moving Byzantium

Volume 2

Edited by
Claudia Rapp and Johannes Preiser-Kapeller

The volumes of this series are peer-reviewed.

Claudia Rapp / Yannis Stouraitis (eds.)

Microstructures and Mobility in the Byzantine World

With 6 figures

V&R unipress

Vienna University Press

Bibliographic information published by the Deutsche Nationalbibliothek
The Deutsche Nationalbibliothek lists this publication in the Deutsche Nationalbibliografie;
detailed bibliographic data are available online: https://dnb.de.

**Publications of Vienna University Press
are published by V&R unipress.**

© 2024 by Brill | V&R unipress, Robert-Bosch-Breite 10, 37079 Göttingen, Germany,
an imprint of the Brill-Group
(Koninklijke Brill NV, Leiden, The Netherlands; Brill USA Inc., Boston MA, USA; Brill Asia Pte Ltd,
Singapore; Brill Deutschland GmbH, Paderborn, Germany; Brill Österreich GmbH, Vienna, Austria)
Koninklijke Brill NV incorporates the imprints Brill, Brill Nijhoff, Brill Schöningh, Brill Fink,
Brill mentis, Brill Wageningen Academic, Vandenhoeck & Ruprecht, Böhlau and V&R unipress.

Cover image: Paul Klee: Hauptweg und Nebenwege, 1929, Köln, Museum Ludwig,
Inv.-Nr. ML 76/3253, © Rheinisches Bildarchiv Köln, rba_d039386_01.
Printed and bound by CPI books GmbH, Birkstraße 10, 25917 Leck, Germany
Printed in the EU.

Vandenhoeck & Ruprecht Verlage | www.vandenhoeck-ruprecht-verlage.com

ISSN 2940-3529
ISBN 978-3-8471-1497-0

Contents

John Haldon

Claudia Rapp / Yannis Stouraitis

Microstructures and Mobility in Byzantium: An Introduction

The movement of individuals, groups, and peoples has always been part of human history. Indeed, the key texts that shaped the thinking of medieval Byzantium – the Old Testament, the New Testament, and Homer's *Odyssey* – are built on the premise of movement. The book of Exodus recounts the movement of the ancient Israelites out of Egypt, where they had been of inferior civic status and, according to their story, performed forced labour. Under the leadership of Moses, they reached the promised land of Canaan after forty years of wandering, hardships, and internal strife. Following Jewish tradition, the Byzantines interpreted this as a tale of liberation brought about by divine guidance, but we can also read it as a tale of mass migration in search of better working and living conditions. The Gospels depict Jesus of Nazareth as a wandering preacher and miracle worker with extraordinary powers, who shunned societal conventions and a sedentary lifestyle. As modern readers, we observe (although the Byzantines apparently did not) that the element of mobility is underlined by the fact that Jesus was born in a temporary shelter in Bethlehem, and later grew up in Nazareth with his mother Mary and her husband Joseph, and the need of his family immediately afterwards to seek refuge in Egypt from King Herod's persecution.

The Old Testament stories and the Gospels were familiar to everyone in Byzantium, regardless of social status, as they would have been heard in the liturgy or in sermons and seen in pictorial representations on the walls of churches. Those who were privileged enough to receive a higher education were taught to read and interpret the verse epics of Homer, the *Iliad* and the *Odyssey*. Odysseus, the protagonist of the latter, was shipwrecked after the Hellenes succeeded in capturing Troy (ancient Ilion). He spent ten adventurous years of moving from place to place by sea, until he finally returned to the island of Ithaca where he was reunited with his faithful wife Penelope. The Neoplatonists, who deeply influenced Byzantine theology, saw in Odysseus' meanderings a metaphor for the human soul in search of union with the divine.[1]

These stories from the deep wells of the history they considered their own were well known to the Byzantines. But the movement of an entire people of shared language and religion in search of better living conditions, the need of safety that forces a family to move, and the long way home of an individual in the aftermath of warfare – these are events that we still see today.

Writing these words in the spring of 2023, in the midst of the destruction wrought by Putin's war on Ukraine that has resulted in the displacement of several millions of people (mostly women and children), eight years after hundreds of thousands of people tried to make their way to the safety and prosperity of Europe in the wake of the wars in Syria and Afghanistan (mostly young men), one cannot help but wonder whether the word 'migration' has by now become a politicised term loaded with specific connotations (largely negative).

Yet, migrations as a distinct phenomenon have been an object of study in their own right for several decades. Much has been written on the slave trade that supplied the Caribbean and South and North America with African workers and transatlantic labour migrations from Europe to North America. Migrations of this kind do not appear in the historical record of Byzantium, though any large-scale construction project would have required mass migrations of skilled artisans and unskilled labourers. Instead, earlier generations of Byzantinists have been mostly concerned with migration *within* the Byzantine Empire, whether as a result of an imperial policy of forced re-settlement or by religious and ethnic groups acting on their own initiative, although often under duress.[2] Internal migration (German: 'Binnenmigration') was the key word, and this often included the in–migration of Armenians from the eastern borderlands, which was presented as a success story of resourcefulness and social advancement.[3]

Yannis Stouraitis has created a useful diagram based on the reasons for migration, distinguishing between voluntary and involuntary migration, with various sub-categories.[4] What such a diagram cannot show is the issue of scale: involuntary migration as a result of warfare or due to imperially-ordained forced re-settlement affects larger numbers of people than voluntary migration required by one's station in life. Both, however, were an integral part of the history of Byzantium across the centuries.

---

1 Lamberton, *Homer the Theologian*.
2 For forced migration, see, for example: Rapp, Zwangsmigration in Byzanz; Stouraitis, Migrating in the Medieval East Roman World; Ditten, *Ethnische Verschiebungen*.
3 Charanis, *Armenians in the Byzantine Empire*; also his collected essays in Charanis, *Studies on the Demography of the Byzantine Empire*; Ahrweiler and Laiou, *Studies on the Internal Diaspora of the Byzantine Empire*; Ditten, *Ethnische Verschiebungen*.
4 Stouraitis, Migrating in the Medieval East Roman World, 143.

TYPES OF MIGRATION

INVOLUNTARY				VOLUNTARY	
impelled or forced movement					
NATURAL CATASTROPHE	STATE COERCION		WAR	EDUCATIONAL	PROFESSIONAL
				PILGRIMAGE	ECONOMIC
	Military	Religious	Deportation · Refugees		
	Political	Economic/ Demographic	Military · Economic		

Like the medieval historians whom we depend on as sources of information, the perceptions of modern scholars are all too often determined by scale. When large groups of people labelled with ethnonyms (the Armenians), identified by their regional origin (the Cypriots), or compartmentalised as heretics (the Paulicians), are described by Byzantine historians as moving from one region to another, scholars commonly identify this as 'migration'.[5]

But there are other, smaller-scale constellations of people who moved to a different location. Hagiographers report on families leaving for more- or less-distant parts under the pressure of invasion or piracy. Chronicles mention (and art historians confirm) the movement of artisans to new locations where their skills were in demand. The movement of individuals is frequently mentioned across a wide range of written sources, while archaeology and material culture offer tangible evidence for the movement of objects, carried across long distances by their owners, or brought by traders and diplomats. Individuals often moved for professional reasons. Imperial or elite women (often at a very young age) became brides to husbands in distant regions and moved there with their own entourage. Re-location was required of newly-appointed bishops, metropolitans, or patriarchs. Rising through the ranks of the military meant a lifetime spent in training or on campaign. Acquiring the high level of education that was the prerequisite for an advantageous position at the court, in the imperial admin-istration, or in the higher clergy necessitated a move to the large urban centres,

---

5 For general context, see now Preiser-Kapeller *et al.*, *Migration Histories of the Medieval Afroeurasian Transition Zone.*

such as Constantinople and Thessaloniki, and in the early Byzantine period also Alexandria, Antioch, Athens, or Berytus. In contrast to the large groups mentioned above, however, scholars seem hesitant to identify the movement of smaller groups or of individuals as 'migration'.[6]

This is where the concept of 'mobility' comes in. Employing the concept of 'mobility' allows us to widen our perspective and to include a much wider range of people within our purview, whether they moved as individuals, families, clans, or smaller or larger groups. It also shifts the emphasis to the agency of those who move, rather than assuming that they are passive victims of circumstance, warfare, or imperial policy. With such an approach, mobility becomes more visible as a constant element throughout the long history of Byzantium. As a result, Byzantium appears as a much more mobile – and hence dynamic – society than previous generations of scholars have been able to acknowledge.

The term 'mobility' has a further advantage: it allows us to imagine movement not only in geographical terms, from one point on the map to another, but also, in our perception of a hierarchically structured society, as vertical mobility across social strata. Indeed, there is an intrinsic relation between the two: upward social mobility, as we have noted, often requires geographical mobility.

If we wish to study people who are moving, we cannot neglect these social aspects. Here, too, we can benefit from recent trends in modern migration studies that not only bring into focus the fact of movement or displacement from one location to another, but also seek to understand the agency of individuals on the move as they continue to interact with their social networks in their locations of origin while building new networks at their destinations. In fact, the latter is often an extension of the former, as people who have recently arrived in a new place depend on support systems for the exchange of information and a helping hand, and these are most readily offered by the people to whom they are already connected, i.e. migrants of the same background. The emphasis on personal agency in conjunction with mobility thus invites a closer look at microstructures, i.e. groups defined by a common origin, shared language, joint profession, or similar goals.[7]

This is the approach that we were able to explore with an international and multi-generational team of scholars thanks to the award of the Wittgenstein Prize that was granted by the Austrian National Research Fund to Claudia Rapp in 2015 (FWF P-Z288-G25). Yannis Stouraitis was a member of the Vienna team from 2015 to 2017 and has remained an Associated Scholar since then. In addition to

---

6 Relevant passages by Byzantine authors have been assembled in Claudia Rapp et al., Mobility and Migration in Byzantium.

7 For an overview, see Harzig and Hoerder, with Donna Gabaccia, What is Migration History; Hoerder, Cultures in Contact; Hahn, Historische Migrationsforschung.

many events in Vienna, this funding enabled us to invite scholars to join us for dedicated sessions at the International Medieval Congress in Leeds. A special session at the International Congress of Byzantine Studies held in Belgrade in 2016 also explored 'Mobility and Microstructures'. The chapters of this volume represent a cross-section resulting from these conversations.

The current book does not represent an exhaustive treatment of micro-structures and mobility within Byzantine society. The small collection of case studies presented here is, rather, intended as an introduction to the study of those topics, and as stimulation for further research and dialogue. The book consists of chapters which span different periods of Byzantine history between roughly the seventh and the fifteenth centuries, focussing on different regions and paying particular attention to the provinces and the periphery of the empire. Within this broad chronological and spatial framework, the authors explore practices of social advancement of persons from the lower to the higher social echelons, as well as the building of horizontal and vertical solidarities and the interconnectivity of persons and social groups both in Constantinople and the provinces. Moreover, they pay particular attention to the physical mobility of individuals and objects.

The chapter by Christos Makrypoulias explores a rather under-studied social group: the infantry commanders during the later period of the so-called Mace-donian dynasty.[8] It offers fresh insight into personal agency and social mobility in the lower echelons of society, because service in the infantry as a means of social advancement pertained predominately to low-born men, in contrast to the high-ranking officers who have been the focus of the most important studies on social advancement and were, more often than not, men born into well-estab-lished families.[9] Such cases of social mobility become visible from the tenth century onwards, when authors started to pay more attention to the infantry.[10]

Makrypoulias examines the social position of infantry commanders based on the evidence of the lists of precedence and sigillographic material that testifies to their court titles, which reveal that they could advance considerably in the social hierarchy. In this context, he seeks to clarify the ways in which these men were able to climb the social ladder, bearing in mind also the sudden appearance of information about the infantry in the sources. The beginning of this process can be traced to the relationship between the infantry units and the high ranks of the *doukata* or *katepanata* that begin to be mentioned in the late tenth century.[11] Moreover, the position of infantry commander – given that it could function as a

---

8 On the Middle Byzantine armies, see Haldon, *Warfare, State and Society*.
9 Haldon, Social Élites; Cheynet, Byzantine Aristocracy.
10 McGeer, *Sowing the Dragon's Teeth*, 198–211; Makrypoulias, Boots on the Ground.
11 On the military reform of the *doukata/katepanata*, see Kühn, *Die byzantinische Armee*.

stepping-stone for further advancement in the military hierarchy – emerges as a
prestigious reward which members of the power elite used as a means to attract
supporters to their cause or convince people to change sides in the course of
coups d'état and the great civil wars of that period. The position of these 'new
men' as members of the provincial elite is confirmed by their roles as donors. By
the middle of the eleventh century, infantry commanders appear to be part of the
upper social strata, the office being a starting point even for the establishment of
new military aristocratic families.

Efi Ragia's chapter shifts our attention to the question of the formation of
micro-solidarities within Byzantine society, focusing on four kinds of groupings
in a provincial context: the community of the village; the *phratriai/phatriai*; the
'confraternities'; and the monastic/church communities. Beginning with the
community of the *chorion* (village), Ragia goes beyond the well-studied image of
the *chorion* as the basic fiscal unit from the late-seventh century onwards.[12] She
scrutinises the social aspect of the village as a microcosm of various bonds and
interactions that found their expression in the forging of a coherent community
which was recognised by the state in legal terms and is often seen as acting by
itself as a unit. The latter is made explicit in the case of legal acts where all
members of the village community, irrespective of their social status and professional capacity, appeared as a single body. Within this framework, the question of violence exercised between the members of the village community is
addressed. Particular attention is paid to the role of the soldiers as a group that
acquired power and social prestige within the local community, and was often
able to impose its will by force of arms.[13]

Another kind of grouping addressed in the chapter are the *phratriai* or *phatriai*, extended networks usually based on bonds of blood kinship and marriage
built around persons of elite status, as well as on clientele relationships.[14] Ragia
argues that the *phatriai* were groupings that promoted attachments that cut
across the boundaries of local communities. The elite status of the heads of such
networks made them vehicles of social advancement for their clients and supporters, conveying social capital and political power to their members. The
phatriai could acquire considerable influence both at the local level as well as at
the level of imperial society.

In contrast to the political aspect of the *phatriai*, the 'confraternities' represented a kind of grouping with different characteristics and goals. Ragia delves

---

12 Kaplan, *Les hommes*, 95–101; Laiou, Byzantine Village, 31–54; Kyritses and Smyrlis, Villages,
    439–445.
13 On soldiers and their relationship to land and village communities, see Haldon, *Recruitment
    and Conscription in the Byzantine Army*; *idem*, Military Service.
14 The classic study on the topic of the retinues of elite families is Beck, Byzantinisches Ge-
    folgschaftswesen.

into the terminology of the Byzantine sources in an effort to clarify which terms apply to the phenomenon of 'confraternity' and what information may be deduced about their internal function and social action. These ranged from activities related to the support of the poor to the organised cult of icons and practices of public piety. The last part of the chapter is devoted to monasteries and churches as *loci* where Christians could come together and engage not only in religious practices, but also in socio-political activities. The foundation of churches and/or monasteries by members of the local community offered a meeting point where donations were collected and distributed, fairs were organised, and the poor could seek various kinds of support. Besides being a sacred space where communal religious identity was reasserted, the village church was also a space where transactions took place and people from all social strata could come together and interact as a collectivity.

The chapter by Yannis Stouraitis is dedicated to the microstructures of social action during revolts in the capital of the empire in the High Middle Ages. It begins with an analysis of the literary image of the people as a political body with a leading role in popular uprisings against emperors and takes issue with modern approaches that have tended to accept that image uncritically.[15] Using the iconic revolt of 1042 as a case study, Stouraitis analyses the ideological agenda of elite authors, pointing to the inherent contradictions and inconsistencies of the projected anthropomorphised image of the people, presented as if they acted like a single body with a single will towards a common goal. By deconstructing that literary image, he shows how elite authors instrumentalised the generic elite perception of the commoners as imprudent and fickle in order to present them as the only part of the populace able to commit acts of violence and capable of dragging all other social strata into a conflict with the emperor. This image served to mitigate the central role of members of the senatorial elite and the higher clergy in instigating the violent deposition of an emperor.

The second part of the chapter goes beyond the literary image of 'people vs. emperor' in order to scrutinise which social groups participated in unrest and with what agenda, as well as how and why different social groups took action on such occasions. Stouraitis shows that different groups of people such as the marketplace mob, mercenaries residing in the city, the members of the guilds, the senatorial elite, and the higher clergy could take part in a revolt with different roles and without having the same ideological motives or the same goals. In this context, the group that aimed to depose an emperor needed to have the necessary

---

15 There exist number of modern studies on popular revolts in Constantinople during the Late Antique and Medieval periods: see Cameron, *Circus Factions*; Whitby, Violence of the Circus Factions; Garland, Political Power and the Populace; Bell, *Social Conflict in the Age of Justinian*; Cheynet, Colère du peuple.

networking and economic capacity in order to organise a strong military force capable of overwhelming the defenders of the imperial palace. This was the crucial element that usually distinguished an unsuccessful from a successful attempt at usurpation. The latter was the outcome not simply of popular dis-satisfaction, but of the well-planned and organised escalation of unrest into a small-scale civil war within the capital.[16]

Ekaterini Mitsiou's chapter scrutinises the relationship between mobility and crime, in particular murder, during the first half of the thirteenth century in one of the Byzantine Empire's successor states, the so-called despotate of Epirus. Based on an explanatory model derived from modern criminology, Mitsiou seeks to analyse murder in relation to the movement of perpetrators and victims in the areas of western Greece in the transitional period that followed the sack of Constantinople by the Crusaders. Within this framework she offers an overview of how criminology and forensic science have been applied to the exploration of criminal behaviour in the Middle Ages with examples from western Europe and China.

The main part of the chapter is devoted to the exploration of the micro-structures of murder at the level of the lower social strata, a topic that has previously received little attention in modern research.[17] The main sources of information are court decisions made by church officials, which shed light on the identity of perpetrators and victims and their motives, the crime scenes, and the ways people committed murder or were murdered. The evidence shows that murder often occurred at the place of work, and that perpetrators and victims worked together and knew each other. Trespassing and illegal use of one's land, forests, or grazing areas appear to be among the main reasons that could lead to altercations that ended with killing, an aspect that points to how movement within a geographical area could play a role in the act of murder. Other cases of killing pertained to domestic abuse and strife among family members, or were a result of a strained relationship between lords and peasants.

Christos Malatras deals in his chapter with the question of personal agency in the process of social advancement in Late Byzantine society.[18] Beginning with the period after the Arab conquests, higher social status had been increasingly linked to good ancestry in Byzantium, a development that culminated with the emer-gence of the Komnenian elite in the twelfth century, which was an elite based on kinship relations to the imperial family.[19] In Palaiologan Byzantium, aristocratic

---

16 On a typology of Byzantine civil wars see Stouraitis, Civil War.
17 The focus has instead been on the murder of emperors, see Markopoulos, Αίμα στο παλάτι; Stouraitis, Mord als Mittel zur Machtergreifung.
18 On the structure of Late Byzantine society, see Matschke and Tinnefeld, *Gesellschaft im späten Byzanz.*
19 Magdalino, *Empire of Manuel I Komnenos,* 320–321.

status by birth was not confined to those related to the family of the ruling dynasty. Higher education remained a main vehicle for the acquirement of a higher social status. However, persons of good ancestry had greater access to wealth and thus better chances to achieve such an education than members of the lower strata. Within that framework and in the absence of a rigid stratification system based on hereditary or legal divisions, upward mobility in Late Byzantine society still remained a possibility for people who were not born to elite families.

In this context, Malatras scrutinises the role of patronage in facilitating upward social mobility. He shows how adherence to a patron, in the form of friendship or political alliance and support, or in the form of entering a powerful person's service, were the main avenues open to people who wished to improve their social and economic status. Offering service to a powerful person was the most popular and effective way to achieve social advancement in Late Byzantium. The bonds of allegiance between a servant and a patron were strong and created a reciprocal relationship where the one party improved their social position and the other secured long-lasting loyalty. However, persons who profited from a relationship of patronage could also distance themselves from their patron once they had achieved a certain social status. Upward mobility often required more than one patron, as exemplified by the career of Michael Gabras which Malatras presents as a case study. The most successful form of patronage was, of course, patronage that came from the emperor himself.

The chapter by Florence Liard shifts our attention to material culture and a relatively new area of research, namely the pottery traditions of the Late Medieval Mediterranean, which can shed light on social boundaries and microstructures in Byzantium. The case studies she presents offer insights into a bottom-up approach to glazed pottery traditions in Constantinople, the provinces, and on the periphery of the Byzantine Empire in the transitional period between the twelfth and the fourteenth centuries. Based on archaeological and archaeometric evidence, Liard seeks to reconstruct workshop production outputs, pottery commercial networks, and local demands. She enquires about the modalities of sharing aesthetic tastes and decoration techniques both at the regional and the long-distance level.

The evidence of the practices of production and distribution of glazed pottery provides important information on craftsmen and pottery consumers with regard to their everyday life, social behaviour, and the social and cultural bonds between them. Moreover, it provides insights into the process of re-negotiation of collective identities and social cohesion, as well as into social interactions and boundaries in a world that had undergone major changes in political, territorial, and cultural terms. Liard shows that this changing world was marked by internal flexibility and diversity, with Byzantine traditions being adopted, adapted, and perpetuated by Latin groups across Europe and western Asia in the period after 1204.

The chapter by Bruno de Nicola takes us to Mongol-dominated Anatolia in the second half of the thirteenth century, which represented a peripheral region from the viewpoint of the contemporary centres of power in Constantinople, Tabriz, and Baghdad. This region was inhabited by Greek-speaking Christians, semi-nomadic Turkmen, and Persianised urban elites.[20] The author makes use of a collection of twenty-four letters in order to complement the scarce information we have about this region, which is treated only marginally in the major contemporary Byzantine and Persian chronicles. The evidence of that compendium of letters, probably written in the mid-thirteenth century, allows for the reconstruction of the journey of a physician named Saʿd al-Dīn al-Ḥaqq to Kastamonu, Sinop, and a number of other cities in northern Anatolia. The account offers insights into the mobility of people from certain social classes in Islamic Anatolia and sheds light on various aspects of the social, cultural, and economic life of the region.

De Nicola pays particular attention to the itinerary of the trip, the physical landscape, and the anthropogeography of the locations visited by the traveller. The physician appears to have been offering his services to a society where the co-existence between Christian and Muslim communities facilitated the movement of professionals across religious and cultural boundaries. Professional ambition as well as personal and spiritual interests appear as the main motives for the movement of individuals in thirteenth-century Anatolia. Within this framework, the letters testify to the multicultural environment of commercial locations such as Sinop and highlight the networks that promoted the interconnectivity of cities such as Kastamonu, Sinop, Sivas, Niksar, Samsun, and the region close to Trabzon.

The concluding chapter of the book, the afterword written by John Haldon, provides some general methodological observations about mobility, micro-structures, and personal agency in the Byzantine world against the background of the various insights offered by the individual chapters. Haldon's remarks are intended to bring to attention the important gains that current research has made so far and to point towards potential fruitful avenues for future research. It is our hope that the chapters of this volume serve as a contribution to this process, as they draw on a wide range of evidence, from material culture to documentary texts, and from legal treatises and epistolography to historical narratives. They demonstrate that investigating microstructures and personal agency through the

---

20 The classic – but now rather outmoded – study on Late Medieval Anatolia is Vryonis, *The Decline of Medieval Hellenism in Asia Minor and the Process of Islamization.*

lens of mobility can offer valuable insights into the inner workings of Byzantine and neighbouring societies.

Bibliography

Ahrweiler, Helene and Angeliki Laiou (eds.), *Studies on the Internal Diaspora of the Byzantine Empire* (Washington, DC, 1988).

Beck, Hans-Georg, Byzantinisches Gefolgschaftswesen, *Bayerische Akademie der Wissenschaften, Philologisch-Historische Klasse, Sitzungsberichte* (1965) 3–32.

Bell, Peter, *Social Conflict in the Age of Justinian: Its Nature, Management, and Mediation* (Oxford, 2013).

Cameron, Alan, *Circus Factions: Blues and Greens at Rome and Byzantium* (Oxford, 1976).

Charanis, Peter, *The Armenians in the Byzantine Empire* (Lisbon, 1963).

Charanis, Peter, *Studies on the Demography of the Byzantine Empire* (London, 1972).

Cheynet, Jean-Claude, La colère du peuple à Byzance (Xe–XIIe siècle), *Société française d'histoire urbaine* 3 (2001) 25–38.

Cheynet, Jean-Claude, The Byzantine Aristocracy (8th–13th Centuries), in: Jean-Claude Cheynet (ed.), *The Byzantine Aristocracy and its Military Function* (Aldershot, 2006) 1–43.

Ditten, Hans, *Ethnische Verschiebungen zwischen der Balkanhalbinsel und Kleinasien vom Ende des 6. bis zur zweiten Hälfte des 9. Jahrhunderts.* Berliner Byzantinistische Arbeiten 59 (Berlin, 1993).

Garland, Lynda, Political Power and the Populace in Byzantium Prior to the Fourth Crusade, *Byzantinoslavica* 53 (1992) 17–52.

Hahn, Sylvia, *Historische Migrationsforschung* (Frankfurt am Main, 2012).

Haldon, John, *Recruitment and Conscription in the Byzantine Army c.550–950: A Study on the Origins of the stratiotika ktemata* (Vienna, 1979).

Haldon, John, Military Service, Military Lands, and the Status of Soldiers: Current Problems and Interpretations, *DOP* 47 (1993) 1–67.

Haldon, John F., *Warfare, State and Society in the Byzantine World, 565–1204* (London, 1999).

Haldon, John F., Social Élites, Wealth, and Power, in John F. Haldon (ed.), *The Social History of Byzantium* (Malden, MA./Oxford, 2009), 168–211.

Harzig, Christiane and Dirk Hoerder, with Donna Gabaccia, *What is Migration History?* (Cambridge, UK/Malden, MA., 2009).

Hoerder, Dirk, *Cultures in Contact. World Migrations in the Second Millennium* (Durham/London, 2002).

Kaplan, Michel, *Les hommes et la terre à Byzance du VIe au XIe siècle. Propriété et exploitation du sol.* Byzantina Sorbonensia 10 (Paris, 1992).

Kühn, Hans-Joachim, *Die byzantinische Armee im 10. und 11. Jahrhundert. Studien zur Organisation der Tagmata*, Byzantinische Geschichtsschreiber, Ergänzungsband 2 (Vienna, 1991).

Kyritses, Demetrios and Kostis Smyrlis, Les villages du littoral Égéen de l'Asie Mineure au Moyen Âge, in: Jacques Lefort, Cécile Morrisson, and Jean-Pierre Sodini (eds.), *Les*

Villages dans l'Empire byzantin (IVe–XVe siècle), Réalités Byzantines 11 (Paris, 2005) 437–451.

Laiou, Angeliki, The Byzantine Village (5th-14th Century), in: Jacques Lefort, Cécile Morrisson, and Jean-Pierre Sodini (eds.), *Les Villages dans l'Empire byzantin (IVe–XVe siècle)*, Réalités Byzantines 11 (Paris 2005) 31–54.

Lamberton, Robert, *Homer the Theologian. Neoplatonist Allegorical Reading and the Growth of the Epic Tradition* (Berkeley, 1989).

Magdalino, Paul, *The Empire of Manuel I Komnenos, 1143–1180* (Cambridge, 2002).

Makrypoulias, Christos G., Boots on the Ground: Byzantine Infantry in the Eleventh Century, in: Georgios Theotokis and Marek Meško (eds.), *War in Eleventh-Century Byzantium* (London, 2021) 241–266.

Markopoulos, Athanasios, Αίμα στο παλάτι. Ανταγωνισμοί για τον βυζαντινό θρόνο, in: Spyros Troianos (ed.), *Έγκλημα και τιμωρία στο Βυζάντιο* (Athens, 1997) 257–272.

Matschke, Klaus-Peter and Franz Tinnefeld, *Die Gesellschaft im späten Byzanz. Gruppen, Strukturen, Lebensformen* (Cologne/Weimar/Vienna, 2001).

McGeer, Eric, *Sowing the Dragon's Teeth: Byzantine Warfare in the Tenth Century*, Dumbarton Oaks Studies 33 (Washington, D.C., 1995).

Preiser-Kapeller, Johannes, Lucian Reinfandt, and Yannis Stouraitis (eds.), *Migration Histories of the Medieval Afroeurasian Transition Zone. Aspects of Mobility between Africa, Asia and Europe, 300–1500 CE*, Studies in Global Social History (Leiden/Boston, 2020).

Rapp, Claudia, Zwangsmigration in Byzanz. Kurzer Überblick mit einer Fallstudie aus dem 11. Jahrhundert, in: Thomas Erl (ed.), *Erzwungene Exile. Umsiedlungen und Vertreibungen in der Vormoderne, 500-bis 1850* (Frankfurt am Main/New York, 2017) 59–76.

Rapp, Claudia *et al.* (eds.), *Mobility and Migration in Byzantium. A Sourcebook* (Göttingen, 2023).

Stouraitis, Yannis, Der Mord als Mittel zur Machtergreifung anhand von Quellenbeispielen aus der mittelbyzantinischen Zeit, in: Mihailo Popovic and Johannes Preiser-Kapeller (eds.), *Junge Römer – Neue Griechen. Eine byzantinische Melange aus Wien* (Vienna, 2008) 223–334.

Stouraitis, Yannis, Civil War in the Christian Empire, in: Yannis Stouraitis (ed.), *A Companion to the Byzantine Culture of War, ca 300–1204* (Leiden 2018) 92–123.

Stouraitis, Yannis, Migrating in the Medieval East Roman World, ca. 600–1204, in: Johannes Preiser-Kapeller, Lucian Reinfandt, and Yannis Stouraitis (eds.), *Migration Histories of the Medieval Afroeurasian Transition Zone* (Brill, 2020) 141–165.

Vryonis, Speros, *The Decline of Medieval Hellenism in Asia Minor and the Process of Islamization from the Eleventh through the Fifteenth Century* (Berkeley/Los Angeles/London, 1971).

Whitby, Michael, The Violence of the Circus Factions, in: Keith Hopwood (ed.), *Organised Crime in Antiquity* (London, 1999) 229–53.

Christos G. Makrypoulias

Ranks to Riches: The Social Mobility of Middle Byzantine Infantry Commanders

There are two ways of tackling the question of upward social mobility in the Middle Byzantine period. One is to treat it as the usual case of groups of people taking advantage of networks of family and kinship; the other is to view it as a romantic rags-to-riches story, one of unknown individuals exercising their personal agency in order to climb the ladder of a highly stratified society.[1] Either way, researchers who study social mobility in Byzantium tend to focus on the careers of court officials and high-ranking military commanders,[2] and most of the latter had risen through the ranks of the cavalry, which formed the backbone of both the tagmatic guard units in Constantinople and the provincial armies of the *themata*.[3] Little attention, however, has been paid to the position of infantry commanders in the social hierarchy. The primary aim in this paper is to redress

---

1 A comprehensive overview of Byzantine social history may be found in the various chapters collected in Haldon, *Social History of Byzantium*; see also Ragia, Social Group Profiles. For the important role played by family ties and kinship in social mobility, see Herlong, *Kinship and Social Mobility*; Ludwig, Social Mobility in Byzantium; Leidholm, *Elite Byzantine Kinship*.

2 See Haldon, *Warfare, State and Society*, 270–274, on how the officers of the Middle Byzantine army became a major part of the provincial elite after the seventh century; c.f. Cheynet, Aristocratie byzantine, 284–298, who describes the Byzantine elites of the eighth and ninth centuries as owing their social position mainly to kinship, but also open to *homines novi* who advanced thanks to the (usually military) services they rendered. Byzantine aristocratic families tracing their origins back to ninth-century military commanders include the Argyroi and the Doukai (c.f. Theophanes Continuatus, *Chronographia*, IV.16.6, ed. Featherstone and Signes Cordoñer, 236), but the best-known case is that of the Phokades: see Cheynet, Les Phocas. For the evolution and social status of a mid-level cavalry office, that of *tourmarches*, see the excellent study of Wilson, Subaltern's Fate.

3 For the internal organisation, administration, and social stratification of the cavalrymen of the *tagmata* prior to the tenth century, see Haldon, *Byzantine Praetorians*, 276–337. Middle Byzantine narrative sources habitually use the term καβαλλαρικὰ θέματα to describe provincial levies, indicating that the latter consisted almost exclusively of mounted troops; see Haldon, *Warfare, State and Society*, 197–198 and 344, n. 28. In addition to the texts cited there, c.f. also *De re militari*, 1.161–163 and 3.20–23, ed. Dennis, 252 and 264, where there is a clear distinction between the infantry and the soldiers of the *themata*, implying that the former were either independent of the thematic organisation or only marginally connected to it.

that imbalance. Instead of the well-established Byzantine families whose pro-
genitors had distinguished themselves as cavalry commanders in the eighth and
ninth centuries, I propose to study social mobility from the point of view of the
low-born men who tried to use their service in the infantry of the later Macedonian era as a stepping-stone to promotion, social advancement, and integration.

The lack of scholarly interest in Middle Byzantine infantry officers and their
social status should not come as a surprise, since Middle Byzantine authors had
little to say on the subject of infantry altogether. Although modern medievalists
are finally moving away from the antiquated notion that the period from the
fourth century onwards was, militarily speaking, an 'age of cavalry',[4] the fact
remains that most of the troops who figure prominently in Greek sources after
the sixth century are men on horseback. It is only in the early 960s that units of
regular infantry (the so-called *taxiarchiai* or *chiliarchiai*, each formation mus-
tering 1,000 men) begin to be mentioned.[5] We know next to nothing, however,
about the recruitment and organisation of Byzantine foot soldiers from the 640s
to the middle of the tenth century. As the late Mark Whittow succinctly put it, 'we
know very little about the infantry save the fact that they existed'.[6]

The only concrete piece of evidence for the existence of organised infantry
units before the 960s is also the first reference to Middle Byzantine infantry
officers: men called δρουγγάριοι τῶν πεζῶν ('*droungarioi* of the foot'), mentioned
in the *Kletorologion* of Philotheos (written in the year 899). We have no way of
knowing whether the *taxiarchai* (also known as *chiliarchai*), the tenth and
eleventh-century infantry commanders who will figure prominently in this
paper, evolved from those earlier officers. What we do know is that the ninth-
century '*droungarioi* of the foot' and the later infantry officers shared a similar
position in the lower echelons of the Byzantine court hierarchy. That much is
evident from the two lists of precedence that mention them. In the aforementioned *Kletorologion*, the '*droungarioi* of the foot' are at the bottom of the

---

4 For some of the main points of this ongoing debate, see Bartlett, Technique militaire; Bennett,
   Myth; Morillo, 'Age of Cavalry'; Bachrach, Verbruggen's 'Cavalry'.

5 See McGeer, *Sowing the Dragon's Teeth*, 198–211, for a brief summary of the military reforms of
   the 950s/960s and the regular infantry they produced. On eleventh-century Byzantine infantry,
   similar in most respects to its tenth-century counterpart, see Makrypoulias, Boots on the
   ground.

6 Whittow, *Making of Orthodox Byzantium*, 172. The *Taktika* of Leo the Wise (c. 904) do
   mention infantry companies of 256 men apiece, as well as a total expeditionary force of 24,000
   infantrymen, both heavy and light (Leo, *Taktika*, IV.58–59, ed. Dennis, 64); but the text copied
   the earlier *Strategikon* (Maurice, *Strategikon*, XIIB, 8–9, ed. Dennis and Gamillscheg, 424, 426,
   428, and 430), which in turn had drawn those figures from Hellenistic/Roman military treatises. On Late Roman infantry units as described in the *Strategikon*, see Rance, Senior Regimental Officers, 395–399; see also *idem*, Maurice's *Strategicon*, on how earlier treatises influenced Maurice's *excursus* on infantry.

list, barely above the rank-and-file soldiers.[7] The so-called *Taktikon Escorial*, dating from the mid-970s, has the *taxiarchai* in the second-to-last place; only the *manglabitai*, a group of low-ranking imperial bodyguards, are listed below them.[8]

One cannot help but wonder, however, whether this less-than-distinguished place of infantry commanders in court hierarchy accurately reflected their social position in general – after all, what the lists of precedence actually tell us is merely that, whenever there was a banquet at the Great Palace, infantry officers were seated farthest from the emperor's high table. Sigillography and data from other sources provide a rather more nuanced picture for the *taxiarchai* of the late-tenth and eleventh century: they are shown holding such mid-level and upper mid-level dignities as *kandidatos* (possibly),[9] *spatharios*,[10] *spatharokandidatos*,[11] and even *protospatharios*.[12] The supreme commanders of infantry, the *hoplitarchai* or *archegetai* (true to the spirit of the reforms of the 960s, there were two of them, one for the East and another for the West),[13] held even higher dignities. A series of lead seals belonging to *archegetai* (only two preferred the term *hoplitarches*) identifies the two of the East as *protospatharios* and *protospatharios epi tou*

---

7 Philotheos, *Kletorologion*, ed. Oikonomides, 161.

8 *Taktikon Escorial*, ed. Oikonomides, 273; on the *manglabitai*, see Haldon, *Byzantine Praetorians*, 189–190 and 464, n. 424.

9 The interpretation of the lead seal of Theodore, *taxiarches* of Lykandos, is somewhat problematic. The original editor, Konstantopoulos, Βυζαντιακὰ μολυβδόβουλλα, 303 (no. 224α), had read on its inscription the family name Melias, as well as the rank of *kandidatos*. The more recent publication, however, renders the commander's last name as Rhomaios and omits the rank: Stavrakos, *Die byzantinischen Bleisiegel*, 340–341 (no. 224).

10 E. g. Elias, *spatharios* and *taxiarches* of Sebasteia: McGeer *et al.*, *Catalogue of Byzantine Seals* 4, 126 (no. 49.1).

11 Jordanov, *Corpus of Byzantine Seals*, 3.1, 384–385 (nos. 1060–1061), 385–386 (nos. 1065–1066) and 386 (no. 1068): several lead seals belonging to the *taxiarchai* Brachamios, Theodore, and Joseph, respectively, all holding the court rank of *spatharokandidatos*.

12 There are many examples of infantry commanders who held this dignity. For instance, in 1022 one Niketas Gonypates, *protospatharios* and *taxiarches* of Crete, is mentioned as the owner of a codex containing the *Miracles of St. Demetrius*: see Oikonomides, Ὁ ταξιάρχης Κρήτης. Though their readings are far from secure, lead seals belonging to the *protospatharios* and *taxiarches* Michael Alyates and the imperial *protospatharios* and *taxiarches* Michael Phytianos are published in Jordanov, *Corpus of Byzantine Seals*, 2, 50 (no. 28) and 425 (no. 738), respectively. Some *taxiarchai* were *protospatharioi epi tou Chrysotriklinou*, like George Tzipoureles, for whose lead seal see Seibt and Zarnitz, *Das byzantinische Bleisiegel*, 100 (no. 2.3.10), and an anonymous *axiarchos* of Ikonion, owner of a seal published by Cheynet *et al.*, *Les sceaux byzantins*, 130 (no. 181). For the term *axiarchos/axiarches* as an alternative spelling of *taxiarchos/taxiarches*, see Cheynet, Note sur l'axiarque.

13 On the duties of the *hoplitarchai/archegetai* and the east/west duality of this and other Byzantine military offices from the 960s onwards, see McGeer, *Sowing the Dragon's Teeth*, 203; Kühn, *Die byzantinische Armee*, 270–272.

Chrysotriklinou, respectively.[14] Another two *archegetai* belonged to the western armies and were of patrician rank.[15] So were two of the three supreme infantry commanders whose surviving lead seals carry no geographical determination: Leontakes Tzintziloukes[16] and Leo Brachamios.[17] The latter, in fact, held the slightly higher dignity of *anthypatos* and *patrikios*, while the last of the three, the *hoplitarches* Constantine Bourtzes, outranked them all, having been awarded the title of *magistros*.[18] In addition to sphragistics, an isolated reference to supreme infantry commanders found in a narrative source confirms their high status.[19] As was to be expected, *archegetai* were also better-placed in the court hierarchy: granted, the *Taktikon Escorial* lists them below the high command of the eastern armies, sandwiched between the thematic *strategoi* of Chaldia and Mesopotamia, but they definitely ranked above the generals of the western *themata*, the new 'Armenian' *themata*, and even some tagmatic commanders.[20]

Once researchers embark on a study of the rise of the *taxiarchai* in Byzantine social hierarchy, they soon come across a stumbling block: the sudden appearance of regular infantry units and their field commanders in the sources gives the impression that the emergence of this new officer corps took place in a vacuum. Of course, this cannot possibly be true, but the aforementioned absence of data on Byzantine infantry before the 960s does create an almost insurmountable obstacle when it comes to ascertaining both their social origins and the reasons behind their meteoric rise in the social hierarchy. The only shortcut available to

---

14 For the lead seals of the *protospatharios* George Maniakes, see Nesbitt and Oikonomides, *Catalogue of Byzantine Seals* 3, 172 (no. 99.1); Stavrakos, Unpublizierte Bleisiegel, 104. Seals belonging to the *protospatharios epi tou Chrysotriklinou* Theodorokanos: Konstantopoulos, Βυζαντιακὰ μολυβδόβουλλα, 152 (no. 594); Jordanov, *Corpus of Byzantine Seals* 1, 30.

15 Theophylaktos Chalkotoubes: Wassiliou-Seibt and Seibt, *Die byzantinischen Bleisiegel* 2, 235–236 (no. 240). Demetrios Apokaukos: Nesbitt and Oikonomides, *Catalogue of Byzantine Seals*, 3 (no. 1.3).

16 Campagnolo-Pothitou and Cheynet, *Sceaux de la collection George Zacos*, 118 (no. 97).

17 Cheynet and Theodoridis, *Sceaux byzantins*, 46–47 (no. 35).

18 Cheynet, Trois familles, 30–31 (no. 7).

19 Although he does not use the specific term, Skylitzes describes Samuel Bourtzes, whose rash actions precipitated the battle of Basilike Libas (June 1050), as 'commander of the infantry forces and in charge of the fortified encampment', precisely the duties of an *archegetes/ hoplitarches* as described in the military manuals; according to the historian, Bourtzes was a *patrikios* at the time (Skylitzes, *Synopsis Historiarum*, ed. Thurn, 470–471). Two unpublished lead seals attributed to the same person refer to him as *anthypatos patrikios* and *vestes:* Cheynet, Trois familles, 34–35 (no. 10).

20 *Taktikon Escorial*, ed. Oikonomides, 265; on late tenth-century Byzantine military organisation, including the new 'Armenian' *themata* (as well as the frontier commands of the *doukata/katepanata* mentioned below), see Krsmanović, *Byzantine Province*.

historians is to try to find some sort of explanation for the latter by first examining how the *taxiarchai* fitted into the military hierarchy.[21]

Thanks to tactical treatises written by actual soldiers (as opposed to armchair generals) during the last decades of the tenth century, we have a rough idea of how the chain of command worked within the new field armies of Nikephoros II and his successors. The entire infantry on campaign – a force of either 12 or 16 *taxiarchiai* was envisaged – came under the overall leadership of the *archegetes*. On the other hand, some sources seem to imply that on occasion, e. g. when facing an Arab raid, even a local general could have control over infantry forces in his area of operations. Although it is by no means certain that the authors had the *taxiarchiai* in mind when describing these dispositions, there are passages that clearly refer to new-model infantry units being placed under the overall command of a *strategos*.

All this, however, fails to address the fundamental issue: how did the new infantry fit into the peacetime establishment of the army. Did the *taxiarchai* continue to be subject to the authority of a central command stationed at Constantinople (the *archegetai/hoplitarchai*) even when not on campaign? Except for one piece of epigraphic evidence that could conceivably point in that direction, there is little to support this conclusion.[22] A closer look at our sources would reveal that, when not part of an expeditionary force led by an emperor or some high-ranking lieutenant of his, Byzantine infantrymen were quartered throughout the empire, subject to a less-centralised command, and with day-to-day logistical matters necessitating some degree of cooperation between infantry commanders and the local thematic administration. Geographical names preserved in the sigillographic, epigraphic, and literary record of the period include Soublaion,[23] Sebasteia,[24] Negido,[25] Lykandos,[26] Kase,[27] Ikonion,[28] and Crete.[29] Granted, this

---

21 For a more extensive treatment of what follows, see Makrypoulias, Boots on the ground, 242–246.

22 An inscription commemorating the restoration of fortifications in eastern Thrace ordered by Emperor Basil II and his brother, Constantine VIII, was commissioned jointly by the two military officers who supervised the works, the *archegetes* Basil Goutos and the *taxiarchos* Elpidios Brachamios: Asdracha, Inscriptions byzantines, 306–308 (no. 89). This collaboration, however, cannot be taken as evidence of an infantry commander taking orders from an *archegetes* in peacetime: the inscription dates from the year 1001–1002, when the Bulgarian army of Tsar Samuel was active as far east as Adrianople, so there is a good chance that Goutos and Brachamios were on campaign at the time.

23 The identification is based on the reconstructed text of an inscription commemorating the complete renovation of the fortifications of the town by the *taxiarches* Nikephoros in 1070–1071: see Cheynet and Drew-Bear, La forteresse de Soublaion.

24 See above, n. 10.

25 For the seal of Basil Palatinos, *taxiarches* of Negido (mod. Niğde), see Cheynet and Theodoridis, Sceaux byzantins, 169–171 (no. 161).

26 See above, n. 9.

sample is not particularly representative, given the fact that six out of these seven places were situated in or around the Central Anatolian plateau; yet it is sufficient to demonstrate that infantry units were dispersed throughout the Byzantine Empire, among both new and older *themata*. A typical example could be Kase, which may or may not have evolved into a small *thema* by the second third of the eleventh century,[30] but the presence of a *taxiarchia* on the island of Crete shows that even second-tier *themata* of the interior received their quota of infantry.

However, as well-supplied with infantry as the older *themata* might have been, modern researchers believe that an even closer connection existed between these troops and the frontier zones of small 'Armenian' *themata* and even smaller *strategides* which after the 960s were grouped together into high commands under a *doux* or *katepano*, reinforced with professional units and detachments of the Constantinopolitan *tagmata* stationed locally. Indeed, some go so far as to view the force of professional foot soldiers created in the 960s as a sort of 'tagmatic infantry'.[31] Though the latter statement is an exaggeration, a surviving lead seal of one Constantine Kourtikes, *taxiarchos* of Moxegas, does attest to the presence of regular infantry units in a frontier district, namely Vaspurakan, after the incorporation of the region into the Byzantine Empire in the 1020s.[32]

Indeed, the link between the high command of the *doukata/katepanata* and the *taxiarchai* seems to have been a strong one from the beginning of their creation. A case in point is Byzantine Italy,[33] where documentary sources not only contain numerous references to *taxiarchai*, but also demonstrate how some of them reported directly to the *katepano*, even though old-style *themata* continued to exist in the region.[34] Similar dispositions may be observed in the *doukaton* of Antioch. In an incident described in the *Life of St Lazaros of Mt. Galesion* and

27 The name of Theodore Balantes (or possibly Bialantes), *taxiarches* of Kase, appears in two inscriptions found in the fortress of Anakopia (mod. Akhali Atoni, Georgia): Bănescu, Les inscriptions byzantines; for clarifications regarding the correct dates of the inscriptions (February-March 1046), see Seibt, Byzantine Thema, 176.

28 See above, n. 12.

29 See above, n. 12.

30 Charalampakis, Toponymy and Prosopography, 28–39.

31 Cheynet, L'armée et la marine, 158.

32 The lead seal probably dates from shortly after the middle of the eleventh century: Seibt, Ταξίαρχος Μωξηγάζ; Jordanov, *Corpus of Byzantine Seals* 2, 245–246 (no. 383).

33 For the position held by infantry commanders in the imperial administrative system of Byzantine Italy, see von Falkenhausen, *Untersuchungen*, 115–116.

34 In a bilingual grant of privileges issued by the *katepano* Gregory Tarchaneiotes in May 999, *taxiarchoi* – referred to as *centuriones* in the Latin text – are listed among various thematic officers and functionaries (Beltrani, *Documenti longobardi*, 11–13, no. IX). In 1001 the *taxiarches* Constantine Kontos was sent to Basilicata as the personal envoy of Tarchaneiotes, in order to settle a boundary dispute between the fortified towns of Tricarico and Acerenza: Guillou and Holtzmann, Zwei Katepansurkunden; von Falkenhausen, *Untersuchungen*, 173.

dated to the early 990s, Armenian soldiers (probably infantrymen, since the saint managed to intercept them even though he was on foot) marching through the countryside of Antioch abducted a peasant girl; they were persuaded to release her only after Lazaros threatened to 'go straight to the *katepano*' and denounce them.[35] A decade later, Nikephoros Ouranos, then *doux* of Antioch, wrote to a correspondent that he had received the latter's letter through a *taxiarches* whom he went on to describe as 'one of our own'.[36] According to both Greek and Arabic sources, the first decades of the eleventh century saw several infantry brigades being moved around by local *doukes* to garrison the various forts along the borderlands of Northern Syria.[37]

This evidence, circumstantial though it may be, indicates a close connection between the *taxiarchai* and the high commands of the *doukata* and *katepanata* that appeared either simultaneously with, or a few years after, the formation of the new-model infantry units. It was this link, forged in the fires of continuous warfare and reinforced by the various administrative ties within this new military hierarchy, that set the ball rolling; it allowed these new officers, many of them *homines novi*, to rub elbows with the scions of the great military aristocratic houses of Byzantium, thus providing commanders of the later Macedonian infantry with an opportunity that would have been unimaginable to their earlier counterparts: the chance to improve their social standing.

The first documented case of collaboration between infantry commanders and military aristocrats away from the battlefield was an affair rather 'Byzantine' in nature: the plot hatched by John Tzimiskes to assassinate Nikephoros II Phokas and ascend the throne. The cabal of army officers who took part in the December 969 coup included at least two *taxiarchai*, Michael Bourtzes and Leo Balantes (or Abalantes), along with a certain Leo Pediasimos, and a fourth conspirator, Sachakios Brachamios.[38] Apart from its role in the political history of the time, the palace coup of 969 may also be used as a case study to illustrate the social origins of late-tenth-century mid-level commanders. The social profile of the conspirators was an interesting mixture of 'new men' and members of established families – not to mention their diverse ethnic backgrounds. Michael Bourtzes was the first member of his family to appear in the historical record. He is mentioned in 968 as the infantry commander in charge of the blockade of Antioch; shortly before the coup, Bourtzes had attracted the ire of Phokas for

---

35 Gregory the Cellarer, *Life of Lazaros Galesiotes*, §15, ed. Delehaye, 513–514. In this context, the term *katepano* probably refers to the *doux* of Antioch and not to a subordinate military commander (*pace* Greenfield, *Life of Lazaros of Mt. Galesion*, 93, n. 75).

36 Darrouzès, *Épistoliers byzantins*, 229 (letter 25).

37 See Makrypoulias, *Boots on the ground*, 256, n. 29.

38 Leo the Deacon, *Historia*, V.6–9, ed. Hase, 84–92; Skylitzes, *Synopsis Historiarum*, ed. Thurn, 279–281.

capturing the city against orders.[39] His ethnicity and place of origin are still a matter of conjecture; some consider the family name to be Arabic, while others believe that he was of Armenian ancestry.[40] Leo Balantes, the man who struck the first blow and whom Tzimiskes used as a convenient scapegoat afterwards, was probably the son of a *tourmarches*, a high-ranking cavalry commander allied to the Phokas clan in 919 and promoted to *patrikios* and *strategos* of Lykandos by 950.[41] Leo Pediasimos – the Greek etymology of whose family name indicates that he was probably of Byzantine extraction rather than a foreigner – was also a *homo novus*, the first member of his family mentioned by name; Tzimiskes later appointed him *doux* of Thessaloniki.[42] Interestingly enough, an eleventh-century *taxiarches* Leo Pediasimos owned a lead seal found in Bulgaria; was he a descendant of the earlier Pediasimos, perhaps a namesake grandson continuing the family business?[43] Finally, the case of Sachakios Brachamios illustrates the degree of ethnic, as well as social mobility in Byzantium. Sachakios is mentioned as an associate of Michael Bourtzes when the latter commanded at Bagras, and would go on to become *anthypatos patrikios* and *strategos*.[44] He belonged to a family that hailed from the Armenian region of Vaspurakan, and was its first prominent member to enter imperial service. In the eleventh century, at least two Brachamioi will begin their illustrious careers by getting entry-level jobs as *taxiarchai*, and we have already seen that another would eventually achieve the high status of *anthypatos patrikios* and *archegetes*.[45]

Further evidence illustrating the prominence of *taxiarchai* at this time is provided by the historian Leo the Deacon. When Bardas Phokas rebelled against John Tzimiskes in 970 to avenge his murdered uncle, he 'began to promise distributions of money, and to offer awards of dignities, appointing *taxiarchai* and *strategoi*, and the glorious positions that an emperor is accustomed to offer generously to his supporters'.[46] Likewise, when Tzimiskes promptly dispatched Bardas Skleros to quell the uprising, the office of *taxiarches* was one of the

---

39 Leo the Deacon, *Historia*, V.4, ed. Hase, 81–82; Skylitzes, *Synopsis Historiarum*, ed. Thurn, 271–273.

40 For a brief history of the Bourtzes family and some prosopographical notes on Michael Bourtzes, see Cheynet, Trois familles, 15–24.

41 See Stephenson, Development in Nomenclature, 210, n. 106.

42 C.f. *Life of St. Phantinos*, §49, ed. Follieri, 436.

43 Jordanov, *Corpus of Byzantine Seals* 2, 336 (nos. 560–561).

44 For an introductory note on the Brachamioi and a brief biographical sketch of Sachakios (Isaac) Brachamios, see Cheynet, Trois familles, 57–59.

45 On the *archegetes* Leo Brachamios, see above, n. 17; c.f. Cheynet, Trois familles, 62 (n. 6): another lead seal with a bust of St Demetrius on the obverse, mentioning a *protospatharios* and *strategos* Leo Brachamios, could belong to the same individual at an earlier stage of his career.

46 Leo the Deacon, *Historia*, VII.1, ed. Hase, 113; Talbot and Sullivan, History *of Leo the Deacon*, 163.

incentives (along with pledges of amnesty, gifts of gold, and offers of appointing *strategoi* and *patrikioi*) dangled before key followers of Phokas to induce them to switch sides.[47]

What is significant for our study is that this elevated position of *taxiarchai* in military hierarchy from the late tenth century onwards is mirrored in their social profile. Now, for the first time in the Middle Byzantine period, we come across infantry commanders in the capacity of local actors. One aspect of this is the occurrence of members of this officer corps as donors, a clear indication that their status as local gentry was beginning to solidify.[48] For instance, in the eleventh century the *protospatharios* and *(t)axiarches* Theophylaktos and his father, the monk Arsenios, paid for the decoration of a cave church in Cappadocia,[49] while at about the same time in Italy a land-owning infantry commander named Calones granted part of his estates to a monk so that the latter could establish a church and a monastery.[50] Sometime prior to 1078, the *taxiarches* Leo Mauroutzikos and his wife founded a church in the town of Gerace in Calabria.[51] Other infantry commanders witness private documents from Chiaramonte.[52] A similar instance is that of a document from 1054, detailing the partition of landed property between the descendants of seven brothers; no fewer than three *taxiarchai* are found in it: the *spatharokandidatos* Konstas of Oursoleon, one of the heirs, along with Andreas Kasires and Georgios, two of the three men who sign as witnesses.[53] The extent to which these officers had risen in status in the provincial elite of Byzantine Italy may be seen by comparing two documents from the region. In a grant of privileges issued by the *katepano* of Italy in 999,[54] the names of the infantry commanders who signed as witnesses were placed below those of the local *tourmarchai*; a few years later, in 1015, when another Italian *taxiarches* notarised a private contract in the town of Oriolo, his signature preceded those of two *topoteretai* (lieutenant commanders, probably his brothers) and a *tourmarches*.[55] Infantry officers who owned manuscripts were also a novel feature, never before seen in the Middle Byzantine period.[56]

---

47 Leo the Deacon, *Historia*, VII.3, ed. Hase, 117.
48 Their work in renovating fortifications, e. g. in Thrace (see above, n. 22), Soublaion (see above, n. 23) and Anakopia (see above, n. 27) is not considered here, since serving officers would undertake such tasks in their official capacity, not as private citizens.
49 Thierry, Un style byzantin schématique.
50 Thomas, *Private Religious Foundations*, 174–175.
51 Ménager, L'abbaye bénédictine, 19.
52 Robinson, History and Cartulary, 189.
53 Mercati *et al.*, *Saint-Jean Théristès*, 31–42 (no. 1).
54 See above, n. 34.
55 Trinchera, *Syllabus*, 16–17 (no. 15).
56 See above, n. 12; c.f. Evangelatou-Notara, *"Σημειώματα" ἑλληνικῶν κωδίκων*, 155 (no. 168), for a manuscript of the *Homilies* of John Chrysostom commissioned by the *spatharokandidatos* and *taxiarches* Pharismanes (perhaps Pharasmanes Apokapes).

The office of *taxiarches* was much more than an entry point into the provincial elite; an even more significant reason why it appears to have been much sought-after was that in many instances it could be a stepping-stone to further advancement within the military establishment. Promotions based on both merit and family connections were common in the Byzantine army, and many an infantry commander took advantage of this to gain even higher offices and titles. What is noteworthy – though it should come as no surprise – is that these promotions were usually into the senior service, the cavalry of the old *themata* and the new *doukata*. Michael Bourtzes, the first individual to distinguish himself as an infantry commander in 968–969, went on to become *doux* of Antioch. We know from two of his lead seals that the aforementioned Constantine Kourtikes eventually left Moxegas, when he was promoted to the office of *strategos* and the dignity of *patrikios*;[57] the career of Basil Palatinos (also promoted to general and raised from *spatharokandidatos* to *protospatharios*) appears to have followed a similar path.[58] The best-documented case of an officer who rose through the ranks of both infantry and cavalry is that of Constantine Bourtzes, who was eventually promoted to *hoplitarches* after having served as *topoteretes* (an office common in both the thematic and the tagmatic military hierarchy) and *taxiarches*, before being appointed *doux* of Antioch.[59]

The reverse was also possible, and far from uncommon: generals of smaller *themata* being promoted to the infantry high command. The two lead seals of Demetrios Apokaukos that refer to him as *strategos* and *archegetes* of the West, respectively, probably indicate a promotion from the former office to the latter.[60] The case of Theodorokanos is rather more complicated, but we may safely assume that he too was promoted from *strategos* to *archegetes* and not vice versa.[61] A similar process that probably took place in the case of George Maniakes, arguably the best Byzantine general of the eleventh century, is indicative both of the degree of upward social mobility an infantry officer might expect as a reward

---

57 See above, n. 32.
58 Laurent, *Les sceaux byzantins*, 150 (no. 145).
59 See above, n. 18; c.f. Cheynet and Theodoridis, *Sceaux byzantins*, 44–45 (no. 33).
60 Seibt and Zarnitz, *Das byzantinische Bleisiegel*, 93–94 (no. 2.3.4); for the lead seal identifying him as *archegetes*, see above, n. 15. C.f. Cheynet, Par saint Georges, par saint Michel, 118.
61 Earlier scholarship had placed Theodorokanos (see above, n. 14) in the first half of the eleventh century; c.f. McGeer *et al.*, *Catalogue of Byzantine Seals 5*, 34 (no. 11.1), probably belonging to the same person, since this '*strategos* of Artach' and the *archegetes* share the same dignity, that of *protospatharios epi tou Chrysotriklinou*. It was assumed that Theodorokanos had served as *strategos* (of Artze, according to an alternative reading of his seal) between 975 and 979, following which he was promoted to *archegetes* of the East before Emperor Basil II transferred him to the Balkans in the early 990s: see *Prosopographie der mittelbyzantinischen Zeit*, s.v. Θεοδωροχάνος #27615. However, a recent study (Seibt, Theodorokanoi, 82–83) reverts to the earlier view that the aforementioned seals belonged to a *strategos* of Artach and later *archegetes* of the second quarter of the eleventh century.

for his meritorious service and of the fact that the infantry remained a second-rate force in the eyes of the educated elite. The lead seal identifying Maniakes as *protospatharios* and *archegetes* of the East is dated to the 1030s, roughly the same period when he is first mentioned in narrative sources as commander of the 'Armenian' *thema* of Telouch.[62] Since we already know from the *Taktikon Escorial* that the supreme commanders of infantry outranked the generals of the various new *themata*, and many of the older ones as well, it is more probable that the seal attests to a promotion from an 'Armenian' *thema* to the infantry high command; Maniakes' service in the infantry, however, seems to have gone completely unnoticed by both Michael Attaleiates and John Skylitzes, our main sources for the period.

Byzantine meritocracy, of course, should not be overstated. Networks of family and kinship played a key role in the social mobility of many infantry commanders. The sources describing the meteoric rise of George Maniakes do not fail to mention that he was 'the son of Goudelios';[63] we do not know who this was, but the fact that the name of his father was important enough for eleventh-century historians to remember shows that personal agency was only one of the factors behind the advancement of Maniakes. The Brachamios family is another case in point. Elpidios Brachamios, who restored fortifications in Thrace in the first years of the eleventh century, is usually identified with the *patrikios* Elpidios who led the opposition against the *doux* of Antioch in 1034.[64] His more famous relative, Philaretos Brachamios, was the eleventh-century equivalent of Michael Bourtzes in social mobility: a lowly *taxiarches* in the 1050s or early 1060s, he went through a *cursus honorum* that included the military ranks of *stratopedarches* and *domestikos* of the East, as well as the dignities of *magistros* and *kouropalates*, to become a semi-independent ruler of Northern Syria and Mesopotamia.[65]

Well-established Byzantine military families were usually associated with service in the cavalry of the *themata* and *tagmata*, but some noble houses had links to the infantry as well. Family ties between infantry commanders and their superiors were not uncommon. The *taxiarches* Andronikos Balantes (interestingly enough, he bears the same family name as the assassin of Nikephoros

---

62 Skylitzes, *Synopsis Historiarum*, ed. Thurn, 381.

63 Skylitzes, *Synopsis Historiarum*, ed. Thurn, 387.

64 See above, n. 22, and Cheynet, Trois familles, 59–60 (n. 2). He may or may not be the same person as the *taxiarches* Elpidios Brachamios whose lead seals are published in Jordanov, *Corpus of Byzantine Seals* 2, 102–103 (nos. 123–124), who dates them several decades after the beginning of the eleventh century. He was probably the grandfather of another Elpidios Brachamios, who was *kouropalates* and *doux* of Cyprus in the second half of the eleventh century. See in general Georgiou, Η χρονολόγηση της υπηρεσίας.

65 Philaretos Brachamios rose rapidly in status thanks to his imperial connections (he was a close friend of Emperor Romanos IV Diogenes); his career is described in Cheynet, Trois familles, 66–73 (no. 13), and Koltsida-Makre, Philaretos Brachamios.

Phokas) agreed to marry his son to the daughter of Melias, a *strategos*. Their decision to form a marriage alliance was so firm that, when the son died before the wedding could take place, Balantes and Melias (illegally) married the former's daughter to the latter's son instead.[66]

The incident mentioned above dates from around the year 1050. By then, the final step in the gradual rise of a number of infantry commanders to the top tiers of society had already been taken, and they were beginning to coalesce into military aristocratic families of their own. The best example of a self-made man who advanced himself through early service in the infantry was probably that of Michael Bourtzes, founder of a new military aristocratic family with all the usual trappings: landed estates, military offices and court titles, access to imperial patronage. The clan, which had a long and distinguished history (as late as 1116, one of its members was serving Alexios Komnenos as a general), even included at least two other members serving in the infantry: Samuel, one of Michael's three grandsons, was a *hoplitarches* in 1050, as was Constantine Bourtzes, also in the eleventh century.[67]

When all is said and done, however, the fact that the office of *taxiarches* served as an entry point into the military aristocracy – whether through merit or kinship – should not be underestimated. Indeed, a recent study has suggested that those in the top rank of subordinate officers (*merarchai, tourmarchai, droungarioi, ek prosopou*), including the *taxiarchai*, depicted St. Nicholas on their seals more frequently than did their high-ranking superior officers, e. g. the *katepano, strategoi, domestikoi*, and *doukai*. Although Wilson is the first to admit that the following is highly conjectural, he believes that Nicholas, as a non-military saint, was more likely to be depicted on seals by military officers who did not come from families with histories of military service; this frequency reflected their status as either lower-ranking or first-generation aristocrats.[68]

Speaking of family names, we would be remiss not to mention here that, unlike their more well-heeled brothers in the cavalry and the high command, some Byzantine *taxiarchai* (perhaps one in five, although this is no more than a ballpark figure) were still using lead seals that bore either no family name at all or a very unusual *unicum*. Given the fact that the rise in the use of family names on lead seals has been linked to the rise of the provincial aristocracy during the last

---

66 Schmink, Vier eherechtliche Entscheidungen.
67 See above, n. 18–19.
68 Wilson, Subaltern's Fate, 65–67. See *ibid.*, 64, fig. 14, for a statistical analysis of the religious imagery of military seals: c.f. the high percentage of seals with St. Nicholas that belong to *merarchai* (50%) and *tourmarchai* (30%), as opposed to those attributed to *katepano, strategoi, domestikoi*, and *doukai* (5–15%); the same table shows that a quarter of the 24 seals belonging to *taxiarchai* were decorated with the bust of St. Nicholas.

decades of the tenth century,[69] should we presume from this lack – also evident in some Italian documents – that well into the eleventh century there were still *taxiarchai* who were trying to work their way into Byzantine high society? Did the upper nobility of Byzantium in the decades before 1071 still view some *taxiarchai* (perhaps foreigners who had yet to assimilate) as low-ranking gentry with nothing more to their credit than their erstwhile participation in the wars of reconquest, much like the *hidalgos* of the Iberian Peninsula?

One final remark remains to be made: although there are instances of infantry commanders with obviously – or at least seemingly – Greek family names (Barys, Chalkotoubes, Dipotamites, Gonypates, Palatinos, Phytianos, Strabotrichares etc.),[70] most of the heavy infantry they commanded (known as *kontaratoi*, i.e. 'spearmen') were of Armenian or Armeno-Georgian extraction, and so were many of the notable families connected to the tenth- and eleventh-century Byzantine infantry, such as the Apokapai, Brachamioi, and others.[71] This is probably the main reason why the increased importance of infantry in Byzantine warfare did not lead to any noticeable social changes similar to those that seem to have taken place in other historical periods.

Two such instances of supposed social change fueled by the rise of the infantry spring to mind: the first is the 'hoplite revolution', a theory which claims that the increasing importance of 'hoplites' (heavy infantrymen protected by large shields and bronze armour) on the battlefield during the seventh and sixth centuries BC prompted the middle class in the city-states of ancient Greece to demand a larger share in the conduct of state affairs;[72] the second is the so-called 'infantry revolution' of the Late Middle Ages, the notion that the emergence of an effective infantry militia in the fourteenth century facilitated the creation of urban commons in Flanders, Switzerland, and Italy.[73]

As was the case in previous centuries, the ethnic background of upper-class refugees did not hinder Armenian upward social mobility and integration into

---

69 Stephenson, Development in Nomenclature.
70 Barys: Stavrakos, *Die byzantinischen Bleisiegel*, 96–97 (no. 36); Chalkotoubes: see above, n. 15; Dipotamites: Jordanov, *Corpus of Byzantine Seals* 2, 127–128 (no. 166); Gonypates: see above, n. 12; Palatinos: see above, n. 25; Phytianos: see above, n. 12; Strabotrichares: Jordanov, *Corpus of Byzantine Seals* 2, 382 (no. 671).
71 On the ethnic background of infantry recruits after the middle of the tenth century, see McGeer, *Sowing the Dragon's Teeth*, 183–184; for the preponderance of Armenians among them well into the eleventh century, see Makrypoulias, Boots on the ground, 244–245 and n. 43.
72 On the 'hoplite revolution', see in general Viggiano, Hoplite Revolution; Konijnendjik and Echeverría, Max Weber.
73 The idea was first proposed by Rogers, Military Revolutions, 247–257; for an alternative view (that it was the emergence of the commons that gave rise to an effective infantry arm, not vice versa), see Stone, Technology.

the Byzantine military aristocracy;[74] the same, however, cannot be said of their men. Severe clashes between Armenian soldiers and local Greek speakers – either civilians or other servicemen, such as sailors – are documented throughout the second half of the tenth century; at the same time, a twelfth-century source describing the situation in Byzantine Greece during the war against the Bulgarians in the first years of the eleventh century demonstrates the hatred of the local populations towards the Armenian infantrymen sent there by Basil II as garrison troops by referring to them as 'the so-called Kontaratoi, beastly murderous people, a group of merciless highwaymen'.[75] It is obvious that, whatever military significance the infantry possessed in the tenth and eleventh centuries, it was little more than a force of foreign mercenaries in the pay of the central government.[76] The fact that a large gap existed between these foot soldiers and local society, whose sons were not part of that force, meant that there was no way for service in the infantry to be converted into political power; therefore, whatever quaint notions might float around in eleventh-century Byzantium, identifying the poor with walking or serving on foot and the elites with horse-riding, were certain to remain nothing more than an interesting aside in one of John Mauropous' Sunday sermons.[77]

It was only in Byzantine Italy, where infantry troops were probably recruited locally, that the men and their commanders (as we have already seen) were deeply embedded in local society, to the extent that in the decades before and after the Norman Conquest the term *kontaratoi* came to be almost synonymous with southern Italian urban militias.

A group of relatively-unknown infantry commanders managing to break into the old-established military aristocracy is a remarkable feat, one that certainly deserves further study. Although the landed magnates whose ancestors had distinguished themselves as thematic cavalry officers in the ninth century continued to rule over both state and society in the tenth and eleventh centuries, the increased importance of the infantry arm gave commanders of the later Macedonian era an opportunity that would have been almost unimaginable to their counterparts in the eighth- and ninth-century Byzantine infantry (if indeed such counterparts even existed): the opportunity to use their position in the military hierarchy to improve their social status. For the high-ranking officers at least, service in the infantry was truly a stepping-stone to upward social mobility.

---

74 See in general Preiser-Kapeller, Aristocrats.
75 A brief account of those clashes may be found in Makrypoulias, Cities, 95 and n. 33. For the passage describing the situation in Byzantine Greece, see Skylitzes, *Synopsis Historiarum*, ed. Thurn, 352; it belongs to one of the interpolations added to the text by Michael, bishop of Devol, in 1118 (now preserved in codex Vindobonensis hist. gr. 74).
76 See above, n. 31.
77 Kazhdan, Hagiographical Notes.

Acknowledgements

This is a slightly revised version of my paper Ranks to Riches: Infantry Officers and Social Mobility in the Middle Byzantine Period, delivered at the International Medieval Congress (Leeds, 3–6 July 2017); it also draws from A Byzantine Band of Brothers: The Tenth- and Eleventh-Century Infantry Commanders, delivered at the 23rd International Congress of Byzantine Studies (Belgrade, 22–27 August 2016). I would like to extend my warmest thanks to Prof. Dr. Claudia Rapp (Project Leader, Moving Byzantium Project, University of Vienna/Austrian Academy of Sciences) for making possible my participation at the 'Moving Byzantium' sessions of the 2017 Leeds International Medieval Congress, which proved a truly amazing scholarly experience.

Bibliography

Primary Sources

Darrouzès, Jean, *Épistoliers byzantins du Xe siècle*, Archives de l'Orient chrétien 6 (Paris, 1960).

De re militari, ed. George T. Dennis, CFHB 25 (Washington, D.C., 2010), 241–335.

Gregory the Cellarer, *Life of Lazaros Galesiotes*, ed. Hippolyte Delehaye, AASS Nov. III (Brussels, 1910), 508–588. English translation: Richard P. H. Greenfield, *The Life of Lazaros of Mt. Galesion: An Eleventh-Century Pillar Saint*, Byzantine Saints' Lives in Translation 3 (Washington, D.C., 2000).

Leo the Deacon, *Historia*, ed. Charles-Benoît Hase, *Leonis diaconi Caloënsis historiae libri decem*, CSHB (Bonn, 1828). English translation: Alice-Mary Talbot and Dennis F. Sullivan, *The* History *of Leo the Deacon: Byzantine Military Expansion in the Tenth Century*, Dumbarton Oaks Studies 41 (Washington, D.C., 2005).

Leo the Wise, *Taktika*, ed. George T. Dennis, CFHB 49 (Washington, D.C., 2010).

Life of St. Phantinos the Younger, ed. Enrica Follieri, Subsidia Hagiographica 77 (Brussels, 1993).

Maurice, *Strategikon*, ed. George T. Dennis and Ernst Gamillscheg, CFHB 17 (Vienna, 1981).

Mercati, Silvio, G., Ciro Giannelli, and André Guillou, *Saint-Jean Théristès* (Vatican, 1980).

Philotheos, *Kletorologion*, ed. Nikos Oikonomides (Paris, 1972), 65–235.

Skylitzes, John, *Synopsis Historiarum*, ed. Hans Thurn, *Ioannis Scylitzae Synopsis Historiarum*, CFHB 5 (Berlin, 1973).

Taktikon Escorial, ed. Nikos Oikonomides (Paris, 1972), 255–277.

Theophanes Continuatus, *Chronographia*, ed. Michael Featherstone and Juan Signes Cordoñer, CFHB 53 (Boston, 2015).

Trinchera, Francisco, *Syllabus Graecarum membranarum* (Naples, 1865).

Secondary Literature

Asdracha, Catherine, Inscriptions byzantines de la Thrace orientale (VIIIe–XIe siècles). Présentation et commentaire historique, *Ἀρχαιολογικόν Δελτίον* 44–46 (1989–1991) 239–334.

Bachrach, Bernard S., Verbruggen's 'Cavalry' and the Lyon-Thesis, *Journal of Medieval Military History* 4 (2006) 137–163.

Bănescu, Nicolae, Les inscriptions byzantines du château d'Ἀνακουφὴ au Caucase (XIe siècle), *Revue des Études Sud-Est Européennes* 18 (1941) 103–108.

Bartlett, Robert J., Technique militaire et pouvoir politique, 900–1300, *Annales. Économies, Sociétés, Civilisations* 41 (1986) 1135–1159.

Beltrani, Giambattista, *Documenti longobardi e greci per la storia dell' Italia meridionale nel medioevo* (Rome, 1877).

Bennett, Matthew, The Myth of the Supremacy of Knightly Cavalry, in: Matthew Strickland (ed.), *Proceedings of the 1995 Harlaxton Symposium: Armies, Chivalry and Warfare in Medieval Britain and France*, Harlaxton Medieval Studies 7 (Stamford, 1998), 304–316.

Campagnolo-Pothitou, Maria and Jean-Claude Cheynet, *Sceaux de la collection George Zacos au Musée d'art et d'histoire de Genève* (Milan, 2016).

Charalampakis, Pantelis, On the Toponymy and Prosopography of Some Minor Military-Administrative Districts in Byzantium: Kas(s)e, *Vindaion, Mauron Oros, *Karadeniz Araştırmaları Enstitüsü Dergisi* 3/3 (2017) 27–49.

Cheynet, Jean-Claude, Note sur l'axiarque et le taxiarque, *REB* 44 (1986) 233–235.

Cheynet, Jean-Claude, Les Phocas, in: Gilbert Dagron and Haralambie Mihăescu (eds.), *Le traité sur la guérilla (De velitatione) de l'Empereur Nicéphore Phocas (963–969)* (Paris, 1986) 289–315.

Cheynet, Jean-Claude, Trois familles du duché d'Antioche, in: Jean-Claude Cheynet and Jean-François Vannier (eds.), *Études prosopographiques* (Paris, 1986) 7–122.

Cheynet, Jean-Claude, L'aristocratie byzantine (VIIIe–XIIIe siècle), *Journal des savants* (2000) 281–322.

Cheynet, Jean-Claude, Par saint Georges, par saint Michel, *TM* 14 (2002) 115–134.

Cheynet, Jean-Claude, L'armée et la marine, in Cheynet, Jean-Claude (ed.), *Le monde byzantin, 2: L'Empire byzantin (641–1204)* (Paris, 2006) 151–174.

Cheynet, Jean-Claude and Thomas Drew-Bear, La forteresse de Soublaion en Phrygie (1070–1071), *REB* 70 (2012) 209–220.

Cheynet, Jean-Claude, Cécile Morrisson, and Werner Seibt, *Les sceaux byzantins de la collection Henri Seyrig* (Paris, 1991).

Cheynet, Jean-Claude and Dimitri Theodoridis, *Sceaux byzantins de la collection D. Theodoridis. Les sceaux patronymiques* (Paris, 2010).

Evangelatou-Notara, Florentia, *"Σημειώματα" ἑλληνικῶν κωδίκων ὡς πηγὴ διὰ τὴν ἔρευναν τοῦ οἰκονομικοῦ καὶ κοινωνικοῦ βίου τοῦ Βυζαντίου* (Athens, 1982).

Georgiou, Stavros G., Η χρονολόγηση της υπηρεσίας του δούκα Κύπρου Ελπιδίου Βραχαμίου, *Βυζαντιακά* 13 (2014) 145–154.

Guillou, Andrè and Walther Holtzmann, Zwei Katepansurkunden aus Tricarico, *Quellen und Forschungen aus italienischen Archiven und Bibliotheken* 41 (1961) 1–28.

Haldon, John F., *Byzantine Praetorians: An Administrative, Institutional and Social Survey of the Opsikion and Tagmata, c.580–900*, ΠΟΙΚΙΛΑ ΒΥΖΑΝΤΙΝΑ 3 (Bonn, 1984).

Haldon, John F., *Warfare, State and Society in the Byzantine World 565–1204* (London, 1999).

Haldon, John F. (ed.), *The Social History of Byzantium* (Chichester, 2009).

Herlong, Mark W., *Kinship and Social Mobility in Byzantium, 717–959*. Unpublished PhD thesis (The Catholic University of America, 1986).

Jordanov, Ivan, *Corpus of Byzantine Seals from Bulgaria, 1: Byzantine Seals with Geographical Names* (Sofia, 2003).

Jordanov, Ivan, *Corpus of Byzantine Seals from Bulgaria, 2: Byzantine Seals with Family Names* (Sofia, 2006).

Jordanov, Ivan, *Corpus of Byzantine Seals from Bulgaria, 3.1* (Sofia, 2009).

Kazhdan, Alexander, Hagiographical Notes 2: On Horseback or on Foot? A 'Sociological' Approach in an Eleventh-Century Saint's Life, *Byzantion* 53 (1983) 544–545.

Koltsida-Makre, Ioanna, Philaretos Brachamios, Portrait of a Byzantine Official: An Unpublished Lead Seal in the Byzantine Museum of Phthiotis (Greece), *TM* 21/1 (2017) 325–332.

Konijnendjik, Roell and Fernando Echeverría, Max Weber, the Rise of the Polis, and the 'Hoplite Revolution' Theory, *Journal of the History of Ideas* 84 (2023) 103–125.

Konstantopoulos, Konstantinos M., *Βυζαντιακὰ μολυβδόβουλλα τοῦ ἐν Ἀθήναις Ἐθνικοῦ Νομισματικοῦ Μουσείου* (Athens, 1917).

Krsmanović, Bojana, *The Byzantine Province in Change (On the Threshold Between the 10th and the 11th Century)* (Belgrade, 2008).

Kühn, Hans-Joachim, *Die byzantinische Armee im 10. und 11. Jahrhundert. Studien zur Organisation der Tagmata*, Byzantinische Geschichtsschreiber, Ergänzungsband 2 (Vienna, 1991).

Laurent, Vitalien, *Les sceaux byzantins du Médaillier Vatican* (Vatican City, 1962).

Leidholm, Nathan, *Elite Byzantine Kinship, ca. 950–1204: Blood, Reputation, and the Genos* (Leeds, 2019).

Ludwig, Claudia, Social Mobility in Byzantium? Family Ties in the Middle Byzantine Period, in: Leslie Brubaker and Shaun Tougher (eds.), *Approaches to the Byzantine Family*, Birmingham Byzantine and Ottoman Studies 14 (Farnham, 2013) 233–245.

Makrypoulias, Christos G., Cities, Citizens and Sieges in the Balkans, 976–1018, in: Miša Rakocija (ed.), *Niš and Byzantium XIV* (Niš, 2016) 89–96.

Makrypoulias, Christos G., Boots on the ground: Byzantine Infantry in the Eleventh Century, in: Georgios Theotokis and Marek Meško (eds.), *War in Eleventh-Century Byzantium* (London, 2021) 241–266.

McGeer, Eric, *Sowing the Dragon's Teeth: Byzantine Warfare in the Tenth Century*, Dumbarton Oaks Studies 33 (Washington, D.C., 1995).

McGeer, Eric, John Nesbitt, and Nikos Oikonomides, *Catalogue of Byzantine Seals at Dumbarton Oaks and in the Fogg Museum of Art, 4: The East* (Washington, D.C., 2001).

McGeer, Eric, John Nesbitt, and Nikos Oikonomides, *Catalogue of Byzantine Seals at Dumbarton Oaks and in the Fogg Museum of Art, 5: The East (continued), Constantinople and Environs, Unknown Locations, Addenda, Uncertain Readings* (Washington, D.C., 2005).

Ménager, Léon-Robert, L'abbaye bénédictine de la Trinité de Mileto, en Calabre, à l'époque normande, *Bollettino dell'Archivio Paleografico Italiano*, n.s. 4/5 (1958–1959) 9–94.

Morillo, Stephen, The 'Age of Cavalry' Revisited, in: Donald J. Kagay and L. J. Andrew Villalon (eds.), *The Circle of War in the Middle Ages* (Woodbridge, 1999) 45–58.

Nesbitt, John and Nikos Oikonomides, *Catalogue of Byzantine Seals at Dumbarton Oaks and at the Fogg Museum of Art*, 1: *Italy, North of the Balkans, North of the Black Sea* (Washington, D.C., 1991).

Nesbitt, John and Nikos Oikonomides, *Catalogue of Byzantine Seals at Dumbarton Oaks and the Fogg Museum of Art*, 3: *West, Northwest, and Central Asia Minor and the Orient* (Washington, D.C., 1996).

Oikonomides, Nikos, Ὁ ταξιάρχης Κρήτης, *Ἀριάδνη* 5 (1989) 119–124.

Preiser-Kapeller, Johannes, Aristocrats, Mercenaries, Clergymen and Refugees: Deliberate and Forced Mobility of Armenians in the Early Medieval Mediterranean (6th to 11th Century A.D.), in: Johannes Preiser-Kapeller *et al.* (eds.), *Migration Histories of the Medieval Afroeurasian Transition Zone*, Studies in Global Migration History 39/13 (Leiden, 2020).

Preiser-Kapeller, Johannes, Lucian Reinfandt, and Yannis Stouraitis (eds.), *Migration Histories of the Medieval Afroeurasian Transition Zone*, Studies in Global Migration History 39/13 (Leiden, 2020).

Ragia, Efi, Social Group Profiles in Byzantium: Some Considerations on Byzantine Perceptions about Social Class Distinctions, *Byzantina Symmeikta* 26 (2016) 309–372.

Rance, Philip, *Campidoctores Vicarii vel Tribuni*: The Senior Regimental Officers in the Late Roman Army and the Rise of the *Campidoctor*, in: Ariel S. Lewin and Pietrina Pellegrini (eds.), *The Late Roman Army in the Near East from Diocletian to the Arab Conquest*, BAR International Series 1717 (Oxford, 2007) 395–409.

Rance, Philip, Maurice's *Strategicon* and 'the Ancients': The Late Antique Reception of Aelian and Arrian, in: Philip Rance and Nicholas V. Sekunda (eds.), *Greek Taktika: Ancient Military Writing and its Heritage* (Gdańsk 2017) 217–255.

Robinson, Gertrude, History and Cartulary of the Greek Monastery of S. Elias and S. Anastasius of Carbone, *Orientalia Christiana* 15 (1929) 121–275.

Rogers, Clifford J., The Military Revolutions of the Hundred Years' War, *The Journal of Military History* 57 (1993) 241–278.

Schmink, Andreas, Vier eherechtliche Entscheidungen aus dem 11. Jahrhundert, *Fontes Minores* 3 (1979) 221–279.

Seibt, Werner, Ταξίαρχος Μωξηγάζ – ein byzantinischer Kommandant in Mokkʼ um die Mitte des 11. Jahrhunderts?, *Handes Amsorya* (1993) 145–148.

Seibt, Werner, The Byzantine Thema of Soteroupolis-Anakopia in the 11th Century, *Bulletin of the Georgian National Academy of Sciences* 6 (2012) 174–178.

Seibt, Werner, The Theodorokanoi. Members of the Byzantine Military Aristocracy with an Armeno-Iberian Origin, *Studies in Byzantine Sigillography* 13 (2019) 81–91.

Seibt, Werner and Marie Louise Zarnitz, *Das byzantinische Bleisiegel als Kunstwerk* (Vienna, 1997).

Stavrakos, Christos, *Die byzantinischen Bleisiegel mit Familiennamen aus der Sammlung des Numismatischen Museums Athen*, Mainzer Veröffentlichungen zur Byzantinistik 4 (Wiesbaden, 2000).

Stavrakos, Christos, Unpublizierte Bleisiegel der Familie Maniakes: Der Fall Georgios Maniakes, *Studies in Byzantine Sigillography* 8 (2003) 101–111.

Stephenson, Paul, A Development in Nomenclature on the Seals of the Byzantine Provincial Aristocracy in the Late Tenth Century, *REB* 52 (1994) 187–211.

Stone, John, Technology, Society, and the Infantry Revolution of the Fourteenth Century, *The Journal of Military History* 68 (2004) 361–380.

Thierry, Nicole, Un style byzantin schématique de Cappadoce daté du XIe siècle d'après une inscription, *Journal des Savants* (1968) 45–61.

Thomas, John Philip, *Private Religious Foundations in the Byzantine Empire*, Dumbarton Oaks Studies 24 (Washington, D.C., 1987).

Viggiano, Gregory F., The Hoplite Revolution and the Rise of the Polis, in: Donald Kagan and Gregory F. Viggiano (eds.), *Men of Bronze. Hoplite Warfare in Ancient Greece* (Princeton, 2013), 112–133.

von Falkenhausen, Vera, *Untersuchungen über die byzantinische Herrschaft in Süditalien vom 9. bis ins 11. Jahrhundert* (Wiesbaden, 1967).

Wassiliou-Seibt, Alexandra-Kyriaki and Werner Seibt, *Die byzantinischen Bleisiegel in Österreich*, 2: *Zentral- und Provinzialverwaltung* (Vienna, 2004).

Whittow, Mark, *The Making of Orthodox Byzantium, 600–1025* (Berkeley, 1996).

Wilson, Lain, A Subaltern's Fate: The Office of Tourmarch, Seventh through Twelfth Century, *DOP* 69 (2015) 49–70.

Efi Ragia

Mutual Interest Groups in a Provincial Context

In his seminal work *People and Power in Byzantium*, Alexander Kazhdan suggested that research on Byzantium needed to escape from studying the institutions and shift to the people within them.[1] In the same year, he proposed a number of 'microstructures' that need to be examined for their significance in the context of Byzantine society. He defined these as groupings that worked below the surface of Byzantine history and could have influenced the evolution of Byzantine society or might have contained at least a part of the identity, beliefs, self-expression, and self-representation of people that belonged to the lower social strata: family, confraternities, monasteries, and villages or towns may be seen as such 'microstructures'.[2] Byzantium indeed inherited from antiquity a society that was multi-faceted, organised in groups or circles of people that partly overlapped each other. These worked as satellites around the main institutions and provided people with the necessary options for organising their daily and social life according to volition, ability, and perhaps social standing. Professional corporations, particular cults, expanded family networks, and clientele networks, are groupings that can be detected in the sources. While social position per se is important for the type of individual social self-projection, these circles that were inherent in, or interwoven with, ancient ways of life provided ancient societies with mobility below the surface and empowered individuals to pursue their interests and goals despite the apparent rigidity of the institutions and social stratification of the Roman empire.[3]

The present study focuses on groupings that have observed in non-urban Byzantine settings, whether in villages or rural towns outside Constantinople: namely, the village itself, the *phratriai/fatriai*, confraternities, and monasteries or churches built by individuals or communities. These are examined as clusters

---

1 Kazhdan and Constable, *People and Power*, 17.
2 Kazhdan, Microstructures, 3–11; *ODB*, s.v. Microstructures, 1371 (M. Bartusis).
3 The best treatise on Roman society is still Alföldy, *Römische Sozialgeschichte*, supplemented by Aries and Duby, *History*. Peachin, *Social Relations*, is a good starting point for understanding basic Roman social structures.

where particular bonds were forged among the participants, resulting from their common responsibilities, services or goals, and beliefs. The study is far from exhaustive – the absence of the main social unit, the family, is conspicuous, but impossible to address in a single paper. The information collected from the source material about social life in the provinces is both scanty and complex. Therefore, in order to avoid generalisations, the research presented here will take into consideration material about such mutual interest groups that concerns their operation in Constantinople, including legislative and sigillographic material. Although testimonies from the provinces are the starting point, the internal organisation of these groups, the rules or principles that regulated their formation, function, placement and role within a wider social context dominated by the centralised state, and the position of individuals within them, are the main areas focused on in this analysis. To achieve this, the present study attempts instead to interpret the complicated source material, and to suggest methods of approach that might be useful for future research.

The village: mutual interest groups in an agrarian context

The village (*chorion*) is the dominant grouping in the provinces. As a fiscal unit, the village is well known from the various archival, legal, and narrative sources.[4] However, as a small settlement with a small population, the village is a social microstructure as well, and a variety of relationships develop among its inhabitants. Because of this unity, the peasants (called *choritai* in the sources) are primarily obliged to exploit the lands and the natural resources belonging to the village and for this reason they enter into various relationships with their co-inhabitants, whether relatives or non-relatives. Thus, the *chorion* in reality fosters the growth of multiple links among the peasants, which develop outside the family. This observation explains why the state sees the village communities not only as macrostructures facilitating the collection of revenues, which is obvious in tax registers and *praktika*, but also as microstructures that contain a vast array of relationships, which are the subject of close examination in legislative sources, because they are important for social coherence.[5]

---

4 Kaplan, *Les hommes*, 95–101; Laiou, Byzantine Village, 31–54; Laiou-Thomadakis, *Peasant Society*, 33; Lemerle, *Agrarian History*, 37–38, 41, 76f.; Kyritses and Smyrlis, Villages, 439–445; Cheynet, *Le monde byzantin* 2, 235–238. The most succinct definition of the *chorion* is found in Dölger, *Finanzverwaltung*, 126, but Lefort, Rural Economy, 236–240, 275f., 281f., reassesses the research of the past few years and the direction it has taken.
5 See, for example *Novels of the Macedonian Emperors*, ed. Svoronos and Gounaridis, no. 4, esp. lines 80–90. This Novel of Constantine VII deals generally with social differences found inside villages and is rife with social terminology.

The state is not interested in the social roles of individuals and the relationships among them *per se*, but in their legal roles. This is apparently the reason why we find such information in the sources. For the state, a village is not simply inhabited by individuals, but by legal persons (*prosopa*) with an attached legal capacity according to their position, i. e. owner, dependent cultivator, slave.[6] The village itself is a juridical person, which acts collectively and lays claims to other persons, inside or outside the community, or other villages. The best-known example of such legal and collective action is the purchase of *clasmatic* land (fallow land, abandoned for over thirty years) from the state by the village of Hierissos in Chalkidike, dated to before 942. This affair, which lies at the origin of the foundation of Mt. Athos as a monastic community, caused multiple administrative complications, and some aspects relevant to this study will be discussed below.[7] However, even before the tenth century, the Farmer's Law makes provision for the possibility of dispute among entire villages, or with a single owner, over land exploitation. In these cases, the village itself is a community with legal agency.[8] In 995, the inhabitants of the *chorion* Siderokausia, close to Hierissos in Macedonia, dragged the monks of Kolobou monastery to the court of the *krites* of the theme of Strymon and Thessaloniki. In the document they are called *to koinon olon* (the entire community), or *koinotes* (community), or *to plethos* (the crowd), because so many of them had complaints against Kolobou.[9]

The disputes were solved with the aid of witnesses, who were normally chosen from among the elder or more trustworthy village dwellers. The settlement was quite often an affair of oral communication, negotiation, and agreement.[10] In the Farmer's Law, there is no hint that the assistance of legal experts called *nomikoi*, who were normally attached to a church or a bishopric, was required. Even when our documentation increases (tenth to eleventh centuries), it is far from certain that the rural communities had the assistance of a *nomikos*, or that there was easy access to a bishopric where legal assistance could be found. The free settlement of disputes between the implicated parties would at least spare them from the cost of appealing to the authorities. In these cases, the agreements took the form of an 'understanding among gentlemen'. Upholding them was predicated on the re-

---

6 Oikonomides, *Fiscalité*, 54. Oikonomides observes that in later times the *prosopa* are identified in documents with the rich and/or *dynatoi* (the powerful). However, the distinction and characterisation into *prosopa* is of Roman provenance and indicates the legal capacity of individuals. See Ragia, Social Group Profiles, 324–327.

7 *Actes du Protaton*, ed. Papachryssanthou, nos. 4.9–11, 5.1–4, 11–13; Lemerle, *Agrarian History*, 162. On the handling of the *clasmatic* lands by the state, see Oikonomides, Verfalland, 161–168. Neville, *Authority*, 94–98, sees the villages as 'collections of households'.

8 Ashburner, Farmer's Law, 98, nos. 2 and 7.

9 *Actes d'Iviron I*, ed. Lefort *et al.*, nos. 9.4, 23, 26, 28, 46. See Laiou, Byzantine Village, 47; Lefort, Rural Economy, 280, 284; Kaplan, *Les hommes*, 193–194, 201.

10 Papadatou, Επίλυση, 40–43.

spect of the parties involved for each other and the witnesses, and, in addition, the acknowledgement of the validity of the process. Such settlements could also be in a written form, whereby the documents are called 'assurance' (*asphaleia*) or 'resolution' (*dialysis*). These documents are common for ending private disputes, and are binding for all participants, but belong to the private sphere (they are not public acts produced in public procedures, e.g. in courts).[11]

A good example of such an *asphaleia* comes from the archive of the monastery of Megiste Lavra and dates from 1008. The document details the dispute about the use of a piece of land bought by the monastery of St. Akindynos from the peasants of Radochosta. It was drafted by a private individual, who signed with his best-known public qualification as 'nephew of the *tourmaches* and *spatharokandidatos* Nikolaos'. The peasants placed their *signa* at the top of the document (fourteen families are represented), and at the end the witnesses added their signatures: the aforementioned *spatharokandidatos* Nikolaos, a *droungarios*, an *oikodespotes*, and three clerics. Thus, although the village apparently lacked the services of a *nomikos*, its inhabitants completed, as a community, a perfectly lawful act that reveals the co-existence and collaboration of the members of the village from different levels of its social spectrum: village commoners, title-holders, owners of property (*oikodespotai*), and clerics of the parish.[12] In the case of 942, the peasants of the village of Hierissos and the monks of Mt. Athos decided to end the dispute between them about the land they both claimed, and came together under the auspices of the archbishop of Thessaloniki. The corresponding *asphaleia* is preserved in the Protaton archive of Mt. Athos.[13] In 1293, the peasants of Neochorion, near Smyrna (mod. Izmir) in western Asia Minor, committed themselves to never trespass on the land of the monastery of Lembos. The document begins with the names of the leading figures of the village and is characterised as 'letter of promise' (*hyposchetiki graphe)* by the peasants themselves.[14]

In modern bibliography, the common activities of the village inhabitants are given little attention in comparison with joint tax liability. While there is no way of knowing how much time and labour these activities required, it is obvious that they were very important for community life. According to the Farmer's Law, a

---

11 See Papadatou, *Επίλυση*, 43–48, and 34–35, 36, regarding the terminology.

12 *Actes de Lavra I*, ed. Lemerle *et al.*, no. 14; Lemerle, *Agrarian History*, 164–165; Kaplan, *Les hommes*, 194; Neville, *Authority*, 96. With this document the village confirms the purchase of land close to the castle by the monks of St. Akindynos and proceeds to its delimitation (*periorismos*) because it had not been applied before (which was the reason of the dispute). See generally Kaplan, *Les hommes*, 198–203, on the significance of the most distinguished inhabitants of the village as agents for legal actions, and specifically Laiou, Peasant as Donor, 117–118.

13 *Actes du Protaton*, ed. Papachryssanthou, no. 4; Kaplan, *Les hommes*, 193.

14 *MM IV*, 231–232, no. 145. The case is dated to 1293.

village could claim as community property buildings that had been erected by individuals on their own initiative on community land, on condition that the *choritai* would reimburse the owner for his expenses. As is explicitly stated, this practice led to *koinonia*, which means that the community effectively became partner, or co-owner, of the asset.[15] From the documents of the archives of Mt. Athos, we learn that the peasants, based on ancient custom, also claimed the co-exploitation of land allotted to monasteries. In this case, they made certain that their right was recorded in official documents. Around 920, the peasants of Hierissos had collectively rented land of two thousand *modioi* from the monastery of Kolobou. In the village of Dobrovikeia in Macedonia, two mills are indicated as community installations.[16] In this context, apart from pasturelands, wine and oil presses would have been very important, but our evidence is scanty. The Farmer's Law mentions that undivided, free (therefore communal) land could at some point be divided and allotted to farmers.[17] The farmers also claimed access to springs and rivers, and reacted strongly when the use of water was restricted by the intervention of other individuals or villages. In these cases, the law supported the farmers; there are at least three cases concerning the use of water which record sentences passed against the initiatives of individuals and monasteries which were harmful to communities: in Siderokausia (close to Hierissos), in Crete, and in the Strymon area.[18] Conversely, the Farmer's Law contains no restriction with relation to the building of such installations, on condition that the *choritai* would not suffer. The community could divide, and allocate to peasants, common land belonging to the *chorion*, and the new owners could erect mills on their plots without risking the danger of other peasants raising claims based on the former, common status of the land.[19] Thus, in Siderokausia the community, *to plethos*, decided to allow the priest of the parish to rebuild his mill on the land that was given to the village, after his claims were rejected by the monks of Kolobou.[20] The procedures relating to the ownership of the little monastery of Spondai on the island of Kos suggest that the peasants used the water that belonged to it when the monastery was abandoned. Later,

---

15 Ashburner, Farmer's Law, 107, no. 81; Lemerle, *Agrarian History*, 43–44.

16 *Actes de Lavra I*, ed. Lemerle *et al.*, no. 2; *Actes d' Iviron I*, ed. Lefort *et al.* no. 1, 30.26, 31. See Lefort, Rural Economy, 280, 308. In *Actes de Lavra I*, ed. Lemerle *et al.*, no. 3, the sale of *clasmatic* land is secured on condition that the ancient rights of the farmers be maintained.

17 Ashburner, Farmer's Law, 102, no. 32.

18 *Actes d'Iviron I*, ed. Lefort *et al.*, nos. 9.46–47; *MM VI*, 95–97 no. 23 (1118); *Actes de Chilandar*, ed. Petit,167–168 no. 76, 238–239 no. 115. See Laiou-Thomadakis, *Peasant Society*, 62, and, specifically on the case of Chilandar monastery: Laiou and Simon, Of Mills and Monks, 1–50. On the management of waters see: Gerolymatou, La gestion de l'eau, 195–205.

19 Ashburner, Farmer's Law, 108, nos. 82, 83; Lemerle, *Agrarian History*, 43. According to stipulation 83, if a mill damages the fields, its function should be suspended.

20 *Actes d'Iviron I*, ed. Lefort *et al.*, nos. 9.55–58; Kaplan, *Les hommes*, 205.

they made sure that Spondai was given to the monastery of St. John Theologos of Patmos. Presumably, the monastery would be a better landlord than the local bishop or a random owner. Among the documents pertaining to this complicated affair, we find a *deesis* (petition) of the peasants to the emperor. This remarkable document begins with the signatures of no fewer than eighty-three farmers, clerics, and officials of Kos.[21]

Thus, there can be no doubt that common agrarian exploitation fostered the growth of solidarity within village populations. However, separate units also develop within populations, because of social differentiation and inequality. Notwithstanding any factors encouraging solidarity, social difference was indicated above in the case of the village of Radochosta, where people of different social positions came together in the role of witnesses. Social and civic aspects of communal life, such as legal procedures, were organised by state officials and also by churches, the latter usually possessing the staff responsible for these tasks. The leading witnesses were always people from the upper social stratum and the elderly of a *chorion*. Therefore, their social position and old age enhanced their credibility, as the legislation required, and they signed first.[22] But the numerous signatures which appear below those of the notables involve a wide range of individuals of specific social standing in procedures that had to be recognised by co-villagers, neighbours, and the state itself. Already in the Farmer's Law there is mention of the *martyres* (witnesses) or the *akroatai* (witnesses, or judges), without further specification. Their involvement in cases of civic law is necessary for validating the procedures.[23] The title of the aforementioned *deesis* of the inhabitants of Kos declares that it is made by 'the inhabitants of the island of Kos, the military and the entire community (*to koinon tou laou*), and the servants and slaves' of the emperor, which neatly corresponds to the distinction of these groups in the order of signatures.[24] In 1296, the inhabitants of Kometissa were required to attest to the boundaries between lands belonging to the monasteries of Vatopedi and Chilandar. The most important among them (twenty-one individuals) are mentioned by name, and two of them were signaled because they were over seventy years of age. As in the aforementioned cases, the farmers are differentiated as 'the priests, the elders (*gerontes*), the proprietors (*oikodespotai*),

---

21 *Patmos Inscriptions 2*, ed. Nystazopoulou-Pelekidou, no, 75. See in detail Gerolymatou, Origines, 387–399.

22 See Ragia, Social Group Profiles, 324–327, 330–331, with references. When the 'upper social strata' are discussed in such a limited context, aristocratic provenance is not an essential condition. See also Laiou, Byzantine Village, 47–48; Kyritses and Smyrlis, Villages, 445–446; Kaplan, *Les hommes*, 193–194.

23 Ashburner, Farmer's Law, 98, nos. 3, 7; 106, no. 67.

24 *Patmos Inscriptions*, ed. Nystazopoulou-Pelekidou, no. 75.α-β.

and the rest of the people (*loipos laos*)', or, inclusively 'the younger and the older' (*mikroi kai megaloi*).[25]

Communal feeling ultimately legalises these actions, and places the legal procedures and even the economic activity in a community framework. However, as the tax burden of abandoned land and its exploitation was shared by the village community, it is not surprising that economic and social activities overlap at least partly within a *chorion* and in the context of joint fiscal liability.[26] For example, members of the same family could expect a share in the inheritance, but if they did not divide it among themselves, they were effectively co-owners of their farms. Transmitting property from generation to generation could over time result in an accumulation of legal rights on small parcels of land. The division of the properties tied to supporting military service illustrates this process.[27] The cartulary of the Theotokos of Lembos monastery near Smyrna (mod. Izmir) also contains related evidence dated to the thirteenth century. John Chante, with his brothers Michael and Basil (and Basil's wife and son) and his sisters Maria and Kale, sold twenty-two olive trees; Kale Tyrannina and five co-owners alienated a significant plot of land. In Priene, a piece of land was sold by its seven co-owners, who placed their *signa* at the top of the sale contract along with those of their wives, brothers, sons, and daughters; only two of the owners have the same surname. Had the document not been mutilated it might have been similar to that found in a document of Lembiotissa regarding a mill: 'because there are too many of us and we are not able to put to good use the functions of the water mill and we have strife among ourselves, we abandoned it and it was ruined'. In this case, it was fifteen co-owners belonging to at least three families, including children, brothers, and sons- and daughters-in-law, who decided to sell the mill and end the strife. When such accumulation of rights occurs, alienating the property seems indeed to be the only solution.[28]

When there is information about communal resources – i. e. the exploitation of fallow land, or natural water springs – questions relating to cooperation practices and labour issues among the villagers independent of familial ties also emerge. In the Farmer's Law, the communities are made up of owners, lessees or *paroikoi*, and the poor, but they are all indiscriminately called *georgoi* (farmers)

---

25 *Actes de Vatopédi*, no. 26.

26 The fiscal process relating to abandoned land and its fiscal obligations is ancient and was known as *epibole*. In later sources, we find the term ἀλληλεγγύως referring to joint tax liability. See Dölger, *Finanzverwaltung*, 128–130; Lemerle, *Agrarian History*, 7–8, 79–80; Oikonomides, *Fiscalité*, 55–56; Kaplan, *Les hommes*, 188.

27 Ragia, Social Position, 148–151, 159–160.

28 *MM IV*, 64–65, no. 19; 174–175, no. 98; 196–197, no. 113; *Hiéra-Xérochoraphion cartulary*, ed. Wilson and Darrouzès, 39, no. 14. See Laiou, Byzantine Village, 49–52; Lefort, Rural Economy, 244–245, 247–248; Kyritses and Smyrlis, Villages, 447–448.

because what binds them together is the cultivation of the village lands.[29] Multiple stipulations concern paid workers who found employment as shepherds (*poimen misthotos*), and slaves (*douloi*); these categories apparently make up the lower social strata in a *chorion*.[30] In the monastic archives of the tenth to eleventh centuries, we find examples of cooperation among farmers that are not pre-dicated upon social equality within the *chorion*. In 1076/7, the monastery of Peristera in Thessaloniki agreed to buy the vines the *paroikoi* had planted on lands that Peristera claimed for itself. Interestingly, a total number of thirty peasants signed with their *signa* at the beginning of the document as co-owners of the vines and guarantors of the agreement with the monastery. It has been suggested that the number of the individuals involved in this sale represents the total number of the inhabitants of the *chorion*. However, it only relates to part of the village, since the priests appear on behalf of the inhabitants.[31] Similarly, in the *asphaleia* of the Protaton (942) that we have seen above, the 'hegoumenoi [of local monasteries] with the peasants on behalf of the entire community of the country [of Hierissos]' proceeded to this arrangement with the monks of Mt. Athos regarding the fallow lands of Hierissos.[32] It is impossible to know whether the land mentioned in the act of Protaton is the same land as that bought by thirteen peasants of Hierissos before 942. These peasants were not of equal social status, and their plots varied from fifty to two hundred and fifty *modioi*. Nonetheless, the administrative case involving them was one and the same. Apparently, the peasants had bought the land by paying a lump sum to the state and divided the plots among themselves according to their financial situation.[33] Thus, within the communities themselves, there are elements that break the unity and create separate circles of co-operation and solidarity according to shared interests, which may only partly overlap in the context of a *chorion*.

The introduction of the institution of *pronoia*, along with the expansion of estate exploitation, favoured such mutual interest groups that were effectively separate from the *chorion*, and diluted social differences within the land grants of the *pronoia* holders. The village of Bare, with its attached *proasteia* close to

---

29 Ashburner, Farmer's Law, 98, nos. 2, 9, 10; in nos. 11, 12, 14, and 18, poor farmers are mentioned (ἀπορήσαντος γεωργοῦ, 'impoverished farmer'). This category is not the same as the well-known *penetes* (poor) of the tenth century, a category that was defined by law. See Ragia, Social Group Profiles, 326–331, 341–348, with bibliography.
30 Ashburner, Farmer's Law, 102, no. 34; 103, nos. 45–47; 106, nos. 71, 72. Shepherds guarding cows and oxen are called *agelarioi: ibid.*, 101, nos. 23–29.
31 *Actes de Lavra I*, ed. Lemerle *et al.*, no. 37; Lemerle, *Agrarian History*, 165.
32 *Actes du Protaton*, ed. Papachryssanthou, no. 4.7–8. Four peasants from Hierissos and one from Ravenikeia along with the abbots of three local monasteries represented the community.
33 *Actes de Xéropotamou*, ed. Bompaire, no. 1. In 956, the plots were given to the monastery of Xeropotamou because the land had been sold at half its price. See Oikonomides, Verfalland, 165–166.

Miletus in Asia Minor, was granted to Andronikos Doukas in 1073. Only fourteen families were registered in the *praktikon* as inhabitants of the *chorion* of Bare. The remaining cultivators lived either in the *proasteia* (estates, of which six were granted to Doukas) or in the surrounding villages, and were listed separately. It is telling that the *proasteion* of Prinos was 'found uninhabited', but the village of Prinos, to which the *proasteion* had originally belonged, was not part of the grant.[34] Thus, although the economic engagement of the peasants appears to divide them and form into clusters according to the *proasteion* they inhabited and cultivated, they are still seen as an entity that served the particular financial interests of Andronikos Doukas specifically. The examples, of course, multiply in the thirteenth century, as the *praktika* (registers of properties and workforce) of the Athonite monasteries begin to increase. Although entire villages had been granted to the great monasteries, the cases where village unity broke down because the farmers were given as a workforce to different beneficiaries are more telling. The monastery of Xenophon only had four *paroikoi* in the village of Hierissos, which belonged primarily to the Lavra, but also partly to Iviron; and Esphigmenou only possessed half the village of Portarea before the emperor Michael VIII Palaiologos also granted it the other half. In the *pronoia* system, farmers from different settlements worked for a single beneficiary, who could change in the course of time. The succession of *pronoia* beneficiaries resulted in the reshuffling of the agrarian workforce and the re-formation of those clusters of cooperation among the farmers.[35] Thus, the importance of social boundaries among the peasants decreased, because their workforce only mattered in the context of each allocation. While the village remained a stable social unit, the *pronoiai* were made, but also regularly dissolved, and the farmers of new *pronoiai* often came from different villages. Therefore, the unity of the village broke down in favour of the financing of the *pronoiai*, and the separate interest groups formed among the peasants served different ends that transcended the limits of the *chorion*.[36]

Several examples illustrate the theoretical framework described above. In an agrarian context, the process of exploiting or claiming land is almost a natural phenomenon. The farmers tended to expand their activities. The most noted cases of mutual interest groups with the purpose of expansion are those of the Sampsenoi (*paroikoi* of the Sampson estate in western Asia Minor) and the tax

---

34 *Patmos Inscriptions* 2, ed. Nystazopoulou-Pelekidou, no. 50. See Lefort, Rural Economy, 305. On the villages of Bare and Prinos, see Ragia, Κοιλάδα, 141–142, 198, and 408–409, 450–451 on the *episkepsis* of Alopekai.
35 *Actes de Xénophon*, ed. Papachryssanthou, no. 12; *Actes d'Ésphigménou*, ed. Lefort, no. 6. Many more examples can be detected in the archival material of the period. See Ragia, Agrarian Policy, 513–515, 519–520.
36 C.f. Cheynet , *Le monde byzantin* 2, 222–225, 238–241 and Lefort, Rural Economy, 240–243.

contributors of the *pronoiarios* Syrgares, near Smyrna. Both date from the beginning of the thirteenth century. I have dealt extensively with the Sampson case
elsewhere. In 1211, the Sampsenoi were condemned by the court for their un-
authorised expansion outside their own fields.[37] Some of the tax contributors of
Syrgares, who came from the village of Potamos and occupied the location
Sphournou for more than twenty years (c. 1212 until 1235/6), were partially
vindicated in their claim to the land. Their case was examined on multiple levels.
Upon completion, the related acts formed a separate dossier in the Lembiotissa
archive, which shows that farmers could become particularly assertive when it
came to claiming their own rights and protecting their own interests. It is worth
noting that the farmers of the neighbouring villages, Rouze and Drous, testified
against them, apparently because they too claimed the same piece of land. Some
of them – if not all – were even *paroikoi* of Syrgares.[38]

In the *pronoia* system, the income allotted to the *pronoiarioi*, which is established by a *praktikon* of delivery, comes from sources that usually display a
narrow geographical dispersion. The *pronoiarioi* themselves were usually not of
aristocratic provenance. Most of them came from a middle social stratum, but
they differed fundamentally from the agrarian population, because they were in
the service of the Byzantine state. Therefore, their social standing was quite
different from that of the farmers.[39] In reality, then, the expansion of the funding
system of the *pronoia* in the twelfth century consolidated the protection that the
privileged beneficiaries of a *pronoia* income, such as Syrgares, could offer to the
farmers, and framed it in a context different to that of the *archontike prostasia*.[40]
In the eleventh century, before the expansion of the *pronoia* system, Kekaumenos
described this form of *prostasia* and the cases where an *archon* (to be understood
better as a member of the aristocracy rather than a person of authority) might
intervene. In Kekaumenos' work, the aristocratic descent of the *archon* is taken
for granted, but he describes the relationship of an *archon* with 'the people' (*o

---

37 *Cartulary of St Paul, Latros*, ed. Gastgeber and Kresten, 46–71 no. 1; Ragia, *Λάτρος*, 165–190.
    Also see below.
38 *MM* IV, 32–43, no. 7. On the parties involved see esp. *MM* IV, 34, no. 7.3; 38, no. 7.4. The
    decision is in accordance with a stipulation of the Farmer's Law. See Ashburner, Farmer's
    Law, 100, no. 21; c.f. Lemerle, *Agrarian History*, 179–180. In the final decision of the met-
    ropolitan bishop of Smyrna, the right of the farmers to claim reimbursement was acknowl-
    edged and Lembos was obliged to concede the allotment of a parcel of land where the
    Potamenoi could re-erect their huts.
39 Lemerle, *Agrarian History*, 222f. Still valuable is Ahrweiler, Concession, 103–114, esp. 109–
    112 about this type of reimbursement and its distinctions. The relatively recent monograph of
    Bartusis, *Land and Privilege*, collects all the information, scrutinises the evolution of the
    institution, and analyses the different grants.
40 Saradi, Prostasia, 69–117, 314–351; Ragia, Social Group Profiles, 331–341, with references.
    Also see, in a different spirit, Kyritses and Smyrlis, Villages, 447.

laos tes choras), not with the *paroikoi*.[41] The *pronoiarioi*, however, were not aristocrats, and the *pronoia* created bonds of a legal-economic nature between the peasants and the *pronoia* holder, which was not a necessary condition in the previous period. On the contrary, from the twelfth century onwards, the *pronoiarioi* were called to represent and defend the taxpayers whose taxes had been included in their grant of land. Asia Minor again offers eloquent examples. Irene Botaneiataina Doukaina Komnene, beneficiary of the Sampson estate in the twelfth century, was called upon by the abbot of the monastery of Hiera to restrain her *paroikoi* from trespassing on the land of the monastery; Irene Branaina was called to adjudicate in the Sphournou case; the uncle of Michael VIII Palaiologos, George Angelos, rushed to represent his own *paroikoi* against the monastery of Patmos. When one of the peasants of Bare, close to Smyrna, appealed to Syrgares regarding the exploitation of a significant number of olive trees, the latter duly called upon 'the most prominent landholders of his *pronoia*' (*tous oikodespotas tes pronoias autou*) to come to a decision. It is interesting that the expression employed here is almost identical to expressions of the tenth to eleventh centuries, but it is applied in the context of a *pronoia*, meaning within the framework of a simple *praktikon* relating to income delivery, not in connection with a *chorion*.[42] We also see the contributors to the *pronoiai* of different beneficiaries, those of Syrgares and the governor (*prokathemenos*) of Smyrna, Konstantinos Alopos, acting as witnesses in the same process.[43]

It becomes clear, then, that the allotment of *pronoiai* resulted in mobilisation of farmers, enabling an increase in cultivation. The result of this type of mediation is particularly evident in the case of the Sampsenoi. The following comment, found in the acts relating to their affairs, is unique in the Byzantine sources: 'the *paroikoi* of the Sampson estate have always been powerful because they have been supported, dominated, and commanded by important people and relatives of the emperors'.[44] The involvement of the notables in such cases of trespass did not alter the outcome of the processes, nor did they replace the state and its

---

41 Kekaumenos, *Consilia et Narrationes*, ed. Spadaro, 182 ch. 133. See Ragia, Social Group Profiles, 336–337.

42 *MM IV*, 81–85, no. 38 and c.f. 239–244, no. 150; *Hiéra-Xérochoraphion cartulary*, ed. Wilson and Darrouzès, 31–34 no. 9; *Patmos Inscriptions 1*, ed. Vranouse, no. 30. Another soldier, Kalegopoulos, was forced to renounce the claim of his own *paroikoi* on the exploitation of the river. See generally Laiou-Thomadakis, *Peasant Society*, 62–63, although the author makes no distinction between village inhabitants and farmers paying their taxes to *pronoiarioi*. Of all these documents, only that of Hiéra is a private document drafted by one of the estate managers of Sampson on the orders of Anna Botaneiataina; the rest were drafted after the corresponding public procedures. See Ragia, Κοιλάδα, 422.

43 *MM IV*, 38, no. 7.IV.

44 *Hiéra-Xérochoraphion cartulary*, ed. Wilson and Darrouzès, 13–15, nos. 1, 2; 19–20, no. 5.12–14; Ragia, Κοιλάδα, 455–457; Ragia, Didyma, 142.

employees, or even the peasants who could plead their own case. Nonetheless, it emboldened the peasants, although the interest groups formed only represented one part of the community to which they belonged; specifically, the part which had been allocated to the beneficiaries.

Violence, agrarian communities, and the soldiers

Another aspect that needs to be addressed in the context of agrarian communities is the question of the expanded family and its ties, and its relation to the existence of soldiers and the exercise of violence in the community. Romanos I Lakapenos' Novel of 928 signals the existence of violence coming not from the powerful, but from the *synchoritai* (co-villagers). Either themselves, or through the actions of their relatives, the peasants are noted for their occasional violence against their neighbours. According to the law, these actions were even 'premeditated' (*ek pronoias*).[45] As there is no corroborating evidence about this assertion from the same period, we have to wait for the archive of the Lembiotissa monastery, which dates from the thirteenth century and contains precious information regarding the violence that might develop in the context of agrarian communities. When the monastery was renovated by John III Vatatzes in the 1220s, it was found that the peasants of the village Prinovaris claimed a field of the neighbouring village of Bare, which had been allocated to the Lembiotissa. They found a suitable opportunity to usurp it in the abbot's absence and 'came with bows and many weapons and sowed the field with all the oxen pairs of their village in a single day'.[46] In a similar fashion, Soterichos Pothos and his brother-in-law Manteianos, who were family to a certain Konstomares, and 'their relatives', threatened the monks of Lembiotissa with murder if they dared go into the disputed plots and vineyards. While there is no evidence that they ever realised their threats, it is by such means, after they had sowed the fields and planted vines, that they managed to hold on to the land apparently from 1235 to at least 1260. In 1256 the emperor noted in an *horismos* that 'other locals' had also seized the opportunity and tried to seize other assets of the monastery.[47]

The most blatant case of violence in the agrarian communities of Smyrna concerns the *paroikoi* of the *parakoimomenos* Konstantinos Doukas Nestoggos,

---

45 *Novels of the Macedonian Emperors*, ed. Svoronos and Gounaridis, 66.55–60 (no. 2). The Novel essentially re-establishes within a logical legal context the rights of relatives and neighbours regarding estates in the alienation process (the *protimesis*), on which see Papagianni, Protimesis, 1071–1982.

46 *MM IV*, 187–189, no. 107, esp. 188. The document dates to 1228.

47 *MM IV*, 247–248, no. 154. Documents no 120–125 (*MM IV*, 206–213) also concern the same case and somewhat clarify the kinship among the members involved in this dispute.

a very powerful man in Michael VIII Palaiologos' government. The farmers beat up the monks; killed a horse worth eighteen gold coins; broke into the monastery's warehouses and stole oil, olives, and wheat; destroyed a load of the monastery's olive oil by breaking the vessels; stole cheese; let their livestock free in the pastures at night; and, just before harvest in August of the year 1276, burned the monastery's vines. In the reports a murder is also mentioned, and life-threatening situations involving a lance and the drawing of a knife as well. This may be considered yet another example of a type of solidarity developed under the influence of a powerful man, but it is also an example of the kinds of actions to which conflicting economic interests could lead farmers. This makes the remarks of emperor Romanos I Lakapenos seem relevant still in the late thirteenth century. We do not learn anything about the punishment of the *paroikoi*, but Nestoggos himself, to whom the monks initially appealed, did not care enough to chastise his *paroikoi*, perhaps because he was protecting his farmers' interests.[48]

In the context of the village community, soldiers are recognised as potentially powerful and even dangerous, as is explicitly stated in Novel 4 of Constantine VII.[49] The soldiers of the middle Byzantine period live in their villages; they are practiced in the use of weapons, enjoy tax reliefs, receive reimbursements and awards for their service, and have a share in the spoils of war. In the tenth century, many soldiers present themselves to the army together with their *hyperetoumenoi*, who are to be understood as assistants or squires. According to Constantine VII, there was a distinction between soldiers who were attached for operational reasons to the service of the military commanders and officers, and those who came from outside the army, in particular those who 'belonged to a village community' (*tes koinotetos*), who were simple peasants.[50] At about the same time, Nikephoros II Phokas, in *De velitatione bellica*, stated that 'the soldiers' households and those of the soldiers serving them [*tōn hyperetoumenōn autois*] and everyone about them should enjoy complete freedom' from the payment of taxes.[51] The soldiers' status, their social position, and their image in the sources, is certainly a complicated issue, but it is clear that Nikephoros Phokas claimed soldier status for the *hyperetoumenoi*, who Constantine VII explicitly thought that they belonged to the village communities. These hints suggest the creation of obligations and possibly the establishment of clientele

---

48 *MM IV*, 257–260, nos. 163–164. See Ragia, Agrarian Policy, 542–543.
49 *Novels of the Macedonian Emperors*, ed. Svoronos and Gounaridis, 102.82–83 (no. 4), and no. 5, which establishes well the social and economic differences among soldiers. It is worth underscoring the fact that by 947 the soldiers of the Scholae or Tagmata (professional corps) were included among the *dynatoi* (the powerful). See *Novels of the Macedonian Emperors*, ed. Svoronos and Gounaridis, 120.39–40.
50 *Novels of the Macedonian Emperors*, ed. Svoronos and Gounaridis, 126.149–157 (no. 5).
51 Dennis, *Three Byzantine Military Treatises*, 216.37–39.

networks in the provinces, which may connect either the *choritai* to soldiers within the community, or soldiers of the community with officers outside of it.[52]

Analysing the bonds created among the soldiers of the region of Smyrna based on the archive of Lembiotissa is a subject in its own right. It is, however, worth underscoring that bonds of collegiality among soldiers or even with the peasants because of their profession were usually strengthened by marriage. Therefore, it is not surprising that they appear to form strong groups within their villages and to belong to the notables of the province. Often, groups of soldiers act as witnesses to procedures, while it is implied or even stated that they belong to the decision-making group in the investigations. This was the case when the monasteries of Lembiotissa and Stylos decided to settle a dispute between themselves in 1266. In 1280, the soldiers made up a group distinct from the landowners of the village of Mantaia in the settlement of the dispute of a certain Phokas with the monastery. Violence is also attested in the case of the soldier Varycheir, Nikephoros Pharissaios, and their relatives, who rejected the settlement with the Lembiotissa and even 'drew their swords' against the monks over a piece of land. The documents relating to this affair, which has a long history, are dated to 1259, but we find Pharissaios among the judges of the dispute of 1280, along with a person we have already seen above, also in connection with acts of violence, George Manteianos.[53]

But it is a single piece of advice to an abbot, dated to the twelfth century, that exemplifies what Constantine VII reports in tenth century. The soldiers settled in the lands allotted by the *sebastokrator* Isaakios Komnenos to the monastery of Kosmosoteira in Thrace had apparently exhibited shameless and disobedient behaviour, 'emboldened, perhaps, by their military calling'. Isaakios, however, advised the abbot to treat them politely and even invite them to his table, because 'with their support he should be strong enough to drive off those who have settled themselves around our villages and wish out of greed to attack them with violence [...]. For these soldiers are capable of being of assistance to the monastery, and of warding off evildoers, and are extremely beneficial'.[54] Obviously, these soldiers trusted in their own position and the use of their weapons, and solidarity among them was strengthened by the fact that Isaakios first, and then the monastery, substituted for the state as collectors of their taxes.[55] Isaakios readily realised that they could serve the monastery by using their strength and their weapons. This is in fact an example of social interdependence in the making.

---

52 Ragia, Social Position, 165–166.
53 *MM IV*, 93–94, no. 38; 128–129, no. 60; 153–157, nos. 62–64.
54 *Typikon of the Kosmosoteira*, ed. Papazoglou, 145.2004–218; Thomas and Hero, *Byzantine Monastic Foundation Documents* 2, 846.
55 Lemerle, *Agrarian History*, 237–238. The author implies that the soldiers were landowners themselves.

The phratriae/fatriae

In the *Life of St. Euthymios the Younger* (tenth century) we read: 'His parents were of good family (*eupatrides*) and righteous at the same time, and urged each other on in virtue to such an extent that each was competing to see which one would carry off the first prize of virtue from the other; for they did not envy each other's advancement (*anabaseos*), but zeal spurred them on, and their rivalry was a positive one (*eris... agathe*) and a group (*fatria*) formed around them that was spiritually beneficial and desirable not only for those who lived in the same village, but also for those who had as their lot a life and property far away'.[56] The uniqueness of the extract lies in the fact that the author frames the military or social-military targets of the family (*anabasis*, promotion, or social advancement in a more general sense) in an ancient context (*eupatrides, fatria*). Further on in the *Life* it is specified that Euthymios' family is in fact subject to the military *strateia*.[57] As a term, *anabasis* characterises those rising through the ranks in the military or civil administrative offices.[58] The question whether the *fatria* refers to the nuclear family of St. Euthymios or to his extended family living in the same village or in the wider area is open to interpretation. The doubt derives from the fact that in antiquity the *phratria* was a family-based religious association, which united extended families around a particular cult,[59] while the competition de-scribed in the *Life of St. Euthymios the Younger* concerns two different fields of social distinction, the military and the religious. It is hard to believe that this competition would be even remotely commendable within an exclusively familial context; on the contrary, it appears that this particular family was apparently an example for the inhabitants of Galatia because it strove for the military and social distinction for itself and its surrounding *fatria*.

The *phratria/fatria* in Byzantium is an interesting research topic, mostly be-cause of the interweaving of the ancient Greek, family-based *phratria* with an-cient Roman concepts which include notions of clientele relationships and po-litical subversion, and in particular the Roman *factio*. As such, the *fatria* can be found all over the empire, although it is not exclusive to aristocratic contexts. We shall even see below that the problem is also related to the Roman *collegia*, whose subversive activities were condemned by Roman laws. For this reason, the term is

---

56 *Life of Euthymios the Younger*, ed. Petit, 16.20–26; Greenfield and Talbot, Holy Men of Athos, 9–11. I have removed the description from 'advancement' to conform with the military and social (not spiritual) connotations of the extract.

57 *Life of Euthymios the Younger*, ed. Petit, 16.28–29.

58 C.f. Procopius, *Historia arcana*, ed. Haury and Wirth, 151.30–152.17; Psellos, *Chronographia*, ed. Reinsch, 119–120 ch. 29.13–16, 219 ch. 28.7–8. The term is rather rare and the *Life of Euthymios the Younger* provides one of the few examples.

59 Pollucis, *Onomasticon*, ed. Bethe, 171.9–14.

ambivalent in almost all sources and environments in which it appears. The *factio* is addressed, for example in the sections of the *Basilica* relating to crimes, where the term is directly translated from the *Digesta*, but is also recognised by Canon Law: 'the crime of conspiracy or *phratria* is also punished by secular laws'.[60] The sentence for 'conspiracy or *phratria*' is in most cases death – for example, for cases occurring in the army,[61] or against a member of the senate. In these cases, it is combined with property confiscation and also affects the descendants of those convicted.[62]

The ambivalence and inconclusiveness of the sources regarding the correct interpretation of the term *fatria/phratria* also appears in the Lexica. In Hesychius' Lexicon, the *phratores* are recognised as relatives, but they are also called *hetairoi* or *symmachoi* (comrades, allies), although the *fatria* is qualified as *syntagma* or *systema* (corps or corporation, guild).[63] Hesychius was probably the source for Photius' *Lexicon*, the *Suda*, and other sources, where the *symmoria* (crew, or even gang) is explained as *syntagma* or *fatria*.[64] Stephanus Byzantius, however, is much more analytical and explicit: according to his entry, *phratria, phratriazo,* signified the wider family and included its common meals, which took place in honour, commemoration, or remembrance of its common origin and religious background.[65] For the Romans, nevertheless, the name also signified a *kinema* (movement, conspiracy, or even revolt). This difference between the ancient Greek and Roman perceptions of the value of the wider family is recorded in Cassius Dio. It is possible that his text influenced later interpretations by abandoning the attempt to distinguish between the wider family and conspiracy, as he combines the *phratriai* with the *hetaireiai, adelphotetes,* and *systemata*.[66] Apparently, already by the fourth century the term *fatria* had

---

60 *Digesta*, ed. Krueger, 48.19.11; *Basilica*, ed. Scheltema *et al.*, 60.51.11; *Acts of Chalcedon*, ed. Schwartz,161.24–25. The *Ecloga*, ed. Burgmann, contains an entire chapter, no. 17, titled περὶ φατριαστῶν.

61 Maurice, *Strategikon*, ed. Dennis and Gamillscheg, 94.19–22.

62 *Corpus Iuris Civilis*, II, ed. Krueger, 9.8.5; *Basilica*, ed. Scheltema *et al.*, 60.36.19.

63 Hesychius, *Lexicon*, ed. Latte *et al.*, Φ no. 234: φατρία· σύνταγμα, σύστημα; no. 848: φράτορας· τοὺς τῆς αὐτῆς μετέχοντας φρατρίας, συγγενεῖς; no. 849: φράτορσιν· ἑταίροις, συμμάχοις. Also see no. 880: φρήτηρ· ἀδελφός, and c.f. nos. 233 and 882.

64 *Synagoge*, ed. Cunningham, 450 σ. 296: συμμορία· σύνταγμα ἢ φατρία; C.f. 495, φ. 59: φατρία· σύνταγμα. C.f. Photius, *Lexicon*, ed. Theodorides, 583 nos. 289, 290; 584 no. 291; *Suda*, ed. Adler, 704.11–20 (Σ 136).

65 Stephen of Byzantium, *Ethnica*, ed. Billerbeck and Neumann-Hartmann, 48–49 no 99.

66 Cassius Dio, *Historiae Romanae*, ed. Boissevain, 10.1–6: λέγονται δὲ καθ᾽ Ἕλληνας αἱ κουρίαι φρατρίαι καὶ φατρίαι, οἰονεὶ ἑταιρεῖαι ἀδελφότητες συναλλάγματα συστήματα, παρὰ τὸ τοὺς φρατριάζοντας φράζειν ἢ φαίνειν ἀτρέπτως καὶ ἀφόβως ἀλλήλοις τὰ ἴδια βουλήματα· ὅθεν καὶ φράτορες οἱ πατέρες ἢ συγγενεῖς ἢ διδάσκαλοι, οἱ τῆς αὐτῆς φρατρίας μετέχοντες. τάχα δὲ καὶ ἀπὸ τῆς Ῥωμαϊκῆς μετηνέχθη λέξεως τοῦ φράτερ, ὃ δηλοῖ τὸν ἀδελφόν. Cassius Dio was known in Byzantium mostly through the *Epitome* of John Zonaras and that of John Xiphilinos. See: Kruse, Xiphilinos' Agency, 193–223.

acquired negative connotations despite its reference to the family. This may be attributable to the influence of Christianity, which considered that the family could deter individuals from devoting themselves to God,[67] but in any case, this is a subject that requires further exploration.

Casual references found in the Byzantine sources refer to both meanings of *fatria*. Among them the *hetairiotis fatria* of Caesar Bardas stands out; this refers to his fearsome armed retinue.[68] Specific references to *fatriai* within the Byzantine army are rare, but the Byzantines were well aware of this phenomenon. The Continuator of Skylitzes mentions that the soldiers originating from Cappadocia deserted the battle of Mantzikert 'in *fatriai* and *symmoriai*'.[69] In the case of the Turks looting Asia Minor the same author relates that their '*fatriai* and squadrons' acted in the manner of 'thugs and thieves'.[70] However, the *fatria* which concerns the family is undoubtedly a feature of the nobility. We have seen above that St. Euthymios' parents are specifically characterised as *eupatrides*, nobles.[71] At about the same time, a different text, also from the ecclesiastical environment, makes mention of the '*fatria* of the so-called Skleroi'.[72] Niketas David qualifies the relations inside this type of formation by noting that St. Eugenios was an associate by 'homeland, family, and *fatria*, and indeed by familiarity growing from friendship' with St. Eustratios.[73]

From the tenth century onwards, when the social and political dominance of the aristocracy solidifies the references to the *fatriai* of the nobles multiply. The most interesting among them are undoubtedly John VI Kantakouzenos' reference to his own 'glorious *fatria* of relatives and friends',[74] and the extensive comparison of Nikephoros Botaneiates' lineage with that of Nikephoros Bryennios by Michael Attaleiates: the ancestors of Bryennios were 'unknown' and Bryennios himself was of 'base' origin compared to the 'noble' emperor, whose nobility was founded on many generations of service in the higher military

---

67 See *Catenae patrum*, ed. Cramer, 159.29–160.2: Θεόδωρος δέ φησι· τινὲς πατριὰν ἀνέγνωσαν, οὐ συνιέντες τὸ κείμενον. ἔστι δὲ φρατρία. Πατριὰ μὲν γὰρ ἡ συγγένεια λέγεται, φρατρία δὲ τὸ σύστημα. ἐν δὲ τοῖς οὐρανοῖς συγγένεια οὐδεμία, συστήματα δὲ καὶ πολλά.

68 *Life of Basil*, ed. Ševčenko, 64.20.

69 *Skylitzes Continuatus*, ed. Tsolakis, 149.25–26.

70 *Skylitzes Continuatus*, ed. Tsolakis, 138.26–139.1: ...καταλιπὼν ἕτερον λαὸν ὄπισθεν διὰ τὸ καὶ ἑτέρους Τούρκους καταληίζεσθαι τὴν ρωμαϊκὴν γῆν κατὰ φατρίας καὶ μοίρας διαιρουμένους καὶ κατατρέχοντας λωποδυτῶν τρόπον καὶ κλεπτῶν καὶ τὸ προστυχὸν ἅπαν ἀφανίζοντας καὶ ληίζοντας. C.f. Attaliatae, *Historia*, ed. Tsolakis, 107.28.

71 See Ragia, Social Group Profiles, 348–350, on the meaning of the term εὐπάτριδες.

72 *Chronicle of Monemvasia*, ed. Kislinger, 202.59–60, and 40, 47 (commentary).

73 Halkin, Éloge, 139: πατρίδος καὶ γένους καὶ φατρίας καὶ δὴ καὶ τῆς κατὰ φιλίαν οἰκειότητος πάνυ τῷ Εὐστρατίῳ κοινωνός ἦν.

74 Kantakouzenos, *Historiae*, ed. Schopen, 2, 313.22–23. In this extract, Kantakouzenos admits that he could boast in everything that made a man proud, 'illustrious descent, wealth, glory, people to serve him, fair offspring, *fatria*, and relatives'.

offices. Attaleiates goes as far as to claim that Bryennios' ancestors weren't even worthy of 'taking the position of servants' of Botaneiates' ancestors.[75] Without doubt, then, the existence of the *fatria*, meaning the extended family, including relatives by blood and marriage, as well as supporting networks that existed or were created over time, was one of the features of the aristocracy.[76] The extent of the *fatriai* of the nobles and the importance attached to them in the sources corresponded not only to the social level of the families, but also to the social depths to which they could reach and the expansion of their influence throughout the social and political fabric of the empire.

The phenomenon of the *fatria* was, then, well known in Byzantium, despite the fact that the source material is rare, inconclusive, and even ambivalent. Two leading Byzantine jurists, Zonaras and Balsamon, both indicate that oath-giving was a constituent element of any conspiracy, which is thus neatly to be distinguished from a typical *fatria*. 'A conspiracy is when some scheme against others and are bound together by oath', wrote Zonaras, but 'a *fatria* is malicious consultation (*kakotheles diaboulion*), when some agree to do criminal acts'. But Zonaras adds that 'the civil law punishes the *phratriastai* and the conspirators alike'.[77] The discussion, then, essentially concerned these aristocratic social networks and their potential concurrence with conspiracies, and in this context the line between them, which for the law is the act of oath-giving, fades away as any attempt to legalise these networks remains unsuccessful.[78] Balsamon himself provides us, fortunately, with an example of how such ambivalence could be put aside when it came to the constituent element of a true conspiracy, oath-giving. It appears that at the end of the twelfth century it was indeed discussed whether those *fatriai* formed for a beneficial purpose, e. g. for aiding in the defence against an enemy, should be handled with leniency. Balsamon ruled that all conspiracies should be condemned; however, the decision of Alexios II Komnenos regarding the amnesty granted to those who had formed a *fatria* for the protection of his kingship was a 'special case' and warranted the exercise of 'royal mercy'.[79] Despite the severity of Balsamon's verdict, even the instance he is referring to demon-

---

75 Attaleiates, *History*, ed. Tsolakis, 221.14–27.

76 See in general and with a different perspective Beck, Byzantinische Gefolgschaftswesen, 3–32.

77 Rhalles-Potles, Σύνταγμα 1, 264. See generally Bourdara, Καθοσίωσις, 137–138.

78 On the importance of oaths, see Cheynet, Foi et conjuration, 265–279. Also see Rapp, *Brother-making*, 25–26.

79 Rhalles-Potles, Σύνταγμα 1, 382–383. For handling such cases, Balsamon quotes *Basilica*, ed. Scheltema *et al.*, 60.36.3, which deals with conspiracy against senators. See for the movements against Alexios II: Cheynet, *Pouvoir*, 110–111, 427–430; Brand, *Byzantium*, 34–37 and 324 note 14. Brand noted that Andronikos I officially forgave Maria Komnene and all the conspirators against Alexios II when he first came to power. The document of Balsamon apparently refers to the affair of the Porphyrogennita's conspiracy and the rioting of the mob in Constantinople.

strates the tolerance of the Byzantine government to aristocratic practices. It would seem, as the events of the period show, that it was possible to use one's own *fatria*, enlarge it, and direct its actions to serve specific political ends, and still be acquitted from the charge of conspiracy – if, of course, one was on the winning side, or if the emperor decided for any reason (philanthropy or political gain) to show his lenience, mercy, and magnanimity. In any case, the last quarter of the twelfth century is riddled with internal strife and politically subversive movements, both in the capital and in the provinces.

Lastly, one of the most interesting testimonies about the *fatriai* comes from the fourteenth century. Kantakouzenos reports that the *demos* of Didymoteichon was divided into *fatriai* for taking care of the moat and preparing the city for the eventuality of attack. This piece of information may be regarded as implying that a form of social organisation by *fatriai*, seen as distinct groups within a larger social setting, was well established and accepted in the provinces by the fourteenth century.[80] It seems, then, possible that a similar reference by Nikephoros Gregoras to the *fatriai* of the *demos* of Thessaloniki does not relate to political parties per se, but to social groupings which, because of the circumstances, had acquired a political role in events. In other words, Gregoras' information may imply that the political content attached is a secondary constituent of a *fatria*, which pre-exists any political goals that might be adopted at some point because of some specific pursuit of its leading members or because of particular circumstances.[81] A similar expression, 'into *demoi* and *fatriai*' found in the text of Niketas Choniates relating to the events of 1204 in Asia Minor confirms that this kind of atypical organisation was common in the provinces, outside the Byzantine capital.[82] But, unlike the case of Didymoteichon where they joined forces for a common cause, the *demoi* and *fatriai* in Asia Minor, according to Choniates' opinion, prevented the population from forming a united front against the Latins.

---

80 Kantakouzenos, *Historiae*, ed. Schopen, 2, 289.13–15: διανενεμημένης δὲ τῆς τάφρου κατὰ φατρίας παντὶ τῷ δήμῳ, ὥστε ἀνορύττειν, καὶ τοῖς ἐν τῷ κλήρῳ τῆς ἐκκλησίας πᾶσι παρείχετο μερίς.

81 Gregoras, *Historiae*, ed. Bekker and Schopen, II, 658.17–20. The *fatria* in the context of a *demos* may be connected to professional corporations, as indicated by Choniates, *Historia*, ed. van Dieten, 524.71–72, trans. Magoulias 287–288, which relates the episode of Kalomodios. When Kalomodios was arrested, the 'people of the market' (*agoraioi*) gathered their *fatriai* and demanded his release from patriarch John Kamateros.

82 Choniatae, *Historia*, ed. Van Dieten, 625.33–34: κατὰ δήμους καὶ φατρίας διέστησαν...; trans. Magoulias, 343: 'they divided into parties and factions'.

Confraternities

Although it is generally believed that confraternities existed in Byzantium, the evidence about them is scarce, and the problem much more complicated than it appears at first.[83] Confraternities were well known in the west and were quite common in the Greek provinces under Italian and French rule.[84] Since the research on this subject is relatively new and only a niche research topic, the absence of clear references in the sources makes it necessary to limit discussion to observations and questions, rather than providing clear-cut answers. The questions arising relate to the characteristics of these groups, e. g. their goals and how the 'confraternities' functioned. Even more obvious questions arise about the terminology that indicates their existence, and their identification in the sources.[85] In fact, the material is so difficult to identify and interpret, and its chronological range so wide, that it must be kept in mind from the onset that in all the questions and answers that follow, we must always be cautious when evaluating the evidence and conservative in our interpretations.

A number of terms found in the sources indicate the organisation of such groups or the members participating in them: *philoponoi/philoponia, spoudaioi, syntrophoi, philikoi, diakonia/diakonos*, and the rarer term *adelphotes*. In the Middle Byzantine period we also find *presbeia*, which is specifically connected with religious processions of miracle-working icons and will also be discussed below. We also need to be aware that the origin of these terms is different. The first two terms are quite common in the context of civic evergetism,[86] and there are number of Roman inscriptions mentioning the *spoude* and *philoponia* (σπουδὴ καὶ φιλοπονία) of important city benefactors.[87] The term *adelphotes* in

---

83 See Beck, *Kirche*, 138–139; Angold, *Church and Society*, 387–391; Baun, *Tales*, 373, where the evidence is summarised; Kazhdan, Microstructures, 6; and *ODB*, 494, s.v. Confraternities (M. Bartusis and A. Kazhdan).

84 Panopoulou, Συντεχνίες, 13–20; Wipszycka, Confréries, 257–258; Horden, Confraternities, 25–31; Rapp, *Brother-making*, 17–21.

85 Only a fraction of this is treated by Wipszycka, Confréries, 259.

86 Hesychii, *Lexicon*, ed. Hansen and Cunningham, Φ no 520: φιλοπονία· σπουδαῖα ἔργα; no 521: φιλόπονος· φιλεργός, σπουδαῖος. On evergetism, see primarily Brown, *Making of Christianity*, 53–71; Brown, *Poverty and Leadership*, 1–44. Brown primarily suggested that the evergetism of the rich and noble of the Roman Empire was channelled to the Church when Christianity was legitimised in the fourth century.

87 What follows is a random selection: *Priene Inscriptions*, ed. Blümel *et al.*, nos. 57.4, 5, 70.33, 72.7, 74.21; *Smyrna Inscriptions II.I*, ed. Petzl, no. 603.14; *Ephesos Inscriptions Ia*, ed. Wankel, nos. 6.17, 33–34; *Ephesos Inscriptions III*, Engelmann *et al.*, nos. 614.b12, 690.10; *Ephesos Inscriptions VII.2*, ed. Meriç *et al.*, nos. 3728.10, 3853.7. The inscriptions date from the second century BC onwards and contain expressions such as: φιλόπονον ἑαυτὸν παρεχόμενος (Priene), σπουδαῖον ἐπαινεῖσθαί τε καὶ τῆς καθηκούσης ἀξιῶσαι τιμῆς (Priene), τὸ περὶ τὴν πόλιν σπουδαῖον, γονέων σπουδαίων περὶ τὴν πατρίδα (Ephesos). Σπουδὴ in a civic context may be found together with ἐπιμέλεια, πρόνοια, or similar expressions. Σπουδὴ is also often found in legal contexts

Byzantium normally signifies the relationship that leads to social bonds (*koinonia*), a situation that involves important legal bonds and obligations. For this reason, the term *adelphotes* appears only rarely in the sources to indicate something other than monastic communities.[88] The *syntrophoi* and *philikoi*, on the other hand, appear to come from the alleged Roman 'precursor' of the confraternities, the *collegia*. While groups described with these terms function in many cities, belonging to such a group is not commonly part of the public image of individuals and this distinctly differentiates the *spoudaioi* of early Byzantium from those of the previous era, where the *polis/civitas* honoured these individuals for their services. Indeed, I have only found one inscription referring to two *spoudaioi* who financed the construction of a tomb apparently for themselves and for a third person in Tyriaion in Galatia. The funerary monument itself evidently had nothing to do with their benefactions in Tyriaion.[89]

It is rather far-fetched to believe that none of these terms indicates a 'confraternity'. However, these observations draw a neat distinction between the Byzantine 'confraternities' and their alleged Roman precursors, the civic *collegia* and the *fatriae*, which exhibited a well-documented public group projection in a civic setting, notwithstanding the fact that in this context the terms *philoi*, *phratores*, and even *hetairoi, hetaireia* are common. *Diakonia*, on the other hand, is a generic Greek word for providing services or performing duties. Therefore, it is quite widespread and, in my opinion, should be examined and interpreted every time it occurs in the context in which it is found.[90] Laurent calls the *diakonia* 'an organisation for helping the destitute and the weak'.[91] In his commentary on the *Lives of Eastern Saints*, Brooks noted that a *diakonia* or deaconry is 'a house established by the church for the care of the sick and poor under the superintendence of the deacons'.[92] According to Baun, 'the Late Antique and medieval confraternity [...] most usually functioned as a devotional and burial society for its members'.[93] Magdalino observed that 'the *diakonia* would thus seem to have been a para-monastic, urban lay confraternity similar in compo-

---

relating to litigations with other cities and embassies (which I have not included here). In Priene and Smyrna benefactors are hailed for transcribing public records in 'leather books' (first century BC).

88 C.f. *Basilica*, ed. Scheltema *et al.*, 12.1.61: Τοῦτο γὰρ ἐκ τοῦ φυσικοῦ δικαίου ὥρμηται λογισμοῦ διὰ τὸ τὴν κοινωνίαν ἔχειν ἐν ἑαυτῇ τρόπον τινὰ ἀδελφότητος δίκαιον. Also see *Rule of St. Basil*, PG 31, 1000 B: ποταποὺς χρὴ εἶναι τοὺς τὰ πρὸς τὴν χρείαν οἰκονομοῦντας ἐν τῇ ἀδελφότητι.

89 *Sultan Daği Inscriptions*, ed. Jonnes, no. 388: Τύνβος εἰσπουδέων μακάρων ὧν τὰ ὀνόματα Φλ. Ἀλέξανδρος κὲ Αμιης διακονήσης ἀνεστήσαμεν τὸν τίτλον μνήμης χάριν κὲ Μεινου (sic).

90 The concept of *diakonia* and its association with *philanthropia* has been examined by Constantelos, Diakonia, 1–27.

91 *Corpus des sceaux V2*, ed. Laurent, 125–126.

92 John of Ephesus, *Lives*, ed. Brooks, 669 and note 3.

93 Baun, *Tales*, 372 and 375. Note that Baun's definition is based mostly on evidence coming from the west.

sition, organisation, and scope to other types of pious association which are known to have existed at the time: the groups of zealots (*spoudaioi, philoponoi*), whom we encounter in the world of John Moschos and his contemporaries'.[94] The editors of the Dumbarton Oaks Seals have recently suggested that the *diakoniai* are 'lay service organisations' attached to churches and/or charity establishments.[95]

To the extent that the terminology relating to confraternities is considered to have its origins in the early Christian context, rather than in the Roman civic environment which continued uninterrupted in the early Byzantine period, and is inescapable when examining the existing material on professional groups and *fatriai*, the present analysis is different. In fact, the little that we know about the internal organisation of these groups is strikingly similar to the late Roman professional corporations when it comes to the organisation of their social life.[96] We shall also see below that the *diakoniai* were legal persons that paid taxes and received fees and bonuses, while many were associated with the great charity establishments of the capital. There is no reason to assume that all *diakoniai* are indeed 'confraternities' in the western medieval sense. In other words, the typical 'confraternity' may or may not exist as a parallel group of volunteers next to an organisation such as a *diakonia*, or a *presbeia*.

It appears that the Byzantine 'confraternities' executed their tasks so quietly that they have actually left very little evidence behind. In modern research, the subject is mostly associated with the *lousmata* (baths) of the poor, and the management of burial of the disadvantaged, the poor and the itinerant, mostly in Constantinople, which, however, complicates the issue further. In these cases, the service is specifically in return for tax exemptions, and the actual burial is not

---

94 Magdalino, Diakonia, 180.

95 See *Catalogue of Byzantine Seals 5*, ed. McGeer *et al.*, 75 and 76 regarding Blachernae and Petrou respectively.

96 Aries and Duby, *History*, 189–191; Arnaoutoglou, Roman Law and *collegia*, 28–43; Perry, Collegia, 499–515, esp. 508–511. A *collegium* may be a professional or religious group; there are no real restrictions regarding members' entry, but apparently no women were admitted. It is possible that every *collegium* venerated a particular deity, in the case of professionals one that was seen as a protector of the profession. But in Roman times a *collegium* could be instituted in the context of a household, notwithstanding the status of its members, free or otherwise, with the purpose of the protection of the house. The *collegia* elected their archons on an annual basis and, apart from venerating their deity, they organised common symposia and cared for the burial of their members. As a rule, the Roman authorities were cautious toward them, but eventually they became a considerable force because of their support of the archons (senators and others) of the Roman polity. The *collegia* in the east appear to be have been organised mostly on a professional basis. Kazhdan, Microstructures, 5–6, includes the Byzantine guilds among those formations worth studying for their inner organisation, but without any link to the confraternities.

performed by the benefactors themselves, but by specialised staff.[97] In early Byzantine times, funds for burying the deceased who were too poor or had no one to care for them were provided through the system of *munera*, which aimed at the uninterrupted function of the cities. It appears that by the fourth century the Church had taken over organising this service: we see this in Ephesos and Constantinople, and we can assume that the same development took place in other cities of the empire, although we cannot be sure when this occurred. In Aphrodisias, the inscription 'place of Loukas, philoponos', was found just north of the inscription of 'Tryphon, chief *decanus*' (*archidekanou*) to the east of the church of the Archangel Michael. While the office of Tryphon points to a group, or *collegium*, of *decani*, who are known to have been undertakers,[98] Loukas' inscription strongly suggests that he may have been working in association with them and the church of the Archangel Michael, perhaps also with regard to burials, although other tasks cannot be excluded, e. g. taking care of the sick. There is no indication of a group of *philoponoi* in Aphrodisias, but it is quite probable that they were working individually. Apparently, Loukas could be found in this spot hiring out his good services.

Some of the reports found in the source material on the *lousmata* (baths) relate to this form of benefaction or service in a civic context. In the sixth century we learn of the *neoteros argyroprates*, Andronikos from Antioch, who participated in the '*baths of the brothers*' (*lousmata tōn adelphōn*) along with other colleagues. The participation of only one professional group in the function of the *lousma* points to a specific charge assigned to the *argyropratai* by the city of Antioch, rather than to a 'confraternity', in which participation, as we shall see, is generally open, not limited to people coming from specific backgrounds. It is interesting that the wives of the *argyropratai* also took part in the service, taking care of women. In this instance, the narrative provides us with the much-wanted terminology *philoponia tou lousmatos* (the charity of the baths). The civic context where Andronikos and his wife performed this charity is further accentuated by the fact that he was one of the younger members (*neoteros*) of the *argyropratai*. Andronikos and his wife were obliged to spend three nights of the week at the *lousmata* (according to what is probably the oldest version of the text, not four, as the edited text has it). The narrative clearly places the activity in a general religious context, without connecting it with the veneration of a particular saint or feast, and qualifies it as 'eagerness for good works' (*spoude eis tas philoponias*),

---

97 Leontaritou, Ἀξιώματα, 147–160; Dagron, Confréries, 155–182; Patlagean, *Pauvreté économique*, 192; Dagron, Urban Economy, 424; Herrin, From Bread and Circuses, 278.

98 *Ephesos Inscriptions VII.2*, ed. Meriç *et al.*, no. 4135; *Aphrodisias Inscriptions*, ed. Roueché, nos. 187, 188 and 229, 231–232 (commentary). See Leontaritou, Ἀξιώματα, 152, 1.54–157; Horden, Confraternities, 36–37.

which clearly recalls late Roman inscriptions.[99] Andronikos had divided his wealth into three parts, of which he gave one part 'to the poor'. It has been suggested that the donation covered the payment of the expenses of the *philoponia*, but there is no specific information in the text regarding the economic aspect of the charity, although there is reason to believe that it was rather expensive for the sponsors.[100]

The guild of the *argyropratai* of Antioch on the Orontes probably used public baths for performing the charity at night, when the installations were not operating for the public. In Middle Byzantine times, the baths were probably run by individuals or directly by monasteries.[101] Some of the testimonies clarify the status under which the *lousmata* operated in tenth- to eleventh-century Constantinople. In the tenth century, a linen workshop was obliged to deliver its tax to the '*diakonia* of the *lousma* of Germanos'. Apparently, then, this *diakonia* had been allotted a yearly income, which was in reality the workshop's *telos*, a tax.[102] Another *diakonia* of a *lousma* which belonged to a certain Xylinites owned, or exploited, a forge and delivered its tax to a silk-trading workshop.[103] In the eleventh century, we hear of a '*douleia eis ta louma*' (sic), which was sold to an individual for 18 gold coins. This office, apparently one of the lowest, but which, however, would bring a significant income to its holder, is known because the seller regretted his decision and claimed back the office; in reaching his verdict, Eustathios Rhomaios calculated the office's price and the expected profits per year, and included a yearly interest. The decision is included in the collection of

---

99 The edition dates from 1901 and the text appears to be modelled on middle Byzantine models of piety (the manuscript is dated to 993). Other manuscripts, however, from the eleventh century, retain the early Byzantine view with crucial details that have been carefully removed from the earlier manuscript because they were no longer relevant. The reconstruction of the text would be as follows (I have italicised the earlier additions): ἀλλ' ἦν αὐτῶν σπουδὴ εἰς τὰς φιλοπονίας μετὰ καὶ ἄλλων φιλοχρίστων ἀργυροπρατῶν. Κατὰ Κυριακὴν οὖν καὶ Δευτέρα [Monday is added in the Middle Byzantine version] καὶ τετράδα καὶ παρασκευὴν ἀπὸ ἑσπέρας ἕως πρωὶ ὑπῆγεν ὁ Ἀνδρόνικος εἰς τὰ λούσματα τῶν ἀδελφῶν, ὁμοίως καὶ ἡ γυνὴ αὐτοῦ εἰς τὰ λούσματα τῶν γυναικῶν τῆς φιλοπονίας. See *Life of Daniel of Sketis*, ed. Clugnet, 47–48, 61.

100 Herrin, From Bread and Circuses, 281–283. On this affair, see also: Horden, Confraternities, 35; Magdalino, Diakonia, 179–180; Berger, Das Bad, 26–27. One part of Andronikos' assets was channelled 'to the poor' (εἰς λόγον τῶν πτωχῶν), one part 'to the monks', and the rest '[he kept as] his own holding and for his workshop'. Horden characterises the group to which Andronikos belonged as 'a guild within a guild'. On the story of Andronikos see *Life of Daniel of Sketis*, ed. Clugnet, XIX–XXII.

101 Magdalino, Diakonia, 165–188. Also see Berger, Das Bad, 56–71.

102 Oikonomides, Boutiques, 345 no. 2.

103 Oikonomides, Boutiques, 346 no. 5, 347–348, 353–354; Dagron, Urban Economy, 425. The fiscal function is known as *logisimon* (or *logisima solemnia*, taxes allotted in someone's favour). The full terminology is difficult to find in the sources and is sometimes simply missing altogether. See Oikonomides, Fiscalité, 182–185; Dölger, Finanzverwaltung, 146–147; Ahrweiler, Concession, 105–107.

judicial decisions and opinions commonly known as the *Peira*.[104] Yet another *diakonia*, which administered two baths, is known in Thessaloniki in the twelfth century. Emperor John II Komnenos allocated it to the monastery of the Pantokrator. The *diakonia* also received rents and owned unspecified assets. Thus, this *diakonia* was an establishment that managed a part of the imperial possessions in the city.[105] Again, none of these Middle Byzantine references to bath-associated *diakoniai* suggests that they were run by organised *adelphotetes*. In other words, a bath does not necessitate the existence of a 'confraternity'. These *diakoniai* seem, rather, to have been operated by private individuals and/or monasteries, while a number of *lousmata* must have been incorporated in the public domain. Interestingly, baths belonging to the private sector (such as those of Germanos and Xylinites) and public baths (such as the one attested in Rhomaios' decision and that of the Pantokrator) are not mutually exclusive. Indeed, both private and public baths functioned alongside each other in tenth- to twelfth-century Byzantium. In this context, 'confraternities' associated with the charity of the baths of the poor may have made use of a bath, private or public, but there is no way of knowing this detail unless this particular piece of information is provided by some source, and there is no reason to assume that all baths were used by confraternities.

The earliest references of *spoudaioi* and *philoponoi* in a Christian context indicate the action of fervent Christians who are mentioned in the sources for their chaste way of living, including acts of charity to the poor and the sick, and/or their participation in processions and vigils. The *spoudaioi* and *philoponoi* always show their 'eagerness for good works'.[106] They were groups dedicated to churches and/or saints, mostly in a civic framework, but distinct from early monastic groups – at least in their origins.[107] Eventually these groups may have developed to become actual monasteries, but there is not enough evidence to suggest that this happened everywhere, although individuals belonging to these groups may have been tonsured or joined the clergy at a later stage in their lives. They are attested to have operated in Egypt, Palestine, Syria, Cyprus, and Constantinople.[108] In the absence of further evidence, perhaps it is in this context that

---

104 *Peira*, ed. Zachariae von Lingenthal, ch. 38 no. 74; Oikonomides, Boutiques, 352–354; Magdalino, Diakonia, 181–182. Magdalino suggests that it is to be identified with the 'diakonia of the *protos*', known from the sigillographic record, although there is no convincing argument supporting this interpretation. On the *protoi* see below.
105 *Typikon of the Pantokrator*, ed. Gautier, 121.1538–1539: ἡ διακονία τοῦ Κράμβεως μετὰ τῶν δύο αὐτῆς λοετρῶν καὶ ἐνοικικῶν καὶ λοιπῶν δικαίων.
106 Wipszycka, Confréries, 260–263.
107 Wipszycka, Confréries, 268–270.
108 Petrides, Philopones, 341–348; Petrides, Spoudaei, 225–231; Vailhé, Philopones, 277–278. On the monastery of the Spoudaei in Constantinople see also Janin, *Constantinople Byzantine*, 41, 429.

we can place the inscription relating to *spoudaioi* found in Tyriaion, discussed above, although there is no indication which service they performed.

John of Ephesus is thorough and detailed regarding the groups dedicated to the service of the baths and the poor instituted by Paul of Antioch. He founded such groups not only in Constantinople, but also in Chalkedon, Nikomedia, Cyzicus, Prusias, Herakleia, 'and as far as the sea of Pontus'.[109] According to John of Ephesus, 'the object of his zeal was to carry the poor and the old and sick persons by night and he would take them and bathe and anoint them, and mend and change the clothes of those who were in need, and take them and give them to drink each one according to what was suited for him, and he would give small coins as was suited for each one of them. And thus before daybreak in company with others who shared his enthusiasm with him he would carry him and would go and lay him in his place (and he used to do this not to men only but also to women) for a long time'.[110] In Constantinople these groups developed into the foundation of two establishments, and Paul of Antioch appears to have been managing large amounts of money.[111] It is, however, rather doubtful that this happened in every city he visited, while the discussion as to whether the service of the baths belonged exclusively to Monophysites remains inconclusive.[112]

Although Paul's foundations did not survive long, the practice of providing a bath and a decent meal to the poor appears to have continued in Middle Byzantium and was probably complemented with prayers and ceremonies performed by priests. In the Middle Byzantine *Life of Theophano* the *lousma* is called *diakonia tes ptocholousias kai diatrophes tōn penetōn* (service of bathing and feeding of the poor).[113] A related prayer concerns the *lousma* of the Blachernae in Constantinople. The ceremony here took the form of a purification ceremony and the prayers chanted are a supplication for good health and the expulsion of disease. No details are included regarding the status of those bathed, but there is mention of '*the brothers who sponsor the diakonia* (ἐν τῇ διακονίᾳ καρποφοροῦσι) *and take care of the poor*'.[114] A seal dating to the tenth century may be associated with these ceremonies.[115]

---

109 John of Ephesus, *Lives*, ed. Brooks, 668–671, 673–675; John of Ephesus, *Ecclesiastical History, III*, ed. Brooks, 55–56 c. 15, 16.
110 John of Ephesus, *Lives*, ed. Brooks, 672.
111 John of Ephesus, *Lives*, ed. Brooks, 675: '…he also bought clothing and brought it out and distributed it… while not neglecting to send money to other cities round Sycae also for the expenses of that ministration…'.
112 *Corpus des sceaux V2*, ed. Laurent, 125; Patlagean, *Pauvreté économique*, 192; Dagron, Confréries, 176–178; Horden, Confraternities, 40; Janin, *Églises de Constantinople*, 551–552.
113 *Life of Theophano*, ed. Kurtz, 18. C.f. Magdalino, Diakonia, 180; Herrin, From Bread and Circuses, 282.
114 Dmitrievskij, *Opisanie* II, 1043f., 1048. The baths of the Blachernae were built in the sixth century and renovated in the tenth century under Basil II: Janin, *Constantinople Byzantine*,

When it comes to icon worship, the references are clear. The information comes from the *Miracles of St. Artemios* and the *Typikon* of the confraternity of Thebes, and from the Byzantine versions of the text relating to the Maria Rhomaia icon. The texts do not use the same terminology: the following of St. John the Baptist is called *philikon* in the Miracles, while that of Theotokos Naupaktitissa of Thebes is called *adelphotes* and also *hieros choros* or *syntagma*.[116] The confraternity of Maria Rhomaia of Constantinople is mentioned as *diakonia adelphōn*, and among its members we find the '*spoudaioteroi* of the orthodox'. The icon and the confraternity itself are traditionally associated with that of the Theotokos Hodegetria.[117] According to the narrative, Empress Theodora and the patriarch (Methodios or Ignatios) instituted the procession of the icon of Maria Rhomaia together with that of Hodegetria every Tuesday,[118] and thus the two traditions about the icons seem to blend into one. The procession of the Hodegetria was impressive. The clerics and the women following wore their best silken clothing, as is well depicted in the unique mural painting in the church of Blacherna in Arta. But there is good evidence to suggest that even icons as important and celebrated as that of the Hodegetria could be used in honour of individuals or families.[119] Interesting details about the Hodegetria are known from the *Typikon* of the Pantokrator monastery. In the *Typikon*, Emperor John II Komnenos orders that the procession of the Hodegetria should honour the official commemoration ceremonies of the members of the imperial family. The ceremony would begin with an extended supplication while the icon would be

---

218; Magdalino, Diakonia, 177. Janin draws attention to the emperor's ceremonial bath that also took place at the Blachernae, although perhaps in another location. The ceremony included prayers and the emperor took holy water from the pool. The text is preserved in the Book of Ceremonies: *Book of Ceremonies*, ed. Dagron *et al.*, 75–81 (II.12). According to Laurent, the seal belonging to the '*diakonia* of the return of Blachernae' may be relevant to this ceremony. Another seal of this type mentions the 'return of the Holy Apostles' (without any reference to a *diakonia*). See *Catalogue of Byzantine Seals 5*, ed. McGeer *et al.*, no. 31.2; *Corpus des sceaux V2*, ed. Laurent, nos. 1203, 1205. See generally on these processions: Berger, Processions, 73–87; Janin, Processions, 69–88.

115 *Corpus des sceaux V2*, ed. Laurent. no. 1222: Θεοτόκε βοήθει τοῖς διψοῦσι τῆς διακονίας // τοῦ λούσματος λῦτρον ψυχῆς ὁ ἴδιος πλοῦτος. Translation: 'Mother of God help those who thirst for the *diakonia*. The salvation of one's soul with the *lousma* is one's own wealth'.

116 *Typikon of the Naupaktitissa Confraternity*, ed. Nesbitt and Wiita, 364.5, 34, 366.90.

117 Von Dobschütz, Maria Romaia, 202.23.4–5; Patterson-Ševčenko, Servants, 549; Patterson-Ševčenko, Icons, 51. On the Theotokos Hodegetria, its worship, and its association with Maria Rhomaia, see especially Angelidi and Papamastorakis, Μονή Οδηγών, 373–387, with further bibliography. On the financial aspect of icons, see generally Oikonomides, Holy Icon, 35–44.

118 Von Dobschütz, Maria Romaia, 201–202.

119 Acheimastou-Potamianou, Βλαχέρνα, 73–74, 81–93; c.f. Patterson-Ševčenko, Icons, 47. On the Komnenoi and Hodegetria in particular, see: Angelidi and Papamastorakis, Μονή Οδηγών, 379–380.

placed close to the tombs and stay there the whole night throughout the vigil and in the morning during the liturgy and the second supplication. Upon completion, the fees, amounting to a total of fifty gold coins, were distributed: six gold coins to the icon, twenty-four to the men holding the twelve *koudai* (fire brands), two coins for each man carrying the icon (*bastagarioi*) and the rest of the workers (*douleutai*), and what remained was to be distributed to the men holding the *signa*.[120] Thus, the imperial sarcophagi were surrounded during the entire ceremony by twelve brands burning brightly through the night and by the *signa* of the church and veneration of the Hodegetria while those joining the ceremony at whatever stage would witness its magnificence. Attending the ceremony at the tombs of the Komnenoi must have been a grand sight and a unique experience indeed.

It is no wonder then that the worship of the icon of Theotokos Naupaktitissa was modelled on that of the Hodegetria, and it so happens that the charter of its confraternity is one of two charters saved. The confraternity's task was to carry the icon of the Theotokos Naupaktitissa in procession to a different parish community every month. A brother of the confraternity took up the task of preparing its new abode (*stasis*) each time. The monastery of the Naupaktitissa, where the icon was initially placed in the church of the Archangel Michael, was in all probability a *metochion* of the monastery of Steiris, because the abbot of Steiris was to be commemorated in the liturgies of the church.[121] The members of the *adelphotes* placed their signatures at the end of the charter, thus displaying an atypical provincial social hierarchy. The first was the priest of the monastery of Daphni near Athens, Dionysios, followed by *presbyteroi*, by Christophoros Kopsenos who is well-known from the archive of the monastery of Patmos, and by other priests and private individuals, among whom we find only three women, which is to be expected in a purely provincial context. The family names, toponyms, and epithets mentioned in the document betray the provenance of its members from the wider region of Thebes, Athens, and Euboea. Distant prov-

---

120 *Typikon of the Pantokrator*, ed. Gautier, 81.883–83.900. It appears that this use of the word κοῦδα is unique in the Byzantine sources, but fortunately there is one more mention in a popular poem from post-Byzantine Crete, which clarifies its meaning: see *Anonymous Cretan Poem* ed. Panagiotakes, 76.2500–2502: Ἀπείτις ἐγαστρώθηκε ἡ μάννα του τοῦ Ἰούδα, εἶδε κι ἐγέννησε δαυλὸ μὲ τὴ μεγάλη κοῦδα· ἡ κοῦδα ἐλάβριζε φωτιά, τὸ σπίτι ἐκεντήθη. Translation: 'since Juda's mother conceived, she dreamt that she gave birth to a torch with a large *kouda*; and the *kouda* burned bright, the house was adorned'.

121 *Typikon of the Naupaktitissa Confraternity*, ed. Nesbitt and Wiita, 364.23–32, 38–365.44, 373–374, 376 note 23. The hegoumenos of Steiris was commemorated after the metropolitan bishop of Thebes, and was followed by the mother superior of the monastery of the Naupaktitissa. Detailed prosopographical notes follow the edition of the text. See Baun, *Tales*, 375, 377; Neville, *Authority*, 89–90; Patterson-Ševčenko, Servants, 550; and Cutler and North, Service, 207–213, on the iconographic type of the icon.

enance from Asia Minor (Phygela, Anatolikon, Cappadocia) is perhaps also implied.[122] It is noteworthy that neither the abbot of Steiris, nor the abbot of Daphni, nor the mother superior of the Naupaktitissa signed as members of the confraternity, but this seems reasonable considering that their duties would not have allowed them to leave their monasteries. In this case, Dionysios might have been a representative of Daphni, but there does not seem to be a representative of Steiris in the confraternity.

These texts provide hints about such manifestations of public piety becoming a regular phenomenon in the middle Byzantine period, but it is important to note that most of the confraternities would not have performed their tasks under the auspices of the emperor. However, everything we see in the Hodegetria and the Naupaktitissa is already found in the *Miracles of St. Artemios*, even if the term employed – *philikon* – betrays the late Roman influence. In Miracle 18, the clothing of the hero of the story was stolen from his house and because of this he would not follow the vigil of St. John the Baptist. According to the narrative, St. Artemios appeared to him and reproached him for this failure: 'why did you not meet [the procession] and escort the holies (*ta hagia*) with your candle, as it is customary for you, the people of the vigil?'[123] This story indicates that the people actively involved in carrying 'the holies' may have had a 'dress code'. This is suggested also by the depictions of the Hodegetria procession in Arta and elsewhere. It appears that at least the men carrying the icon (the *bastagarioi* of the Pantokrator Typikon) were dressed in brownish-red tunics with long sleeves.[124]

The third confraternity we know well is described in Theodore Studites' Letter 13. Studites calls it *systema* or *adelphotes*,[125] and the scribe of the manuscript calls it *diakonia tōn apronoetōn* (of the destitute). The group centred its charitable activity on the burial of the poor and the foreigners of the capital (e. g. travellers); its members were obliged to participate in commemorations and meals held on specific days of the year, and visit the sick and the imprisoned and provide comfort to them.[126]

---

122 *Typikon of the Naupaktitissa Confraternity*, ed. Nesbitt and Wiita, 366.96–368.169; Cutler and North, Service, 214; Neville, Authority, 72–73. Neville suggests that more women may have been members of the confraternity through their husbands, and thereby also 'sisters' of other members, but certainly objections can be raised to this generalisation. She also identified a fourth female member, Manachos tou Phygellete, which I take to belong to a man coming from Phygela because of the persistent use of genitive throughout the list of signatures.

123 *Miracles of St. Artemios*, ed. Crisafulli and Nesbitt, 114–118. See: Efthymiadis, Lonely Bachelor, 5–12.

124 Patterson-Ševčenko, Servants, 550–551; Patterson-Ševčenko, Icons, 48; Acheimastou-Potamianou, Βλαχέρνα, 88; Angelidi and Papamastorakis, Μονή Οδηγών, 379.

125 Theodore the Studite, *Epistulae*, ed. Fatouros, no 13.10, 19, 45.

126 Theodore the Studite, *Epistulae*, ed. Fatouros, no 13.17–24, 37–38. See Dagron, Confréries, 162–164, 179–181; Baun, Tales, 375–376.

From all these texts mentioned above we may derive details concerning the internal organisation of these groups and the participation of the members and their obligations, but further questions arise. It has been hinted above that the members of these groups were somehow rewarded for their services. Wipszycka has highlighted this aspect based on evidence from Egyptian papyri, where it appears that these 'rewards' could take the form of distributions in kind. This, then, might have provided a particular motive for participation. Participation in such groups was voluntary, and those recruited were of varied social and professional provenances, if social provenance is discussed at all in the sources.[127] John of Ephesus, interestingly, highlights this aspect in the story of the *protector* Isaac: 'for God's sake, and not as a man in need'[128] Isaac joined the 'ministering office of those who bathe the sick at night', and at the same time he 'hired himself out in it [in a *xenon*, hospital], as an attendant of the sick. And he took off all his clothes and sold them and gave to the poor'.[129] In the *Miracles of St. Artemios*, one of the followers of the *philikon* was a money changer, and another probably belonged to the staff of the eparch of Constantinople.[130] The same text indicates that the more distinguished participants in these groups appeared in vigils and ceremonies with their servants or retinues, called in the text 'free service' (*eleftheriki hypourgia*).[131]

Despite their service, the participation of individuals in such charity groups did not have the same consequences for their public image as the participation of individuals in icon processions, and thus the issue of conviviality raised by Horden regarding the groups of Early Byzantium[132] becomes problematic in Middle Byzantium. Devotees of vigils and icon processions might have been proud to appear in public holding candles or torches. But the baths of the poor were something entirely different. The *protector* Isaac, for example, lived in Antioch, and abandoned everything to devote himself to the charity of the baths; from this 'he began to be known and honoured by many'.[133] On the other hand, the most distinguished followers of Paul of Antioch made sure to cover their faces

---

127 Horden, Confraternities, 40–44; Wipszycka, Confréries, 267–268, 275–278; Oikonomides, Holy Icon, 40; Herrin, From Bread and Circuses, 282–283; Caseau, Objects, 630–632. It should also be noted that the distribution of various goods (such as wine or wheat) is ancient practice.

128 John of Ephesus, *Lives*, ed. Brooks, 671: '…in the exercise of discretion and humility for God's sake, and not as a man in need, he had submitted to minister to the sick'.

129 John of Ephesus, *Lives*, ed. Brooks, 669.

130 *Miracles of St Artemios*, ed. Crisafulli and Nesbitt, 116.22, 120.11–13.

131 *Miracles of St Artermios*, ed. Crisafulli and Nesbitt, 102.19.

132 Horden, Confraternities, 26–27, 43–44.

133 John of Ephesus, *Lives*, ed. Brooks, 669.

and conceal their social position during their service at the baths.[134] This does not mean that they were embarrassed, but that the service was diametrically opposed to the Late Roman way of living, which was often pompous and ostentatious in the context of public life. In Middle Byzantium, a rare piece of evidence suggests that the service of the *lousma* may have been passed down from generation to generation and kept within families, but it was possible to send a slave or servant instead of appearing personally. This is what the *protospatharios* Michael did because he 'thought the baseness of the thing as inconsequential'.[135] But it is for the *lousma* that we have unique information regarding the admission of a member to the *diakonia*. It is a 'supplication for making a brother (εὐχὴ εἰς τὸ ποιῆσαι ἀδελφὸν) in the holy lousma', where it is said 'I have not come [here] to be served (διακονηθῆναι), but to serve (διακονῆσαι)... give him the [strength] to perform the observance of the poor impeccably'.[136] With this piece of information, which encapsulates the personal will and commitment of individuals to perform their duties, we are already in the late fourteenth century.

With regard to the internal organisation of the confraternities, there is no convincing evidence about the existence of a real leadership. Rather, it appears that these groups functioned much more on collegiality and mutual respect among the members, even if some of them were recognised as leaders of their group. This is true in spite of the seals that belonged to *protoi* of the *presbeia* (supplication or procession), of which one referred specifically to the Blachernae and one to the Hodegetria, while a third is not specified but presumably also referred to the Hodegetria. The first two seals belonged to patricians and the third to the *protoproedros* Nikolaos Skleros.[137] In my opinion, the seals are confusing. By mentioning the head of the *presbeia* they indicate a hierarchical organisation, but the term *diakonia* or *adelphotes*, which would indicate this organisation or group, is missing; instead, the term *presbeia* refers to the actual religious procession. Another seal of the '*diakonia* of the church of Blachernae', which belonged to a certain Ioannes, seems to verify that *presbeia* and *diakonia* were

---

134 John of Ephesus, *Lives*, ed. Brooks, 673: 'For many even of the great and eminent men of the city, having put off their apparel (σχῆμα) and hoods that concealed their heads and faces, would thus put straps on the necks and carry the chairs of the sick and the poor, and old men and women, and perform all the ministration to them'.

135 *Life of Theophano*, ed. Kurtz, 19: ὁ πατὴρ τὴν διακονίαν πληρῶσαι τῷ υἱῷ ἐνετείλατο· ὁ δέ τισι φροντίσιν ἑτέραις περιασχοληθείς, τὴν πατρικὴν διάταξιν διά τινος οὐκέτου γενέσθαι προσέταξεν, οὐ τὴν τοῦ πατρὸς καταφρονῶν διάταξιν, ἀλλὰ τὴν εὐτέλειαν τοῦ πράγματος εὐς οὐδὲν λογισάμενος. See Berger, Das Bad, 68, 69.

136 Dmitrienskij, *Opisanie* II, 1051. C.f. Rapp, *Brother-making*, 27–29.

137 *Corpus des sceaux V2*, ed. Laurent, no. 1200–1202. The seals date to the eleventh to twelfth centuries. See Angelidi and Papamastorakis, Μονή Οδηγών, 377.

distinct.[138] Ioannes did not specify his qualification on his seal; he could have belonged to the clergy of Blachernae or he could have been a layman associated with the *diakonia*. Of the other seals preserved, only one can with any certainty be identified as bearing a similar title, that of a *protos* of the *diakonia* of Petrou.[139]

It may be of some significance that these are all seals of Constantinopolitan *diakoniai*, because the establishments in the capital were large and complicated.[140] In the *Life of St. Andrew of Crete* we read that the saint was appointed administrator of the orphanage and the Eugeniou. The author calls the Eugeniou a *diakonia* and *euages oikos*; it was a *gerokomeion* or *ptocheion* (for the old and the poor). Establishments such as this may well have relied on lay groups for the performance of their philanthropic activities, but creating a separate space of worship would not be needed, although the possibility cannot be excluded. In any case, its seal appears to confirm that the *diakonia* belonged to the establishment of the Eugeniou, not to a separate lay confraternity.[141]

These seals range chronologically from the sixth to the twelfth centuries. A cleric of the Blachernae church was *praefectus* in one of the *diakoniai* established by Paul of Antioch in the late sixth century.[142] The confraternity of Theodore Studites in the early ninth century was under the guidance of the *prokathegoumenos*; in this case, Theodore himself. The members were expected to follow a particular code of moral behaviour during the ceremonies and the exercise of their duties; if the code was breached, the abbot would impose an *epitimion* and a fine. The confraternity was also obliged to honour the passing of their own

---

138 *Catalogue of Byzantine Seals 5*, ed. McGeer *et al.*, no. 31.1; c.f. the older editions in *Corpus des sceaux V3*, ed. Laurent, no. 1921; *Byzantine Lead Seals*, ed. Zacos and Veglery, no. 2008. Also see Janin, Processions, 88.

139 *Corpus des sceaux V2*, ed. Laurent, no. 1217; *Byzantine Lead Seals*, ed. Zacos and Veglery, no. 1135. *Corpus des sceaux V2*, ed. Laurent, no. 1213 also mentions a *protos* but the reading is uncertain.

140 *Corpus des sceaux V2*, ed. Laurent, nos. 1206, 1207–1211, 1214–1216, 1218–1221; *Byzantine Lead Seals*, ed. Zacos and Veglery, nos. 317, 1127, 1128, 1281, 2008; *Catalogue of Byzantine Seals 5*, ed. McGeer *et al.*, nos. 29–30, 32–34. It is interesting that some of these *diakoniai* are associated with imperial complexes, possessions, or quarters of the capital, such as the Berou, the Eugeniou, or the Maurianou. One of them belonged to the *presbeia* of St. Panteleemon, another to the monastery of St. Theodore. Another 'seal of the *loutron* of hegoumenos Sabas' seems very peculiar and, judging from its phrasing (*loutron* instead of *lousma*) does not indicate a larger group. See Laurent, *Corpus V2*, no 1223.

141 *Life of St. Andrew of Crete*, ed. Papadopoulos Kerameus, 174. See Magdalino, Diakonia, 187, no. 9 and 188, no. 9; also Laurent, *Corpus V2*, no. 1212; Oikonomides, Organisation, 138–141; Detorakis, Άγιοι της Κρήτης, 160–190. In the eleventh century, the *orphanotrophos* was a very important administrative dignitary: Oikonomides, *Listes*, 319. On the Eugeniou see Janin, *Églises de Constantinople*, 566–567; Janin, *Constantinople Byzantine*, 349. Interestingly, it was the *gerokomos*, director of the Eugeniou, who gave the emperors a blessing as they exited the Blachernai *lousma*. See *Book of Ceremonies*, ed. Dagron and Flusin, 81.106–107.

142 John of Ephesus, *Eccesliastical History*, ed. Brooks, 56 ch. 16.

adelphoi with propriety and solemnity. In the *philikon* of St. John the Baptist, the *arcarios* (treasurer) imposed and collected the fines and supplied the materials needed for the procession. He was a simple money changer and had no affiliation with the church of St. Artemios. In the *adelphotes* of the Naupaktitissa there is no internal hierarchy apart from that followed in the signatures. There was a general moral code, which was not nearly as strict as that of Theodore Studites, but there was no authoritative figure to impose a penalty of any kind, apart from giving a private and public admonition. This confraternity was also obliged to provide a solemn burial ceremony for its members and hold the customary com-memorations.[143] It is obvious that in this context the senior and most revered members would have been accorded more authority and prestige. But it is also worth noting that these stipulations are almost identical to those we know to have been followed by the Roman *collegia*.[144]

From the evidence gathered here, it has become obvious that there may have been a significant economic aspect to the activities of a *diakonia*. We have seen that Paul of Antioch managed large sums of money, apparently depending a lot on donations and benefactions. The mere existence of an *arcarios* of the *philikon* of St. John the Baptist means that he managed the finances of the *philikon*. Upon being ordained metropolitan bishop of Crete (eighth century), St. Andrew built a church which he consecrated to the Theotokos of Blachernae. 'And he had a *diakonia* constructed and had water pour into the nipter [basin], securing with his own money the fulfilment of the needs of the place as if pouring from vessels'.[145] Here again, the *diakonia* was endowed with considerable assets by its founder. In the case of the charter of Theodore Studites, the names of the members of the *adelphotes* were followed by the amount of the donation. The 'confraternity', nevertheless, possessed a sum derived *para theo*, which was presumably larger than the contributions of its individual members. This may well have come from private or imperial donations, or both.[146] In the *adelphotes* of the Naupaktitissa we have to assume that the member who took up the task of transferring the icon to a new parish in procession was also the one who covered the expenses. This would be a basic financial arrangement. We should expect then that the internal structure and economic management of the *diakoniai* would become more complex according to the type of the service and its location – the provincial Naupaktitissa is admittedly much simpler than the *diakonia tōn apronoetōn* of Studites, while, as we have seen, the financial relations among the

---

143 Theodore the Studite, *Epistulae*, ed. Fatouros, no. 13.25–57; *Miracles of St Artemios*, ed. Crisafulli and Nesbitt, 116.21–26; *Typikon of the Naupaktitissa Confraternity*, ed. Nesbitt and Wiita, 365.51–79. See Baun, *Tales*, 373–374.
144 See Perry, *Collegia*, 506–508.
145 *Life of St. Andrew of Crete*, ed. Papadopoulos Kerameus, 176.
146 Theodore the Studite, *Epistulae*, ed. Fatouros, no. 13.15, 59.

separate *diakoniai* of Constantinople could become very complicated. Another piece of evidence comes from the *adelphotes* of the Hodegetria in Thessaloniki. The confraternity owned *katallaktika ergasteria* (money-changing workshops) which it exploited under *emphyteotic* lease. Under the condition that they be turned to *myrepsika ergasteria*, it leased them to another lessee, and thus we have the unique document that bears testimony to this transaction, which comes from the year 1400. The representative of the confraternity was its *oikonomos tes adelphotetos*, who was, at the same time, *megas oikonomos* of the metropolis of Thessaloniki.[147]

Lastly, it would be appropriate to suggest here that in some cases the circle of benefactors may have coincided with the members of the confraternity. Still, large confraternities, found in great cities, would not display the same characteristic. The question of numbers, of members, benefactors, and people helped by this activity, is disappointingly beyond our reach based on our meagre information. The same is true about the employees: were the people working for the *diakoniai* – e.g. the *douleutai* and the *bastagarioi* of Hodegetria – members of the *diakonia*? If so, was their employment in the *diakonia* their only one, or did they have a profession they practised when not engaged in it? We might answer in the affirmative or in the negative, according to our assessment of the evidence, but, in conclusion, we should be careful about our interpretations of the material.

Monasteries and churches

In Early Byzantium, the existence of social clusters such as those of the *spoudaioi* and the *philoponoi* bears witness to the fact that ceremonies and rituals were very important as expressions of togetherness in a public context, or even, taking the apparent secrecy of some of these organisations into account, in the context of Christian communities. The churches and the monasteries became the actual meeting points for Christian activities and accommodated a significant part of public and religious life in Byzantium. These buildings provided common space

---

147 *M.M.* 2, 525–527. See Janin, *Centres*, 369, 377–378, 382; Patterson-Ševčenko, Servants, 549–550. The church of the Hodegetria in Thessaloniki is not to be confused with the Acheiropoietos, but the icon itself was closely connected to both the Acheiropoietos and St. Sophia. Angold, *Church and Society*, 388, followed by Baun, *Tales*, 373, 374, suggested that there was also a confraternity of St. Demetrios in Thessaloniki. However, the *paides* mentioned in the discourse of Eustathios of Thessaloniki about the capture of the city by the Normans refer to novices who belonged to the clergy of the church of St. Demetrios, not to a confraternity. See Eustathios of Thessaloniki, *Capture of Thessaloniki*, ed. Kyriakidis, 95.24–25, and 142.3–21 for the *adelphotes*, where the full narration of a miracle performed by the icon is found. This, however, does not mean that there was no such confraternity of St. Demetrios, but only that we need more evidence about it.

for the needs of the confraternities, for bringing people together in common religious rituals that are related to, but do not coincide with, everyday religious rituals and practices.[148] This becomes amply clear in the case of the icon of the Theotokos Naupaktitissa, which was transferred to a different parish and village on the first day of every month. In the charter, there is even provision that, if the weather conditions were not suitable, the icon would be carried there the next day. On that day, then, the members of the confraternity and the peasants probably celebrated the mass together, while special liturgies were held every Wednesday and Friday.[149] The procession, the ceremony of reception, and the liturgies that followed were not just spiritual events for the pious, but also social events for all the inhabitants of the countryside, where expressions of public life were limited or altogether lacking. Such events could even bring together peasants from the surrounding villages, thus reinforcing bonds that already existed because of localism and the propensity to transcend the narrow limits of village settlements.

Therefore, as a building, the village church is a point of reference for the population of agrarian communities. We have seen in the first part of this paper how the inhabitants of a village took responsibility for settling their affairs within the community. The guarantors of the various transactions were normally the personnel of a church, priests and *nomikoi*, who provided their services to the church and the communities. We have to assume, although it is rarely stated, that in these cases most of the transactions took place inside the churches or church complexes. One of these rare references concerns the examination of a dispute that has already been mentioned above. In the Nestoggos case, dated to 1277, the parties involved gathered in the church of St. John the Baptist in the village of Prinovaris. The trial brought together the representatives of Nestoggos; those of another magnate, Komnenos Raoul; 'many locals' of Prinovaris; high clerics of the metropolis of Smyrna; monks of the Lembiotissa monastery; and many *paroikoi* of Nestoggos and Raoul.[150]

An even more explicit testimony from the archives of the monastery of Patmos dates to the beginning of the thirteenth century. The dispute was between a monastery of Latros, St. John of Batos,[151] and the family of Lampones, who disputed the donation of a field. The investigation of the case was delegated to the metropolitan bishop Manuel by the grand duke Theodotos Phokas. The duke's representative in the procedure was John Pissites, who was local, while the *praktor* John Eudaimonitzes represented the state apparatus in the area. Appa-

---

148 Horden, Confraternities, 27. C.f. Cutler and North, Service, 215–216; also Kazhdan, Microstructures, 7.
149 *Typikon of the Naupaktitissa Confraternity*, ed. Nesbitt and Wiita, 364.37–365.51.
150 *MM IV*, 259, no. 164.
151 Ragia, Λάτρος, 101–102; Janin, Centres, 228–229.

rently, all the clerics of the metropolis were present during the hearing: the three priests, the *ekklesiarches*, the exarch, 'and the rest of the priests and deacons'. The local community was represented by eight landowners of the region of Miletus, or, as the bishop put it, by 'almost the entire community'. The bishop scheduled for the hearing to be held on the first of May of 1209. When the *protopapas* (first-ranking priest) of the metropolis testified in favour of the Lampones, abbot Theodosios 'requested that we [the bishop] put the *protopapas* under [penalty of] excommunication', but 'the entire community under [threat of] penance and excommunication proved the Lampones as owners [of the disputed land]'. After the testimony of John Pissites, who was 'born and raised in Palatia' [Miletus], the final decision was in favour of the family. According to the bishop's final remark, 'the people of the monastery of St. John, having been discredited, left, because they were condemned by the testimony and proof of the locals'. What is interesting in this case is the fact that the underlying background of the conflict turned out to be an 'us against them' affair. It is for this reason that the hearing gathered a large audience under the leadership of the local aristocracy, which is underscored several times in the decision. The monastery of St. John was seen as an outsider in Miletus.[152]

In a sense, then, we might even argue that local churches affirm and enhance local identity and self-awareness by providing a common social space as well as a liturgical-Christian one. We see this very clearly when it comes to donor inscriptions that have survived, either carved on stone or painted in wall paintings. A church is not only a sacred place for religious ceremonies or a space in which transactions are carried out, but also a space for the projection of the social identity of the inhabitants of the countryside, whether they belong to the local aristocracy or to the broader peasant class. Donations given by peasants for the building or renovation of churches are a well-recorded phenomenon in Late Antiquity. Elaborate inscriptions record the names of the donors, sometimes the amount of money donated, and the mosaic surface funded by that amount.[153] However, from the sixth century onwards the inscriptions become simpler without any reference to the amounts donated or even the list of donors. One of the few examples comes from the church of St. Tryphon in Troas: 'for the blessing of the villages and…their houses whose names God knows'.[154] The scarcity of inscriptional material in Middle Byzantium could indicate that this habit is lost, but this may be a far-fetched conclusion. During this period, the references in the narrative sources – mostly lives of saints – reveal the generosity of peasants when

---

152 *MM VI*, 153–156. On the complicated social relations revealed in this document and the individuals involved, see Ragia, Κοιλάδα, 426–428.
153 Atzaka, Επάγγελμα, 46–55, 113–115.
154 *Alexandria Troas Inscriptions*, ed. Ricl, no. 187.

a new church or monastery was erected in their region. The most eloquent descriptions are found in the *Life of St. Euthymios the Younger* about the construction of Peristerai on the outskirts of Thessaloniki, and in the *Life of St. Nikon* about his monastery in Lakedaimon, as well as his work on Crete.[155] The descriptions suggest that the building of a new church was indeed a community affair, and many of the inhabitants of the countryside or village contributed to its completion.

In the thirteenth century, the habit of listing the donors by name along with their donations reappears. It is particularly evident in Lakedaimon (especially in Mani), but it is also observed in Thasos, Crete, Naxos, Cyprus, and Epirus. The donations mentioned in these cases do not only concern amounts of money, but also small land plots, olive trees, and vineyards, and thus the inscriptions also become proofs of transactions. It is interesting that in a number of instances the inscriptions mention the *prokritoi* or the *koinos laos*, the *geneai*, *kleronomoi*, and *ktetores*. Kalopissi-Verti, who has studied these inscriptions, discusses the possibility that the individuals named in them were not simply related to each other, but were extended families, 'clans'.[156] In the context of the present study, one might wonder whether these monuments bear testimony to true *fatriai*, as we have seen them above, meaning families with their clientele networks in the provincial setting, where the monuments were created. In other words, we might well wonder if *geneai* is yet another term used locally for signalling the same group based on extended family ties. Be that as it may, this type of social terminology not only points to the social stratification within the communities, but also to the developing demarcation of the social classes in Byzantium, based on descent and inheritance. Thus, these small buildings become spaces for the social self-projection of the families, affirming their status and role within the local communities.

In Late Byzantine times, the names of the donors were listed in the *brebion* of a church or a monastery.[157] Such a *brebion* with names of individuals, without any reference to their benefaction, has come down to us from Epiros, at the end of a manuscript, dated to 1225, that contains mostly prayers and liturgical texts. In the opinion of Prinzing, who published the list of names, this indicates that a confraternity operated in the region of Ioannina. However, this suggestion cannot be maintained. The list begins with the invocation 'remember, Lord, the

---

155 *Life of Euthymios the Younger*, ed. Petit, 39–41 ch. 29; *Life of St. Nikon*, ed. Sullivan, 86–88 ch. 21, 114–118 ch. 35. Donating land and assets is much more common, since countless examples are found in the monastic archives. See Laiou, Peasant as Donor, 107–116.
156 See in detail Kalopissi-Verti, Collective Patterns, 125–136. See also: Laiou, Peasant as Donor, 116–121.
157 A *brebion* is a simple list, an inventory of different things: persons, lands, properties, etc. See ODB, 321, s.v. Brebion (Alexander Kazhdan).

souls of your servants', while one of the following notes maintains the formula that we have seen in Troas: 'whose names the Lord knows; in the book of life; amen'.[158] The expression indicates donors whose names were grouped together in the manuscript to be commemorated during the liturgies. This function of the *brebion*, which, among other things, also listed the names of donors, is well known from an important document in the archive of the Docheiariou monastery: the donor, Manuel Deblitzenos explicitly requested that, in exchange for his generous donations, his name and those of his parents should be included in the *brebion* of the monastery, and gave specific instructions about the commemorations.[159] While inscriptions, whether carved or painted, are meant to be seen, not only by those participating in the ceremonies but also by those visiting the churches for various reasons, the lists of names in the *brebia* represent a more internalised commemoration of identities, located within a Christian liturgical context. In these cases, only those participating in the ceremonies would witness the commemoration of the individuals concerned.

The Novel of Emperor Basil II of 996 already discusses the ties of the population with the churches and the monasteries in their village and the surrounding area. The Novel partly concerns the diminishing of village lands and their appropriation by the local church authorities. The description of the process by which such church estates were created is of particular interest for our subject: '[…] for it happens, as they report, in many of the villages that a villager puts up a church on his own land and grants his own portion of land to it, becomes a monk himself and resides there for the rest of his life, then another villager does the same and another likewise, and in that place there are two or three monks'.[160] The emperor decided that the churches should remain under the bishop's spiritual authority, but that they should be community churches for the peasants.[161] However, the monasteries that were founded in the same way would have to have at least eight monks, otherwise they would not be considered as monasteries by the law.[162] It appears, then, that the foundation of such religious spaces created collectives of limited size within rural communities, and members of the same family as well as other peasants could be tonsured and live in them.[163]

---

158 Prinzing, Spuren, 751–771, esp. 752–756.
159 *Actes de Docheiariou*, ed. Oikonomides, no. 58.4–8. On the Deblitzenoi and the detailed instructions, under penalty of canonical punishment, see Oikonomides, Deblitzenoi, 182.
160 *Novels of the Macedonian Emperors*, ed. Svoronos and Gounaridis, no. 14, 208.102–106; McGeer, *Legislation*, 122.
161 *Novels of the Macedonian Emperors*, ed. Svoronos and Gounaridis, no. 14, 208.117–119.
162 *Novels of the Macedonian Emperors*, ed. Svoronos and Gounaridis, no. 14, 209.133–150. See Lefort, Rural Economy, 283.
163 The most blatant cases of such clusters come from the archive of the Athonite monasteries. At the beginning of the tenth century, there were already many small communities of monks

The significance of such small religious centres for local communities becomes clear in the cases of St. Marina in the village of Genikon, and St. Panteleimon in Mantaia, both close to Smyrna. Apparently, St. Marina was a small church with some *kellia* attached, and owned perhaps some plots of land, because it is mentioned both as church and monastery in the documents. In 1252–1253, the local bishop decided to have the monasteries in his jurisdiction renovated and ceded to the monastery of Theotokos Lembiotissa. The inhabitants of Genikon consented to the donation of St. Marina and signed the act as a community, apparently because they were considered its owners.[164] Small monasteries like St. Marina must have been quite common in the provinces. Built either by individuals on their own estates, as Emperor Basil's Novel describes, or by a group of people, it often became difficult for them to survive unless they came under the protection of a large monastery. A similar case is known from the same archive. Alexios Tesaites inherited the little monastery of St. Panteleimon, which his father had erected on their estate. The monastery was the receiver of donations from the peasants of the village of Mantaia. Tesaites donated it to the Lembiotissa in 1232. By 1274 the mention of a 'highroad to the *panegyris* of St. Panteleimon' testifies to its annual market fair.[165] Thus, the small monastic establishment that was built on a peasant's initiative became a meeting point for the locals because of its fair.

Lastly, a particular aspect of the role of monasteries relates to the feeding of the poor, but this is very different from what we have seen in the case of the *diakoniai*. The feeding of the poor (*diadosis peneton*: distribution to the poor) takes place at the gates of monasteries, either regularly on great feast days, but sometimes also daily, especially in a city as large as Constantinople, and especially in times of famine.[166] Relevant information about this practice in the provinces concerns Thessaloniki and Lesbos.[167] In no other place, however, did it reach the regularity and formality that it reached in the case of the Theotokos Kosmosoteira in Thrace. In the twelfth century the founder of the monastery, Isaakios Komnenos, brother of the emperor, wrote the regulation of the monastery, where he stipulated on which feasts the distribution would take place,

---

living as hermits; in time, they built small churches and *kellia*, thus creating small monasteries that were then sold to the larger monasteries. See in detail Ragia, Μονές, 1511–1541.

164 *MM IV*, 262–266 nos. 167–169; Ahrweiler, Smyrne, 99; Laiou, Peasant as Donor, 112–113.

165 *MM IV*, 56–59 nos. 15–16, 76–77 no. 25, 97–98 no. 40, 107 no. 49, 138–139 no. 70; Ahrweiler, Smyrne, 98; Kyritses and Smyrlis, Villages, 445. On market fairs, see esp. Vryonis, Panegyris, 196–227.

166 Caseau, *Nourritures*, 223 f. Bread and wheat are mostly distributed in these cases. Also see Ragia, Πρόβλημα ρευστότητας, 261–262, with more source references. Most of the monastic foundation documents of Constantinople contain stipulations about the feeding of the poor.

167 *Life of Theodora of Thessaloniki*, ed. Paschalides, 164; *Lives of Sts. David, Symeon, and George*, ed. Van den Gheyn, 209–259, 224–225, 240.21–241.10.

fixed the number of the poor to at least one hundred on the day of the Dormition of Virgin Mary (August 15th) and also dictated the basic stages of the ceremony: 'they [the poor] should be seated on the floor in a line or a circle, to partake of the food in a more dignified way. When they will be filled, [I want them] [...] to rise [...] from their places, to raise their hands and to recite for my sake the 'Kyrie eleison' forty times, and then to go on home. I wish that this particular action of the monks [the distribution of food] at the time of the feast never once cease, nor ever be altered, in the present age'.[168] In this case, there is no indication that a confraternity was involved, and Isaakios certainly did not institute one. The distribution of food was entirely dependent on the monks and the monastery's prosperity, and the ceremony aimed at the forgiveness of Isaakios' sins.

Concluding remarks

Based on the evidence discussed above, it appears that Byzantine society displays significant flexibility and bonding potential within its structures. While there has been a conscious effort throughout this study to avoid the well-known and rather stereotypical understanding of the family and the village as a fiscal unit, it has not been difficult to detect other groupings that either formed within them, or transcended them, to serve particular purposes of economic or social interest. The village fostered cooperation and thereby promoted growth and change. Lemerle has already described how the fiscal processes of Byzantium after the eleventh century undermined the cohesiveness of the villages, meaning primarily the joint liability of the peasants.[169] This study has made clear that the various fiscal practices of the state were conducive to the formation of mutual interest groups, favoured mostly by, and based on, common economic interests that the peasants could assert with vehemence and even, in some cases, actual violence.[170] This process made real changes to, or at least affected, the different social manifestations of status by those residing in a *chorion*, and presumably the perception of social standing in the context of the increasing self-awareness of social position that these practices also favoured. Although the various beneficiaries of imperial privileges served different economic interests, the juridical functions of the village remained in place. The parish churches provided common space, not only liturgical, but also social and juridical. In this context, the

---

168 *Typikon of the Kosmosoteira*, ed. Papazoglou, 45–48, esp. 47.219–48.226; Thomas and Hero, *Byzantine Monastic Foundation Documents* 2, 802–804, esp. 803; Ragia, Marine Products, 458. The abbot should decide how many poor would take part in this ceremony in other celebrations.

169 Lemerle, *Agrarian History*, 189–192.

170 C.f. Laiou, Peasant as Donor, 119.

social differentiation of the Late Byzantine period and the resulting social self-representation became even more pronounced, as we see in the inscriptions relating to collective donations that are explicit about the social standing of the donors. In fact, it is rather surprising that as social differentiation develops after the tenth century and people increasingly manifest their social status, nevertheless, at the same time local communities also gain in self-awareness, and structures like the villages and simple churches become areas for one's social proclamation and distinction, thus uniting what seems to be a fragmented mosaic of social status. It is a remarkable contradiction but also an interesting one that could lead to a new understanding of the social fabric of Byzantium.

It is important that these aspects of mutual interest groups growing inside villages catered to exchanges that took place within the communities and thereby projected social awareness on a local level. Living in a particular settlement defined people's sphere of social action and was an integral part of their identity.[171] In this context, it is understandable why ancient notions of the wider family such as the *fatria* survived in the middle Byzantine period and later. The *fatria* was a vehicle for social self-definition that cut across communities and local borders. It could serve the social promotion of (extended) families and even take up political characteristics. Its potential to expand to include supporters, friends, and clients and thereby to become a large group that might dominate any provincial setting, or even affect the delicate political balances maintained in the capital, was clearly alarming to Byzantine governments. The meagre evidence we have suggests that the *fatriai* were always an inherent feature of the aristocracy, and as such they are not a factor promoting the coherence and unity of society even if they had their own internal strengths; in fact, it appears that they caused trouble to the authorities in Constantinople. However, on a local level they could lead to the self-awareness and self-assertion of the local population against the capital; and they could also provide aid when it was needed, and set up the organisation, support, and defence of local communities.

In these groupings, social equality was by no means a necessary condition, although in some it appears to have been a dominant feature, e. g. among the peasants, who cooperated to expand their areas of cultivation. The *fatriai* display a certain degree of equality among its members, which, nevertheless, could be expected to diminish the more they expand. In these contexts, clientele relations might also appear. We have seen above how the bonding between a *pronoia* holder and his paroikoi might have worked. Clientele relations should be considered as inherent within the *fatriai*. They cannot be excluded in the framework of the confraternities either. Nevertheless, the fact that the confraternities were so

---

171 See for example Kondyli, Meeting the Locals, 75–90, based on the monastic archives relating to the island of Lemnos.

low-profile differentiates them from the *fatriai*. They were both rooted in Antiquity but the confraternities discarded public self-promotion and the ancient way of living and bonding, which was interwoven into the city fabric.

It is not by chance that most of the material that we have comes from Constantinople; the Constantinopolitan *diakoniai* and *presbeiai* of the eleventh and twelfth centuries were groups eager to promote the distinction of their members in the Byzantine capital, on the social, religious, or even political level. On the other hand, discretion and humility in performing their tasks, such as taking care of the poor, are essential qualities of Byzantine *diakoniai*, otherwise our information would have been abundant. To the degree that they are differentiated from their Late Antique predecessors participation in them was not part of the individuals' public image. The few seals that name individuals as heads of *presbeiai* of Constantinople rather confirm that they were the exception to the rule and are explained because of the high status of their holders, while there is reason to think that *presbeiai* and *diakoniai* were not unquestionably one and the same, neither were these terms interchangeable. Many *diakoniai*, such as the Eugeniou, were somehow incorporated into the social and economic system of the empire. Therefore, it would be going too far to consider that each and every reference to a *diakonia* conceals a group of lay people bound together for the performance of a particular charity or religious service, as we see in the *Typika* of Thebes or of Theodore Studites.

We find few groups like these in the provinces, mostly in provincial cities, but religious processions were probably more frequent than we know, even in a country setting, although not many of them would have replicated the organisation of the Theban procession or that of the Theotokos Hodegetria. It appears that the countryside possessed, as we have seen, other modes of expression. The provincial monasteries and churches were hubs of diverse activities, from hosting legal procedures and collecting donations or organising fairs, to feeding the poor.[172] Horizontal groupings such as those discussed here organised social life in a Christian framework. Even though participation was voluntary and therefore limited, their activities were directed towards the communities, and although limited participation becomes a privilege and an honour for the participants, these activities ultimately become inclusive, reaffirming the bonds of the inhabitants with their land and their community. It seems that formations such as the villages and the *fatriai*, or even the ambiguous *geneai*, were, ultimately, mechanisms of survival, because they sheltered and facilitated the expression of social differentiation and/or homogeneity in the provinces. They helped the

---

172 Kaplan, *Les hommes*, 197–198. In the sources, references to processions and supplications to local saints are numerous.

communities to survive, even if this meant that they needed to escape the tight control of Constantinople.

Bibliography

Primary Sources

Acts of Chalcedon, ed. Eduard Schwartz (Berlin 1962), *Acta Conciliorum Oecumenicorum, Concilium universale Chalcedonense anno 451,* vol. 2.1.2.

Actes de Chilandar, première partie, ed. Louis Petit, Actes de l'Athos 5:I (St. Petersburg, 1911) (repr. Amsterdam 1975).

Actes de Docheiariou, ed. Nikos Oikonomides, Archives de l'Athos 13 (Paris, 1984).

Actes d'Esphigménou, ed. Jacques Lefort, Archives de l'Athos 6 (Paris, 1973).

Actes d'Iviron I, ed. Jacques Lefort, Nikos Oikonomides, Denise Papachryssanthou, and Hélène Métrévéli, *Actes d'Iviron I: des origines au milieu du XIe siècle,* Archives de l'Athos 14 (Paris, 1985).

Actes de Lavra I, ed. Paul Lemerle, André Guillou, Nicolas Svoronos, and Denise Papachryssanthou, *Actes de Lavra. Première Partie: des origines à 1204,* Archives de l'Athos 5 (Paris, 1970).

Actes du Protaton, ed. Dénise Papachryssanthou, Archives de l'Athos 7 (Paris, 1975).

Actes de Xénophon, ed. Denise Papachryssanthou, Archives de l'Athos 15 (Paris, 1986).

Actes de Xéropotamou, ed. Jacques Bompaire, Archives de l'Athos 3 (Paris, 1964).

Alexandria Troas Inscriptions, ed. Marijana Ricl, *The Inscriptions of Alexandria Troas,* IGSK 53 (Bonn, 1997).

Anonymous Cretan Poem, ed. Nikolaos Panagiotakes, Παλαιὰ καὶ Νέα Διαθήκη, ἀνώνυμο κρητικὸ ποίημα (τέλη 15ου-ἀρχὲς 16ου αἰ.), Graecolatinitas Nostra, Fonti 6 (Venice, 2004).

Aphrodisias Inscriptions, ed. Charlotte Roueché, *Aphrodisias in Late Antiquity: The Late Roman and Byzantine Inscriptions Including Texts from the Excavations at Aphrodisias conducted by Kenan T. Erim, Charlotte Roueche; with contributions by Joyce M. Reynolds,* Journal of Roman Studies Monograph 5 (London, 1989).

Attaleiates, Michael, *History,* ed. Eudoxos Tsolakis, *Michaelis Attaliatae Historia,* CFHB 50 (Athens, 2011). English translation: Anthony Kaldellis and Dimitris Krallis, *Michael Attaleiates, The History* (Cambridge, Mass., 2012).

Ashburner, Walter, The Farmer's Law, *JHS* 30 (1910) 85–88; *JHS* 32 (1912), 68–95.

Basilica, ed. H.J. Scheltema, D. Holwerda, and N. van der Wal, *Basilicorum Libri LX* (Gröningen, 1945–1988).

Book of Ceremonies, ed. Gilbert Dagron, Bernard Flusin, and Denis Feissel, *Constantin VII Porphyrogénète: Le livre des cérémonies,* CFHB 52.3 (Paris, 2020).

Byzantine Lead Seals, vol. I/1–3, ed. George Zacos and Alexander Veglery (Basel, 1972).

Cassius Dio, *Historiae Romanae:* vol. 1, ed. Ursulus Boissevain (Berlin, 1895) (repr. 1955).

Cartulary of the Monastery of St. Paul, Latros, ed. Christian Gastgeber and Otto Kresten, *Das Chartular des Paulos-Klosters am Berge Latros,* Wiener Byzantinistische Studien 30 (Vienna, 2015).

Catalogue of Byzantine Seals 5, ed. Eric McGeer, John Nesbitt, and Nikos Oikonomides, *Catalogue of Byzantine Seals at Dumbarton Oaks and in the Fogg Museum of Art, 5: The East (continued), Constantinople and Environs, Unknown Locations, Addenda, Uncertain Readings* (Washington, D.C., 2005).

Catenae Graecorum patrum in Novum Testamentum, ed. J.A. Cramer, vol. 6 (Oxford, 1842), (repr. Hildesheim, 1967).

Choniates, Niketas, *Historia*, ed. Johannes van Dieten, *Nicetae Choniatae historia, pars prior*, CFHB 11.1 (Berlin, 1975); English translation: Harry Magoulias, *O City of Byzantium, Annals of Niketas Choniates* (Detroit, 1984).

Chronicle of Monemvasia, ed. Ewald Kislinger, *Regionalgeschichte als Quellenproblem. Die Chronik von Monembasia und das Sizilianische Demenna. Eine historisch-topographische Studie*, TIB 8 (Vienna, 2001).

Corpus des Sceaux V2, ed. Vitalien Laurent, *Le Corpus des Sceaux de l'Empire Byzantin. T.5, vol. 2: L'Église* (Paris, 1965).

Corpus des Sceaux V3, ed. Vitalien Laurent, *Le Corpus des Sceaux de l'Empire Byzantin. T.5, vol. 3: L'Église: Supplément* (Paris, 1972).

Corpus Iuris Civilis, vol. II: *Codex Iustinianus*, ed. Paul Krueger (Berlin, 1892).

Digesta: Corpus Iuris Civilis, vol. I, *Institutiones*, ed. Krueger, Paul; *Digesta*, ed. Mommsen, Theodor (Berlin. 1889).

Dmitrievskij, Aleksei (ed.) *Opisanie liturgitseckij rukopisei*, tom II, *Εὐχολόγια* (Kiev, 1901).

Ecloga, ed. Ludwig Burgmann, *Ecloga. Das Gesetzbuch Leons III. und Konstantinos' V.*, Forschungen zur Byzantinischen Rechtsgeschichte 10 (Frankfurt am Main, 1983).

Ephesos Inscriptions Ia, ed. Hermann Wankel, *Die Inscriften von Ephesos, Ia*, IGSK 11.1 (Bonn, 1979).

Ephesos Inscriptions III, ed. Helmut Engelmann, D. Knibbe, and R. Merkelbach, *Die Inschriften von Ephesos, III*, IGSK 13 (Bonn, 1980).

Ephesos Inscriptions VII.2, ed. Recep Meriç, Reinhold Merkelbach, Johannes Nollé, and Sencer Şahin, *Die Inschriften von Ephesos, VII.2*, IGSK 17.2 (Bonn, 1981).

Eustathios of Thessaloniki, *On the Capture of Thessaloniki*, ed. Stilpon Kyriakidis, *Eustazio di Tessalonica, La espugnazione di Tessalonica* (Palermo, 1961).

Gregoras, Nikephoros, *Historiae*, ed. Immanuel Bekker and Ludovicus Schopen, CSHB 25–27 (Bonn, 1829–1855).

Halkin, François, Éloge des cinq martyrs de Satala, in: Halkin, François, *Saints de Byzance et du Proche-Orient*, Cahiers d'Orientalisme 13 (Geneva, 1986) 133–145.

Hesychius of Alexandria, *Lexicon, vol. IV, T-Ω*, ed. Kurt Latte, Peter Allan Hansen, and Ian C. Cunningham, Sammlung griechischer und lateinischer Grammatiker 11.4 (Berlin/ New York, 2009).

Hiéra-Xérochoraphion cartulary, ed. Nigel Wilson and Jean Darrouzès, Restes du cartulaire de Hiéra-Xérochoraphion, *REB* 26 (1968) 1–47.

John of Ephesus, *Ecclesiastical History, III*, ed. Ernest Walter Brooks, *Ioannis Ephesini Historiae Ecclesiasticae pars tertia*, CSCO Scr. Syri III.3 (Louvain, 1936).

John of Ephesus, *Lives of the Eastern Saints (II)*, ed. Ernest Walter Brooks, PO 18 (1924) 340–698.

Kantakouzenos, John, *Historiae*, ed. Ludovicus Schopen, CSHB 5–7 (Bonn, 1828).

Kekaumenos, *Consilia et Narrationes*, ed. Maria Dora Spadaro, *Cecaumeno, Raccomandazioni e consigli di un galantuomo (Στρατηγικόν)*, Hellenica 2 (Alessandria, 1998).

Life of Basil, ed. Ihor Ševčenko, *Chronographiae quae Theophanis Continuati nomine fertur. Liber Vita Basilii Imperatoris amplecitur*, CFHB 42 (Berlin/Boston, 2011).

Life of St. Andrew of Crete, ed. Athanasios Papadopoulos Kerameus, Βίος τοῦ ἐν ἁγίοις πατρὸς ἡμῶν Ἀνδρέου τοῦ Ἱεροσολυμίτου, ἀρχιεπισκόπου γενομένου Κρήτης, συγγραφεὶς παρὰ Νικήτα τοῦ πανευφήμου πατρικίου καὶ κυέστορος, in: Ἀνάλεκτα Ἱεροσολυμιτικῆς Σταχυολογίας. Συλλογὴ ἀνεκδότων καὶ σπανίων ἑλληνικῶν συγγραφῶν περὶ τῶν κατὰ τὴν Ἑῴαν Ὀρθοδόξων Ἐκκλησιῶν καὶ μάλιστα εἰς τὴν ἐν Παλαιστίνην, vol. 5 (St. Petersburg, 1897) (repr. Brussels, 1963) 169–179.

Life of St. Daniel of Sketis, ed. Leon Clugnet, *Vie et Récits de l'abbé Daniel le Scétiote* (Paris, 1901), I–XXXII, 1–117.

Life of Euthymios the Younger, ed. Louis Petit, *Vie et office de saint Euthyme le Jeune* (Paris, 1904).

Life of St. Nikon, ed. Denis Sullivan, *The Life of Saint Nikon* (Brookline, Mass., 1987).

Life of Theodora of Thessaloniki, ed. S. Paschalides, Ο βίος της οσιομυροβλύτιδος Θεοδώρας της εν Θεσσαλονίκη. Διήγηση περὶ της μεταθέσεως του τιμίου λειψάνου της οσίας Θεοδώρας, Κέντρον Αγιολογικών Μελετών 1 (Thessaloniki, 1991).

Life of Theophano, ed. Eduard Kurtz, *Zwei griechische Texte über die hl. Theophano, die Gemahlin Kaisers Leo VI* (St. Petersburg, 1898).

Lives of Sts. David, Symeon, and George, Joseph Van den Gheyn, *Acta graeca ss. Davidis, Symeonis et Georgii Mytilenae in insula Lesbo*, AB 18 (1899) 209–259.

Maurice, *Strategikon*, ed. George T. Dennis and Ernst Gamillscheg, CFHB 17 (Vienna, 1981).

The Miracles of St. Artemios: a Collection of Miracle Stories by an Anonymous Author of Seventh-Century Byzantium, ed. Virgil S. Crisafulli and John W. Nesbitt, The Medieval Mediterranean 13 (Leiden/New York, 1997).

Novels of the Macedonian Emperors, ed. Nikos Svoronos and Paris Gounaridis, *Les novelles des empereurs Macédoniennes concernant la terre et les stratiotes* (Athens, 1994).

Patmos Inscriptions 1, ed. Era Vranouse, Βυζαντινὰ ἔγγραφα τῆς μονῆς Πάτμου. Α. Αὐτοκρατορικά (Athens, 1980).

Patmos Inscriptions 2, ed. Maria Nystazopoulou-Pelekidou, Βυζαντινὰ ἔγγραφα τῆς μονῆς Πάτμου. Β. Δημοσίων λειτουργῶν (Athens, 1980).

Peira, ed. Karl Eduard Zachariae von Lingenthal, Πεῖρα ἤγουν διδασκαλία ἐκ τῶν πράξεων τοῦ μεγάλου κυροῦ Εὐσταθίου τοῦ Ῥωμαίου, *Ius Graecoromanum*, vol. 4, ed. Ioannes Zepos and Panagiotes Zepos (Athens, 1931) 11–260.

Photius, *Lexicon*, vol. III: *Ny-Phi*, ed. Christos Theodorides (Berlin, 2012).

Pollux, Julius, *Onomasticon*, ed. Erich Bethe, *Pollucis Onomasticon*, fasc. I, *Lib. I–V continens* (Leipzig, 1900).

Priene Inscriptions, ed. Wolfgang Blümel, Reinhold Merkelbach, and Frank Rumscheid, *Die Inscriften von Priene*, IGSK 69 (Bonn, 2014).

Procopius, *Historia arcana*, ed. Jacoby Haury and Gerhard Wirth, *Historia quae dicitur Arcana. Procopii Caesariensis Opera Omnia, v. 3* (Leipzig, 1963).

Psellos, Michael, *Chronographia*, ed. Diether Roderich Reinsch, Millenium Studies 51 (Berlin/Boston, 2014).

Rhalles-Potles, Σύνταγμα των θείων καὶ ἱερῶν Κανόνων των τε Αγίων καὶ Πανευφήμων Ἀποστόλων καὶ των ἱερῶν Οἰκουμενικῶν καὶ Τοπικῶν Συνόδων καὶ των κατά μέρος Αγίων Πατέρων, vol. 1, ed. Georgios A. Rhalles, and Michael Potles (Athens, 1852).

Rule of St Basil: S. Basilii Caesareae Cappadociae Archiepiscopi Regulae fusius Tractatae, *PG* 31 (905–1052).

Skylitzes Continuatus, ed. Eudoxos Tsolakis, Η συνέχεια της Χρονογραφίας του Ιωάννου Σκυλίτση (Thessaloniki, 1968).

Smyrna Inscriptions II.I, ed. George Petzl, *Die Inschriften von Smyrna*, Teil II.I, IGSK 24.1 (Bonn, 1987).

Stephen of Byzantium, *Ethnica*, ed. Margarethe Billerbeck, and Arlette Neumann-Hartmann, *Stephani Byzantini Ethnica*, vol. V: *Φ-Ω, Indices*, CFHB 43.5 (Berlin/Boston 2017).

Sultan Daği Inscriptions, ed. Lloyd Jonnes, *The Inscriptions of Sultan Daği (Philomelion, Thymbrion, Hadrianiopolis, Tyraion)*, IGSK 62 (Bonn, 2002).

Souda, IV ed. Ada Adler, *Suidae Lexicon, pars IV* (Leipzig, 1935).

Synagoge, ed. Ian Cunningham, Συναγωγή λέξεων χρησίμων, *Sammlung griechischer und lateinischer Grammatiker* 10 (Berlin/New York, 2003).

Theodore the Studite, *Epistulae*, ed. Georgios Fatouras, *Theodori Studitae Epistulae*, CFHB 31 (Berlin/New York, 1992).

Three Byzantine Military Treatises, ed. George Dennis, CFHB 25 (Washington, DC., 1985).

Typikon of the Kosmosoteira, ed. Georgios Papazoglou, Τυπικὸν Ἰσαακίου Ἀλεξίου Κομνηνοῦ τῆς μονῆς Θεοτόκου τῆς Κοσμοσωτείρας, Thrakike Bibliotheke 3 (Komotene, 1994).

Typikon of the Naupaktitissa Confraternity, ed. John Nesbitt and John Wiita, A Confraternity of the Comnenian Era, *BZ* 68 (1975) 360–384.

Typikon of the Pantokrator, ed. Paul Gautier, Le typikon du Christ Sauveur Pantocrator, *REB* 32 (1974) 1–145.

Von Dobschütz, Ernst, Maria Romaia. Zwei unbekannte Texte, *BZ* 12 (1903) 173–214.

Secondary Literature

Acheimastou-Potamianou, Myrtali, Η Βλαχέρνα της Άρτας: Τοιχογραφίες (Athens, 2009).

Ahrweiler, Hélène, La concession de droits incorporels. Donations conditionelles, in: *Actes du XIIe Congrès International des Études Byzantines, Ochride 1961*, t. II (Beograd 1964) 103–114.

Ahrweiler, Hélène, L'histoire et la géographie de la région de Smyrne entre les deux occupations turques, particulièrement au XIIIe siècle, *TM* 1 (1965) 1–204.

Alföldy, Géza, *Römische Sozialgeschichte* (Stuttgart, 2011).

Angelidi, Christina and Titos Papamastorakis, Η μονή των Οδηγών και η λατρεία της Θεοτόκου Οδηγήτριας, in: Maria Basilaki (ed.) *Μήτηρ Θεού. Απεικονίσεις της Παναγίας στη Βυζαντινή τέχνη* (Athens/Milan, 2000) 373–387.

Angold, Michael, *Church and Society in Byzantium under the Comneni, 1081–1261* (Cambridge, 1995).

Aries, Philippe and Georges Duby (eds.), *A History of Private Life*, I. *From Pagan Rome to Byzantium*, ed. Veyne, Paul, *Ιστορία της ιδιωτικής ζωής από τη Ρωμαϊκή Αυτοκρατορία στο τέλος της πρώτης χιλιετίας μ.Χ.* (Cambridge Mass./London, 1987).

Arnaoutoglou, Ilias, Roman Law and *collegia* in Asia Minor, *Revue Internationale des droits de l'Antiquité* 49 (2002) 28–43.

Atzaka, Giota, *Το επάγγελμα του ψηφοθέτη (4ᵒˢ αι. Π.Χ - 8ᵒˢ αι. Μ.Χ)* (Athens, 2011).

Bartusis, Mark, *Land and Privilege in Byzantium: The Institution of Pronoia* (Cambridge, 2012).

Baun, Jane, *Tales from another Byzantium. Celestial Journey and Local Community in the Medieval Greek Apocrypha* (Cambridge, 2007).

Beck, Hans-Georg, *Kirche und theologische Literatur im byzantinischen Reich* (München, 1959).

Beck, Hans-Georg, Byzantinische Gefolgschaftswesen, *Bayerische Akademie der Wissenschaften, Philologisch-Historische Klasse, Sitzungsberichte* (1965) 3–32.

Berger, Albrecht, Das Bad in der byzantinischen Zeit, *Miscellanea Byzantina Monacensia* 27 (München, 1982), 56–71.

Berger, Albrecht, Imperial and Ecclesiastical Processions in Constantinople, in: *Byzantine Constantinople: Monuments, Topography and Everyday Life*, ed. N. Necipoglu, The Medieval Mediterranean 33 (Leiden/Boston/Köln, 2001) 73–87.

Bourdara, Kalliope, *Καθοσίωσις και τυραννίς κατά τους μέσους βυζαντινούς χρόνους. Μακεδονική δυναστεία (867–1056)* (Athens, 1981).

Brand, Charles, *Byzantium confronts the West, 1180–1204* (Cambridge MA, 1968).

Brown, Peter, *Poverty and Leadership in the Later Roman Empire* (London, 2002).

Brown, Peter, *Through the Eye of a Needle. Wealth, the Fall of Rome, and the Making of Christianity in the West, 350–550 AD* (Princeton, 2012).

Caseau, Béatrice, Ordinary Objects in Christian Healing Sanctuaries, in: *Objects in Context, Objects in Use. Material Spatiality in Late Antiquity*, ed. Luke Lavan, Ellen Swift, and Toon Putzeys, Late Antique Archaeology 5 (Leiden/Boston 2008) 625–654.

Caseau, Béatrice, *Nourritures terrestres, nourritures célestes: la culture alimentaire à Byzance, Monographies* 46 (Paris, 2015).

Cheynet, Jean-Claude, *Pouvoir et contestations à Byzance (963–1210)*, Byzantina Sorbonensia 9 (Paris, 1990).

Cheynet, Jean-Claude, Foi et conjuration à Byzance, in: Marie-France Auzépy and Guillaume Saint-Guillain, *Oralité et lien social au moyen âge (Occident, Byzance, Islam)*, Monographies 29 (Paris, 2008), 265–279.

Cheynet, Jean-Claude (ed.), *Le monde byzantin, tome 2. L'Empire byzantin, 641–1204* (Paris, 2006).

Constantelos, Demetrios, Origins of Christian Orthodox Diakonia: Christian Orthodox Philanthropy in Church History, *GOThR* 52 (2007) 1–36.

Cutler, Anthony and William North, The Gift of Service: The Charter of the Confraternity of the Virgin of Naupaktos, in: Jean-Michel Spieser and Elisabeth Yota (eds.), *Donation et donateurs dans le monde Byzantin*, Realités Byzantines 14 (Paris, 2012) 207–219.

Dagron, Gilbert, 'Ainsi rien n'échappera à la réglementation'. État, Église, corporations, confréries: à propos des inhumations à Constantinople (Ive-Xe siècle), in: Vassiliki Kravari, Jacques Lefort, and Cécile Morrisson, *Hommes et richesses dans l'empire Byzantin, vol. II, VIII-Xve siècles*, Réalités Byzantines 3 (Paris, 1991), 155–182.

Dagron, Gilbert, The Urban Economy, Seventh-Twelfth Centuries, in: Angeliki Laiou (ed.), *The Economic History of Byzantium: From the Seventh through the Fifteenth Century*, Dumbarton Oaks Studies 39 (Washington, D.C., 2002) 393–461.

Detorakis, Theocharis, *Οι άγιοι της πρώτης βυζαντινής περιόδου της Κρήτης και η σχετική προς αυτούς φιλολογία* (Athens, 1970).

Dölger, Franz, *Beiträge zur byzantinischen Finanzverwaltung, besonders des 10. Und 11. Jhs*, *Byzantinisches Archiv* 9 (München, 1927) (repr. 1960).

Efthymiadis, Stephanos, A Day and Ten Months in the Life of a Lonely Bachelor: The Other Byzantium in 'Miracula S. Artemii' 18 and 22, in: Stephanos Efthymiadis, *Hagiography in Byzantium: Literature, Social History and Cult*, Variorum Collected Studies 989 (Aldershot, 2011) 1–26.

Gerolymatou, Maria, La gestion de l'eau dans les campagnes byzantines (8e-15e siècle), *REB* 63 (2005) 195–205.

Gerolymatou, Maria, À propos des origines des monastères de la Vierge de l'Alsos et de la Vierge tôn Spondôn sur l'île de Cos, *TM* 16 (2010) 387–399.

Greenfield, Richard and Alice-Mary Talbot, Holy Men of Mount Athos, DOML 40 (Cambridge Mass./London, 2016).

Herrin, Judith, From Bread and Circuses to Soup and Salvation. The Origins of Byzantine Charity, in: Judith Herrin, *Margins and Metropolis. Authority Across the Byzantine Empire* (Princeton/Oxford 2013) 267–298.

Horden, Peregrine, The Confraternities of Byzantium, in: W. J. Shiels and Diana Wood (eds.) *Voluntary Religion. Papers read at the 1985 Summer Meeting and the 1986 Winter Meeting of the Ecclesiastical History Society* (Worcester, 1986) 25–45.

Janin, Raymond, *La géographie ecclésiastique de l'empire byzantin*, I: *Le siège de Constantinople et le Patriarcat œcuménique*, t. III: *Les églises et les monastères* (Paris, 1953).

Janin, Raymond, *Constantinople Byzantine. Développement urbain et répertoire topographique*, Archives de l'Orient chrétien 4 (Paris, 1964).

Janin, Raymond, Les processions religieuses à Byzance, *REB* 24 (1966) 69–88.

Janin, Raymond, *Les églises et les monastères des grands centres byzantins*, La géographie ecclésiastique de l'empire Byzantin 2 (Paris, 1975).

Kalopissi-Verti, Sophia, Collective Patterns of Patronage in the Late Byzantine Village: The Evidence of Church Inscriptions, in: Jean-Michel Spieser and Elisabeth Yota (eds.), *Donation et donateurs dans le monde Byzantin*, Realités Byzantines 14 (Paris, 2012) 125–140.

Kaplan, Michel, *Les hommes et la terre à Byzance du VIe au XIe siècle. Propriété et exploitation du sol*, Byzantina Sorbonensia 10 (Paris, 1992).

Kazhdan, Alexander, Small Social Groupings (Microstructures) in Byzantine Society, in: *XVI Internationaler Byzantinistenkongress. Akten II.2, JÖB* 32.2 (1982) 3–11.

Kazhdan, Alexander and Giles Constable, *People and Power in Byzantium: an Introduction to Modern Byzantine Studies* (Berkeley, 1982).

Kondyli, Fotini, Meeting the Locals: Peasant Families in 13th-Century Lemnos, in: *Liquid and Multiple: Individuals and Identities in the Thirteenth-Century Aegean*, ed. Guillaume Saint-Guillain and Dionysios Stathakopoulos, Monographies 35 (Paris, 2012) 75–90.

Kruse, Maria, Xiphilinos' Agency in the Epitome of Cassius Dio, *GRBS* 61 (2021) 193–223.

Kyritses, Demetrios, and Kostis Smyrlis, Les villages du littoral Égéen de l'Asie Mineure au Mo yen Âge, in: Jacques Lefort, Cécile Morrisson, and Jean-Pierre Sodini (eds.), *Les Villages dans l'Empire byzantin (IVe–XVe siècle)*, Réalités Byzantines 11 (Paris, 2005) 437–451.

Laiou, Angeliki, The Byzantine Village (5th-14th Century), in: Jacques Lefort, Cécile Morrisson, and Jean-Pierre Sodini (eds.), *Les Villages dans l'Empire byzantin (IVe-XVe siècle)*, Réalités Byzantines 11 (Paris 2005) 31-54.

Laiou, Angeliki, The Peasant as a Donor (13th-14th Centuries), in: Jean-Michel Spieser and Elisabeth Yota (eds.), *Donation et donateurs dans le monde Byzantin*, Realités Byzantines 14 (Paris, 2012) 107-124.

Laiou, Angeliki and Dieter Simon, Of Mills and Monks: The Case of the Mill of Chantax, in: Angeliki Laiou, Cécile Morrison, and Rowan Dorin (eds.), *Economic Thought and Economic Life in Byzantium* (Farnham, 2013) no X, 1-50.

Laiou-Thomadakis, Angeliki, *Peasant Society in the Late Byzantine Empire. A Social and Demographic Study* (Princeton, 1977).

Lefort, Jacques, The Rural Economy, Seventh-Twelfth Centuries, in: Angeliki Laiou (ed.), *The Economic History of Byzantium: From the Seventh through the Fifteenth Century*, Dumbarton Oaks Studies 39 (Washington, D.C., 2002) 231-310.

Lemerle, Paul, *The Agrarian History of Byzantium from the Origins to the Twelfth Century. The Sources and Problems* (Galway, 1979).

Leontaritou, Vassiliki, *Εκκλησιαστικά αξιώματα και υπηρεσίες στην πρώιμη και μέση Βυζαντινή περίοδο*, Forschungen zur Byzantinischen Rechtsgeschichte, Athener Reihe 8 (Athens-Komotene, 1996).

Magdalino, Paul, Church, Bath and Diakonia in Medieval Constantinople, in: Rosemary Morris (ed.), *Church and People in Byzantium. 20th Spring Symposium of Byzantine Studies* (1986) (Manchester, 1990) 165-190.

McGeer, Eric, *The Land Legislation of the Macedonian Emperors*, Medieval Sources in Translation 38 (Toronto, 2000).

Neville, Leonora, *Authority in Byzantine Provincial Society, 950-1100* (Cambridge, 2004).

Oikonomides, Nikos, *Les listes de préséance Byzantines des IXe et Xe siècles* (Paris, 1972).

Oikonomides, Nikos, Quelques boutiques de Constantinople au Xe s.: Prix, loyers, imposition (cod. Patmiacus 171), *DOP* 26 (1973) 345-356.

Oikonomides, Nikos, L'évolution de l'organisation administrative de l'empire byzantin au XIe siècle (1025-1118), *TM* 6 (1976) 125-152.

Oikonomides, Nikos, The properties of the Deblitzenoi in the Fourteenth and Fifteenth Centuries, in: Angeliki Laiou-Thomadakis (ed.) *Charanis Studies. Essays in Honor of P. Charanis* (New Brunswick N.J., 1980) 176-198.

Oikonomides, Nikos, Das Verfalland im 10.-11. Jahrhundert: Verkauf und Besteuerung, *Fontes Minores* 7 (1986) 161-168.

Oikonomides, Nikos, The Holy Icon as an Asset, *DOP* 45 (1991) 35-44.

Oikonomides, Nikos, *Fiscalité et exemption fiscale à Byzance (IXe-XIe s.)*, NHRF/IBR Monographs 2 (Athens, 1996).

Panopoulou, Angeliki, *Συντεχνίες και θρησκευτικές αδελφότητες στη βενετοκρατούμενη Κρήτη, Tomasso Flanghini* 7 (Athens/Venice, 2012).

Papadatou, Daphne, *Η συμβιβαστική επίλυση ιδιωτικών διαφορών κατά τη Μέση και Ύστερη Βυζαντινή Εποχή*, Forschungen zur byzantinischen Rechtsgeschichte, Athener Reihe 9 (Athens, 1995).

Papagianni, Eleftheria, Protimesis (Preemption) in Byzantium, in: Angeliki Laiou (ed.), *The Economic History of Byzantium: From the Seventh through the Fifteenth Century*, Dumbarton Oaks Studies 39 (Washington, D.C., 2002) 1071-1982.

Patterson-Ševčenko, Nancy, Servants of the Holy Icon, in: Christopher Frederick Moss and Katharine Kiefer (eds.) *Byzantine East – Latin West* (Princeton, 1995) 547–553.

Patterson-Ševčenko, Nancy, Icons in the Liturgy, *DOP* 45 (1999) 45–58.

Patlagean, Évelyne, *Pauvreté économique et pauvreté sociale à Byzance, 4e-7e siècles,* Civilisations et Sociétés 48 (Paris, 1977).

Perry, Jonathan S., Collegia, in: Michael Peachin (ed.) *The Oxford Handbook of Social Relations in the Roman World* (Oxford, 2011) 498–515 (https://doi.org/10.1093/oxfo rdhb/9780195188004.013.0023).

Petrides, Sophrone, Le monastère des Spoudaei à Jérusalem et les Spoudaei de Constantinople, *EO* 4 (1900–1901) 225–231.

Petrides, Sophrone, Spoudaei et philopones, *EO* 7 (1904) 341–348.

Prinzing, Günter, Spuren einer religiösen Bruderschaft in Epiros um 1225? Zur Deutung der Memorialtexte im Codex Cromqell 11, *BZ* 101 (2008) 751–771.

Ragia, Efi, The Inscription of Didyma (Hieron) and the Families of Phokas and Karantinos in Western Asia Minor (12th-13th C.), *BZ* 100 (2007) 131–144.

Ragia, Efi, *Λάτρος. Ένα άγνωστο μοναστικό κέντρο στη δυτική Μικρά Ασία, με λεπτομερή σχολιασμό των εγγράφων του αρχείου της μονής Θεοτόκου του Στύλου* (Thessaloniki, 2008).

Ragia, Efi, *Η κοιλάδα του κάτω Μαιάνδρου ca 600–1300. Γεωγραφία και Ιστορία,* Βυζαντινά Κείμενα και Μελέτες 51 (Thessaloniki, 2009).

Ragia, Efi, Αποταμίευση και διαχείριση χρήματος στο Βυζάντιο (7ος-11ος αι.): πρόβλημα ρευστότητας; in: K. Bourazelis and K. Meidane (eds.), *Αποταμίευση και διαχείριση του χρήματος στην ελληνική Ιστορία* (Athens, 2011) 247–275.

Ragia, Efi, Μονές ως περιουσιακά στοιχεία: Η περίπτωση του Αγίου Όρους (10ος-11ος αι.) in: Vassiliki Leontaritou, Kalliope Bourdara, and Eleftheria Papagianni (eds.) *Antecessor. Festschrift für Sp. Troianos, zum 80. Geburtstag* (Athens, 2013) 1511–1541.

Ragia, Efi, Social Group Profiles in Byzantium: Some Considerations on Byzantine Perceptions about Social Class Distinctions, *Byzantina Symmeikta* 26 (2016) 309–372.

Ragia, Efi, The Circulation, Distribution and Consumption of Marine Products in Byzantium, in: D. Mylona, A. Trentacoste, S. Grainger, and R. Nicholson (eds.), *The Bountiful Sea. Fish Processing and Consumption in Mediterranean Antiquity, Journal of Maritime Archaeology* 13.3 (2018) 449–466 (DOI 10.1007/s11457-018-9213-3).

Ragia, Efi, Agrarian Policy in the Early Palaeologan Period, ca. 1259–1300 from the Archives of Mt. Athos and West Asia Minor, *TM* 25.1 (2021) 503–562.

Ragia, Efi, The Social Position of the Soldiers and the 'Military Lands': an Interpretation (6th-10th Centuries), *REB* 80 (2022) 129–179.

Rapp Claudia, *Brother-making in Late Antiquity and Byzantium. Monks, Laymen and Christian Ritual* (New York, 2016).

Saradi, Helen, On the 'Archontike' and 'Ekklesiastike Dynasteia' and 'Prostasia' in Byzantium with Particular Attention to the Legal Sources: A Study in Social History of Byzantium, *Byzantion* 64 (1994) 69–117, 314–351.

Thomas, John Philip and Angela Constantinides Hero (eds.), *Byzantine Monastic Foundation Documents. A Complete Translation of the Surviving Founders' Typika and Testaments,* Dumbarton Oaks Studies 35 (Washington, DC, 1998).

Vailhé, Siméon, Les philopones d'Oxyrhynque au IVe siècle, *EO* 14 (1911) 277–278.

Vryonis, Spyros, The Panegyris of the Byzantine Saint: A Study in the Nature of a Medieval Institution, its Origins and Fate, in: Sergei Hackel (ed.), *The Byzantine Saint. University of Birmingham Fourteenth Spring Symposium of Byzantine Studies* (San Bernadino, 1983) 196–228.

Wipszycka, Ewa, Les confréries dans la vie religieuse de l'Égypte chretienne, in: *Études sur le Christianisme dans l'Egypte de l'antiquite tardive, Studia Ephemeridis Augustinianum* 52 (Rome, 1996) 257–278.

Yannis Stouraitis

The Historiographical Image of the People and the Microstructures of Revolt in High-Medieval Constantinople

The revival of popular involvement in the political life of Constantinople during the eleventh and late twelfth centuries is a topic that has drawn a lot of scholarly attention.[1] A number of studies have sought to do justice to the important role of popular participation in the politics of the imperial city, often in an effort to respond to and debunk an established – orientalised – view of Byzantium as a political culture of theocratic absolutism where the people had no political influence.[2] While this is a legitimate goal, it has often led to approaches that tend to rather uncritically accept and reproduce the literary image of the city populace as a single political body, acting in an anthropomorphised manner with a single opinion and will towards a single cause.

Even though the Constantinopolitan citizenry was in a far better position to unite in action and exert political influence on the emperor than the provincial populations of the empire, the image of the populace as a distinct political body with common political goals needs to be analysed critically from the viewpoint of authorial agendas, as well as to be problematised in terms of socio-historical and politological analysis. In the current paper, I aim to analyse how and why such an image was constructed in literary terms, and I shall try – to the extent that this is made possible by the available accounts – to scrutinise and highlight the microstructures of popular revolt, which have often been overlooked in the shadow of the literary 'big picture'. For that, I will use as my main case study the most exemplary popular revolt of that period, the uprising of 1042.

Before delving into the narratives of the most iconic Constantinopolitan revolt in the high medieval period, however, one needs to consider an issue which, at first sight, seems to be more philosophical rather than historical, but it is not:

1　Vryonis, Byzantine ΔΗΜΟΚΡΑΤΙΑ; Garland, Political Power and the Populace; Cheynet, colère du peuple. A recent argument about popular involvement in politics has gone as far as to claim that the people were the sovereign political body in the Byzantine political system; see Kaldellis, *Byzantine Republic*.

2　For the impact of Byzantium's orientalised image on modern research on Byzantine political ideology, see Stouraitis, Is Byzantinism an Orientalism?.

namely, who is meant by 'the people'? The political meaning of the term 'people' is ambiguous across all time periods, insofar as it is employed either to mean a whole, integrated body politic, or to refer to that part of the whole which is excluded, *de fac*to or *de jure* depending on the historical era, from politics.[3] This ambiguity is also evident in the discourse of Byzantine historiographers, particularly in the connotations of the different terms that elite authors – rather inconsistently – employ to designate the people of Constantinople. For instance, the term ἡ δέ γε ξύμπασα Πόλις (the entire city) has a distinctly inclusive character, bearing the positive connotation of an integrated body politic, that is, the citizenry as the people.[4] Instead, terms such as *ochlos* and *plethos* bear an evidently derogatory connotation and were mainly intended to distinguish a part of the whole, the commoners; that part of the people that belonged to the lower strata beneath the social elite.

This diachronic biopolitical fracture that, in the words of Giorgio Agamben, 'makes the people what cannot be included in the whole of which it is a part as well as what cannot belong to the whole in which it is always already included',[5] is reflected in the views of Niketas Choniates about the political nature of the Constantinopolitan masses (*plethos*). In his account of the coup of Maria Komnene in 1181, the author makes the following statement about the Constantinopolitan commoners' role in political unrest:

> In other cities the whole multitude rejoices in disorder and is hard to be constrained. The multitude of Constantinople, however, is the most tumultuous of all. It rejoices in rashness and deviates from the right path insomuch as it comprises of citizens of various origins and its mind is, so to say, as variable as its crafts are varied. …At times, it is disposed to sedition at mere rumour and is more destructive than fire, dancing, so to speak, against drawn swords and resisting protruding rocks and soundless swells, while, at other times, cowers frightened at every noise and bends its neck to whomsoever wishes to trample upon it. As a result, it is fairly accused of suffering from an inconsistent disposition and of being untrustworthy. Neither did the inhabitants of Constantinople ever seek to do the best for themselves, nor did they heed others who made proposals for the common good… Their indifference to the rulers is preserved as if it were inborn. Whom they exalt today as a just leader, this one they ridicule before long as a malefactor, demonstrating that they do both without reasoning due to their ignorance of what is best and to their unstable mind.[6]

---

3 Agamben, *Means without End*, 29–30.
4 The same could be the case with the *demos* in certain instances. On the nuanced content of the term *demos* in different periods in Byzantium, see Kontogiannopoulou, Notion of Δῆμος, 102–103.
5 Agamben, Means without End, 31.
6 Choniates, *Historia*, ed. van Dieten, 233,18–234,19; trans. Magoulias, 132.

One might plausibly argue that the derogatory image of the commoners in that statement calls for caution, since the author's comments bear the mark of the political mentality of a well-educated and privileged member of the court elite that was close to the source of political power and decision making.[7] A closer look at the statement, though, demonstrates that Choniates was not keen to condemn any kind of involvement of the common people in political affairs. Rather, he focused his criticism on the character of that involvement. According to him, this was determined by natural instincts instead of sober political criteria, and was lacking an orderly and responsible expression of political stance.

From a present-day viewpoint, one might be tempted to remark, of course, that such criticism would have made much more sense, had the author directed it against the political system itself, since that system lacked any regularised mechanism that would favour a participation of the common people as an orderly political body in the political affairs of the imperial city state. However, Choniates, as an adherent of the political system of imperial monarchy had no concerns of that kind. In his statement, he was more interested in highlighting the main means though which the common people became an agent on the political scene, namely sedition, and the main causes of that phenomenon. Within that framework, the author seems keen to depict the Constantinopolitan commoners' seditious activity as often having an apolitical nature. This is made evident when he argues that they were inclined to revolt with no good reason other than mere rumour, the main result of such activity being destruction, whereas they could as easily remain apathetic and passively endure oppressive policies.[8]

Instead of *a priori* denouncing these comments as a product of Choniates' elitist snobbery, one should instead examine more closely certain issues that they raise. Firstly, by accusing the common people of being just as capable of remaining passive in the face of oppression, the author seems, in fact, not to be condemning the political practice of sedition in itself. Rather, he blames the commoners for lacking understanding of the right political criterion by which to judge when such a practice did make sense politically. Considering Choniates' high level of education, this argument seems to stem from his knowledge of the history of the imperial city. There, one finds rulers who did not face popular resistance through revolt, even though their practices corresponded more with those of an absolute monarch than with those of a good administrator of the state by Choniates' own standards.

---

7 For Choniates' career and social status, see Simpson, *Niketas Choniates*, 15–21.

8 Choniates' statements regarding the commoners' political role seem to correspond with the modern debate about the nature of the activity of the Late Antique circus factions; see Cameron, *Circus Factions*; Whitby, Violence of the Circus Factions; Bell, *Social Conflict in the Age of Justinian*.

Read in this light, Choniates' statement illustrates, deliberately or not, the contingency of the phenomenon of revolt in Constantinople. This had little to do with a regularised means of organised expression of popular will in matters of government. The outbreak of revolt (as well as its outcome) was principally conditioned by various other factors: for instance, how firm a ruler's control over an extended power network was, or what capacity various social groups had at any given time to take advantage of an emperor's weakened power base in order to promote their interests by claiming the throne for their own candidate.[9] Within this framework, Choniates' statement implies that the commoners lacked the ability to act as a political body and to pursue revolt with their own political agenda, aiming to influence political affairs according to their own socio-political interest – which from the author's viewpoint, of course, should coincide with a broader notion of the common interest of the established order as he understood it. This reproachful attitude towards the political role of the people seems to be contradicted by some reports of Byzantine historiographers, Choniates included,[10] about the agency of the commoners in certain Constantinopolitan uprisings.

In what follows, I shall attempt a close reading and analysis of the uprising of 1042 against Michael V in order to examine the projected image of the Constantinopolitan commoners as an agent setting goals and dictating the course of action. My analysis of this iconic revolt will be enriched with evidence from other revolts in high medieval Constantinople in order to attest established patterns of action in Constantinopolitan revolts.

The mediated image of the rebellious people: a deconstruction

The revolt of 1042 is probably the most cited case of a popular uprising in high medieval Constantinople, in which the image of the common people as a conscious political body and a political agent has been highlighted by both medieval authors and modern scholarship. The latter has capitalised on the former's evidence and has provided various interpretations of the revolt.[11] According to Gustave Schlumberger this was a revolt of the court elite.[12] Spyros Vryonis argued that the outcome of the revolt demonstrated the strength of dynastic sentiment,

---

9 For the contingency of the phenomenon of revolt in the Byzantine empire, see Stouraitis, Civil War, 102–105.
10 For instance, see the agency that Choniates attributed to the mob in the case of the violent deposition of Andronikos I: Choniates, *Historia*, ed. van Dieten, 344–347.
11 The most exhaustive modern reconstruction of the events can be found in Lounghis, Χρονικόν.
12 Schlumberger, Une revolution de Palais.

while stressing that the populace had the last word in unmaking the emperor.[13] The aspect of dynastic legitimacy was also emphasised by Ioannis Karayano-poulos.[14] Lynda Garland interpreted the events of 1042 as 'an episode showing the spontaneous reaction of the Byzantine man-in-the-street to any threat to his society or interests and the way in which he saw his empress as a sacred and untouchable figure to be protected at all costs'.[15] For Anthony Kaldellis, the deposition of Michael V is an episode that adds to the evidence that shows the people, the *politeia*, forming and acting as a sovereign political body.[16]

The contemporary histories of Michael Psellos, Michael Attaleiates, and John Skylitzes offer the most detailed accounts of the revolt, and thus constitute our principal sources of information. Of the three, Psellos' account is the lengthiest and most detailed. Due to his age and position at the court – he was imperial secretary at the time, according to his statement[17] – he should be considered as the one who could claim better knowledge of the events. This does not necessarily make him a more reliable source of information than the others. It is, however, reason enough to use his detailed account as a point of departure for a comparative analysis of both the image of the people and the evidence of the microstructures and microdynamics of the revolt in all the contemporary sources.

A distinguishing feature of Psellos' account is the unique insight the author provides into the political background of the revolt. Unlike his two contemporaries, Attaleiates and Skylitzes, he makes interesting statements about who had a political interest in pursuing the deposition of the emperor. Psellos claims that, once Michael had marginalised his uncle, the eunuch John Orphanotrophos, thus becoming sole master of government affairs,

> his intentions were anything but moderate, for his first efforts were directed to a complete reversal of policy: everything had to conform to his wishes. Government officials were treated with no sign of friendliness whatever. The emperor's hostility to them was evident both in his look and in his general attitude. In fact, his arrogant speech and manners terrified them. His ambition centred on one object: to make his realm (the ruled) in very truth 'subject' to himself; most of the officials were to be stripped of their customary privileges and the people were to have their freedom restored; he would then

---

13 Vryonis, Byzantine ΔΗΜΟΚΡΑΤΙΑ, 308.
14 Karayannopoulos, Ιστορία του Βυζαντινού Κράτους, 502–504.
15 Garland, Political Power and the Populace, 24.
16 Kaldellis, *Byzantine Republic*, 90–94.
17 Psellos, *Chronographia* 1:5.27.6, ed. Reinsch, 95. Skylitzes was certainly born after 1040 and cannot have been an eyewitness of the events. For his date of birth, see Kiapidou, *Η Σύνοψις Ιστοριών του Ιωάννη Σκυλίτζη*), 31. Attaleiates, on the other hand, was probably born around 1025, which means that he was old enough to have been an eyewitness at the time of the revolt. However, he was still a student at the time and did not yet hold a position at court; see Attaleiates, *History*, trans. Kaldellis and Krallis, vii.

have the support of the people, who were many, rather than of the nobility, who were few.[18]

Telemachos Lounghis has plausibly argued that these statements point to the emperor's intention to change the political status quo.[19] Considering that the author's narrative strategy was aimed at drawing a negative image of Michael V, as a ruler whose actions were unpopular, the statement makes clear that the emperor enjoyed no popularity among the members of the senatorial elite because his policies threatened to strip them of their privileges. Instead, the commoners experienced a political change intended to set them free from the burden put on them by those same privileges. Therefore, according to Psellos, the lower strata not only had no real interest to wish for the deposition of Michael V in terms of their own political interest, but – as he explicitly states – they became attached to the emperor and their sentiments found expression in certain public actions of goodwill towards him.[20] The latter statement attributes, in fact, agency to the commoners, implying that they were able to understand that the reversal of the political status quo was to their benefit.

In this regard, it is important to bear in mind that, as a member of the elite writing for an elite audience several decades after the events, Psellos had an obvious motive to raise the point about Michael V's different attitude towards the senatorial elite and the lower strata in order to draw and emphasise the image of a bad emperor. This is a key issue if we want to decode the agenda of the elite authors who shaped the retrospective public image of the events through their histories; especially with regard to the lower social strata's role, motives, and actions.

Psellos, Attaleiates, and Skylitzes unanimously present Michael V's action in banishing the empress Zoe from the palace as the principal cause of a spontaneous uprising of the whole city populace, irrespective of social status, against him.[21] Psellos explicitly highlights the violation of dynastic legitimacy as the cause for the radical change of popular attitude towards the emperor. He presents the women of all social strata lamenting the banishment of the empress with the following words:

> Where can she (i.e. Zoe) be, she who alone of all women is free, the mistress of all the imperial family, the rightful heir to the Empire, whose father was emperor, whose

---

18 Psellos, *Chronographia* 1:5.15.3–9, ed. Reinsch, 88; trans. Sewter, *Michael Psellus*, 93.
19 Lounghis, Χρονικόν, 78–80.
20 Psellos, *Chronographia* 1:5.16.5–6, ed. Reinsch, 88.
21 Attaleiates, *History*, ed. Tsolakis, 11.5–25; Skylitzes, *Synopsis Historiarum*, ed. Thurn, 418.15–17.

grandfather was monarch before him – yes, and great-grandfather too? How was it this low-born fellow dared to raise a hand against a woman of such lineage?[22].

Psellos took particular care in his account to emphasise the emotions of grief that allegedly overwhelmed all citizens irrespective of social status when they heard the news about the harsh treatment of the empress.[23] This seems like a suitable narrative technique for an author keen to involve his audience emotionally in the events he recounted; especially if we consider that one of his main aims was to justify the outburst of lethal violence in the capital. However, one cannot help noticing an inherent contradiction in his narrative. Psellos depicts the commoners as that part of the city populace that was willing to overlook their own group's socio-political interest for the sake of the abstract political ideal of 'dynastic constitutionalism'. For the senatorial elite, on the other hand, a revolt for the same cause against an emperor who was hostile to their class interests was a win-win situation. On top of that, in Psellos' narrative the commoners' sudden change of heart takes place in the name of the dynastic right of an empress who was a leading member of the previous power regime under which they had enjoyed no benefits. Psellos testifies to that when, at the beginning of his account of the reign of Zoe's husband, the previous emperor Michael IV, he stresses that that emperor had undertaken no change to the established status quo that favoured the members of the senatorial elite.[24] That very status quo which Michael V sought to change, according to the author.

This aspect of Psellos' account has been largely overlooked by those scholars who have been keen to uncritically buy into the literary image of the commoners as voluntary and unequivocal guardians of an established notion of 'dynastic constitutionalism'; an image which also pervades the accounts of Attatleiates and Skylitzes and which should call for skepticism. The image of the common people as being prone to undertake political action with the aim of deposing an emperor who favoured them for the sake of an empress whose regime had not favoured them, evidently contradicts the earlier picture of them drawn by Psellos, according to which they were capable of understanding that the political change was to their own benefit. Therefore, if we are to believe our most detailed source about the cause of a 'spontaneous' popular insurrection against Michael V, we need to choose between two interpretative approaches to the commoners' political criterion: either they were not as able to grasp and protect their own political interests as Psellos' initial statement claimed, or they were such hardcore ideologues of dynastic legitimacy that they were willing to sacrifice their own

---

22 Psellos, *Chronographia* 1:5.26.8–12, ed. Reinsch, 94; trans. Sewter, *Michael Psellus*, 99.
23 Ibid. 1:5.25.3–13, ed. Reinsch, 93.
24 Ibid. 1:4.10.7–11, ed. Reinsch, 54–55; c.f. Lounghis, Χρονικόν, 78.

well-being in order to unite in action for the defence of some unwritten 'dynastic constitution'.

In my view, both interpretations are evidently problematical, demonstrating that the image of the commoners acting as a leading force in the revolt needs to be addressed with caution as a literary construct intended to serve a certain authorial agenda. Within this framework, we also need to address critically modern scholarship's tendency to accept and celebrate the accounts of Byzantine historiographers as evidence of the common people's ability to form a unitary political body capable of undertaking organised political action towards a common goal. Attaleiates and Skylitzes, in their shorter accounts of the events leading to the outbreak of the revolt, present the emperor as seeking first to measure the reactions of the city populace regarding his intention to banish Zoe. Having misinterpreted the popular sentiment, he decides to banish her to Prinkepos.[25] As Lounghis has plausibly argued, however, this seems to be a manipulated image of the events for two reasons. Firstly, Psellos' account indicates that Zoe had most probably been removed from the palace before the eighteenth of April, something which means that Michael had little interest in measuring the reactions of the people before making his move. Secondly, irrespective of the actual time of Zoe's removal from the palace, the repeated public appearances of Michael without Zoe at his side in the week before Easter should have alerted the people about her political marginalisation, thus prompting their allegedly spontaneous reaction at a much earlier stage.[26] These observations highlight further the need to problematise the constructed image of the city populace as a unitary group bound together by a shared notion of intransigent loyalty to the empress and her dynastic rights.

In this regard, what calls for further analysis is Psellos' motive for attributing the role of the instigator of unrest and violence to the commoners when talking about the reactions of the whole citizenry (ἡ δέ γε ξύμπασα Πόλις) to the news about the empress' fate. Thus, we are informed that after the rumour had spread in the capital, the officials, the clergy and the court began talking about what had happened to the empress.[27] The craftsmen, instead, prepared themselves for greats deeds of daring, and the mob was on the move, motivated by the will to 'exercise tyranny over him who had himself played the tyrant'.[28] These details draw a very interesting picture. Psellos, just like Attaleiates and Skylitzes, is at pains to ethically justify the action of revolt against the emperor, which was

---

25 Attaleiates, *History*, ed. Tsolakis, 10.21–27; Skylitzes, *Synopsis Historiarum*, ed. Thurn, 418. 17–32.

26 Lounghis, Χρονικόν, 84–86.

27 Psellos, *Chronographia* 1:5.25.14–15, ed. Reinsch, 93–93.

28 Ibid. 1:5.25.16–17 and 26.1–2., ed. Reinsch, 94.

impermissible from a legal-political viewpoint.[29] To do so, he highlights the ideal of dynastic legitimacy as the overarching just cause that motivated the whole city to rise up. When it comes to actual acts of violence aimed at deposing the emperor, however, these he carefully attributes exclusively to the intentions and actions of the lower strata – the craftsmen, and especially the mob. The senatorial elite, even though minded against the emperor, is presented as having had no active part in the instigation of the violent process that was about to commence.[30] In a similar vein, Attaleiates presents the patriarch as having been forced by the mob to participate in the uprising[31] – a manipulated image of the events that has very little to do with Alexios Studites' actual role in the revolt, as I shall relate in more detail below.

In contrast to modern interpretations that view the actions of the commoners in the revolt as proof that the people formed the ultimate sovereign political body able to legitimise or delegitimise an emperor, Psellos' contemporary understanding of the situation was very different. Nowhere does the author imply that both the outbreak and the outcome of the revolt reflected and should be perceived as the result of the people's will and authority. Instead, he is keen to attribute the commoners' unlawful actions to the only authority that supersedes human laws, namely God's will, stressing the rebellious multitude's supernatural inspiration.[32] In this ideological context, he recounts that Zoe expressed her gratitude to God for having put in motion a revolt on her behalf,[33] and that the people gave thanks to God for delivering them from the tyrant after Michael's arrest.[34]

Based on the authorial notion that the people acted as an instrument of God – a notion also testified to in Attaleiates' discourse[35] – Psellos' principal aim behind the representation of the commoners as the sole part of the populace capable of acting violently, seems hardly to have been to present them, implicitly or explicitly, as the spearhead of a sovereign political body that stood above the law and was *de facto* entitled to change the emperor when they saw fit. Instead,

---

29 For the legal-political aspects of revolt against the emperor in Byzantium, see Mpourdara, *Καθοσίωσις και Τυραννίς*, 131–147.
30 A similar narrative motif can be found in the account of Niketas Choniates on the deposition of Andronikos I Komnenos: the people are presented as acting violently and in a frenzy like an anthropomorphised mass, while the members of the elite are largely absent from the scene and the patriarch is forced by the people to bless their actions, see Choniates, *Historia*, ed. van Dieten, 342–347; c.f. the relevant insightful comments in Fögen, Das politische Denken der Byzantiner, 54.
31 Attaleiates, *History*, ed. Tsolakis, 12.26–13.3.
32 Psellos, *Chronographia*, 1:5.28.1–2, ed. Reinsch, 95.
33 Ibid. 1:5.32.2, ed. Reinsch, 97.
34 Ibid. 1:5.38.6–7, ed. Reinsch, 100.
35 Attaleiates, *History*, ed. Tsolakis, 12.8.

the statement that the commoners were ready to exercise tyranny, a notion with inherently negative connotations in Byzantine political terminology, seems to have been first and foremost intended to exonerate the senatorial elite. Those who had an actual political interest in the deposition of Michael V were subtly set free of any accusation that they had something to do with the instigation of the legally and politically impermissible act of *crimen laesae maiestatis*, an attempt to depose the emperor. Moreover, the initiative of the commoners to undertake the legally and politically impermissible act of tyranny is justified as caused by supernatural inspiration, which drove them to do what no law-abiding citizen should do. In the symbolic universe of Psellos' account, God punishes with tyranny an emperor who was tyrannical. For this act, unlawful from a secular viewpoint, God's instrument was the mob.

In this regard, the image of the commoners in Psellos' account seems to fully correspond with their derogatory image in Choniates' statement, cited in the first part of this paper. On the one hand, Psellos' report on the sudden change in the behaviour of the commoners towards Michael V coincides with Choniates' view that the common people's political attitude was fickle because 'whom they exalt today as a just leader, this one they ridicule before long as a malefactor'.[36] On the other hand, Choniates' depiction of the commoners as predisposed to sedition at mere rumour, which was more destructive than fire,[37] was their main attribute capable of turning them into God's instrument for the punishment and deposition of a bad emperor in Psellos' account. This is exemplified by the latter's statement that the rebellious commoners,

> seemed different from their former selves. There was more madness in their running, more strength in their hands, the flash in their eyes was fiery and inspired, the muscles of their bodies more powerful. As for prevailing on them to behave in a more dignified manner or dissuading them from their intentions, nobody whatever was willing to try such a thing. Anyone who gave advice of that sort was powerless.[38]

The reference to 'a more dignified behaviour', which the commoners were not capable of, was intended here to contrast their image with that of the members of the elite. The latter, even though opposed to the emperor, were evidently able to behave in a 'more dignified manner' insofar as they are not presented as the ones getting ready to commit violent acts of revolt. The message the author wants to send to his elite audience seems crystal clear: the fickle and seditious nature of the mob made them capable of doing what the prudent and lawful part of the populace, the senatorial elite, could by nature and social position not do.

---

36 Choniates, *Historia*, ed. van Dieten, 234.87–88.
37 Ibid. 234.77–78.
38 Psellos, *Chronographia* 1:5.28.1–7, ed. Reinsch 95; trans. Sewter, *Michael Psellus*, 100.

Based on that, it is possible to make some preliminary conclusions: Psellos, as well as his two contemporaries Attaleiates and Skylitzes, constructed a literary image of the city populace as a unitary political body in order to justify the revolt of 1042 in a manner that corresponded with the political and cultural needs of the social elite whose members constituted the audience of their histories.[39] Michael V, a ruler who had sought to deprive certain factions of the senatorial elite of their privileges, had to be presented as a bad emperor who had turned the whole city against him. In order to provide a plausible reason for the unity in action between those who had a true class interest in deposing the emperor and those who had little such interest, elite authors highlighted an overarching abstract political cause, namely dynastic legitimacy. In this context, the constructed image of a unitary populace enabled elite authors to take advantage of their elite audience's view of the commoners as being politically imprudent and fickle by nature. These 'inherent qualities' of the mob served to create a convenient literary image of the events: the very part of the populace that had little political reason to pursue the emperor's deposition was presented as the part that was most ready and willing to undertake the initiative to do the dirty job of violently deposing him, eventually dragging everyone else into open revolt. This was a narrative which the audience of Constantinopolitan historiography could easily live and identify with at a time, several decades after the events, when the senatorial elite had no urgent political interest in contesting the legitimacy of the person currently sitting on the imperial throne.

The inherent contradictions in the constructed image of the people as a unitary political body in the revolt indicate that such unity, both in ideological and political terms, never existed beyond text – that is, beyond the context of the elite authors' narratives. Therefore, if we are willing to look beyond the evidently propagandistic image of the impudent seditious commoners who ignored their own interests in order to function as the guardians of some unwritten 'constitution' of dynastic legitimacy, there remains one question that we should try to answer: what were the actual roles and the motives of the different social groups in the revolt of 1042?

---

39 On the audience of Byzantine historiography, see Croke, Uncovering Byzantium's Historiographical Audience; Markopoulos, Le public des textes historiographiques à l'époque macédonienne.

Microstructures and microdynamics of a Constantinopolitan revolt

The revolt of 1042 acquired the character of a small-scale civil war in the capital, with an armed group of rebels undertaking organised military action, which culminated in a proper siege of the palace.[40] With regard to this, one needs to keep in mind that in civil strife not every individual or group participating in the acts of violence as they develop will be driven by the same political motives or will pursue the same political goals.[41] Individuals and social groups may have different reasons and different goals for exercising violence once a breakdown of public order has been set in motion. A closer look at the microstructures of the revolt of 1042, as far as these can be discerned underneath the constructed authorial 'big picture' of a popular revolt on behalf of dynastic legitimacy, may shed some light on the different motives and goals of different social groups that participated in one way or the other in the uprising.

As has been pointed out above, Psellos distinguishes between three major social groups when he talks about the reaction of the populace to the news of the empress' banishment: the upper stratum of members of the court, a middle stratum consisting of the members of the guilds, and the lower stratum, the mob of the marketplace. Within this generic tripartite scheme of social stratification,[42] the author also mentions other kinds of social groupings such as the clergy, the women, and the units of foreign mercenaries.[43] Among the three major social groups, the author presents the members of the mob as being the first to have taken violent action, while it is reported that the members of the guilds were in a state of preparation for great deeds of daring. A main difference between these two social groups pertains to the very fact that, while the mob refers to a larger and rather incoherent group, the guilds were much more capable of functioning as a coherent and well-organised social network that could undertake planned action. This is an important issue to consider, when seeking to discern the actual motive of the members of these groups in revolting, as well as their respective goals during the revolt.

When it comes to the nature of the revolt itself, one may distinguish two basic stages. The initial stage pertains to unrest and rioting taking place in the mar-

---

40 For a definition of civil war in Byzantium, in which also certain revolts in the capital can be included, see Stouraitis, Civil War, 92–94.

41 C.f. the insights of historical sociology on civil war, according to which civil strife is not an event where every segment of political life needs to become politicised, but politics can often also become privatised: Malešević, *Sociology of War*, 61–64.

42 A scheme reminiscent of the tripartite distinction of the populace between *megaloi*, *mesoi*, and *mikroi* made by the late-twelfth-century author, Eustathios of Thessaloniki. See Eustathios of Thessaloniki, *Capture of Thessaloniki*, ed. Kyriakidis, 32.8.

43 Psellos, *Chronographia* 1:5.25.14–26.2, ed. Reinsch, 93–94.

ketplace, followed by attacks against the mansions of members of the elite related to the emperor. The mediated image of a spontaneous uprising by an anthropomorphised mob that acted as one body with a single determination, namely to depose the emperor, calls for further examination. A closer look at how unrest broke out, and who did take action at the initial stage and with what purpose, draws a more nuanced picture. Both Attaleiates and Skylitzes report that once the eparch of the city announced at the forum that Zoe had been banished from the palace, one voice was heard that insulted the emperor, and then others followed.[44] A group of people started a fight in the marketplace with the guardsmen of the eparch, but they did not stop there. According to Attaleiates, after they had routed the eparch's men and had forced them to flight,

> they did not disperse, as usually happens to a mixed crowd that lacks a leader, but as though they were led from on high they became even stronger and bolder in their resolution, especially as their numbers were swelling by the hour from those who poured in to join them. Their leading objective was neither to yield nor to show weakness nor to suffer any delay but to depose from power that ungrateful and unfeeling man...[45]

Despite the author's effort to present these events as a spontaneous divinely-inspired reaction of the mob, the determination he attributes to the instigators of the unrest in pursuing the deposition of Michael V instead points to a group of people who acted in a planned and organised manner. That said, it is important to bear in mind that for anyone who wanted to cause unrest and use that as the first step towards open revolt and civil war in the city, the marketplace was a good place to do so for various reasons. To begin with, it was easy to find people there ready to support an uprising for a few coins. The practices through which elite persons or groups could secure the support of parts of the mob for their cause in this way is testified by other similar episodes in the political life of the city. For instance, in the context of the murder of the emperor Nikephoros II Phokas (963–969) by John Tzimiskes and his group of conspirators, Leo the Deacon states that

> Leo the *kouropalates*, Nikephoros' brother, who possessed vast amounts of gold should have scattered it in the streets at the news of his brother's murder to win the favour of the citizens, and should have exhorted them to take vengeance on the usurpers.[46]

Choniates reports in a similar manner how the *kaisarissa* Maria Komnene was able to win over the support of the mob when she fled to Hagia Sophia to escape the wrath of her stepmother and the *protosebastos* Alexios in the early 1180s:

---

44 Attaleiates, *History*, ed. Tsolakis, 11.24–12.3; Skylitzes, *Synopsis Historiarum*, ed. Thurn, 418.34–29.

45 Attaleiates, *History*, ed. Tsolakis, 12.5–10; trans. Kaldellis and Krallis, 23.

46 Leo the Deacon, *Historia*, ed. Hase, 95; trans. Talbot and Sullivan, History *of Leo the Deacon*, 144.

Not only did she excite the pity of the patriarch and the clergy, but she also moved the majority of the promiscuous rabble to such a degree that they very nearly shed tears over her. A good portion of the indigent populace was angry on her account because she had plied them with gifts of copper coins, thereby inciting them to rebellion and showing contempt for the special privileges accorded those who seek asylum.[47]

Such evidence provides ample proof of how someone interested in setting in motion an uprising in Constantinople could do it with the help of people who had no ideological/political motive for revolting. Eustathios, bishop of Thessaloniki, and Niketas Choniates provide additional insight into the mechanisms that elite factions used to orchestrate unrest and stir up the mob. In the context of the coup of Maria Komnene against the *protosebastos* Alexios, Choniates testifies to the role that priests could play in inciting commoners to revolt.[48] In Eustathios' account of Andronikos Komnenos' rise to power, the bishop recounts how Andronikos used certain prominent men among the city mob to disseminate his propaganda. These men are designated as popular demagogues, wicked and eager for revolt, and as able to control and lead the others.[49]

One more reason why the marketplace was an ideal place for staging popular unrest in order to back up a planned revolt was that, once a small, organized group of people set in motion an uprising there, a part of the mob would be ready to take advantage of that and spontaneously participate in the unrest with their own personal agendas. This is testified by Psellos' account. He reports that, once unrest broke out, the mob attacked the mansions of members of the emperor's family.[50] The attack on these houses obviously served the cause of those who had organised and instigated the unrest in the first place with the intention of deposing Michael V. Nonetheless, Psellos' narrative deconstructs Attaleiates' literary image of the entire mob pouring in and joining the revolt driven by the common goal of defending the empress and deposing the emperor.

According to Psellos, all kinds of people participated in the acts of plunder, including young girls and children of either sex.[51] Their main goal, however, was to take booty and put it on the market for sale.[52] Attaleiates' account also testifies to the existence of different groups among the rioters that acted with different motives and aims over the course of the rebellion. The author states that one group of people attacked the palace while another group attacked the houses of the emperor's relatives. The latter's main motive was their lust for plunder, as becomes evident from Attaleiates' statement that they did not even spare the

---

47 Choniates, *Historia*, ed. van Dieten, 232.37–44, trans. Magoulias, 131.
48 Choniates, *Historia*, ed. van Dieten, 234–235, trans. Magoulias, 132.
49 Eustathios of Thessaloniki, *On the Capture of Thessaloniki*, ed. Kyriakidis, 42.19–23.
50 Psellos, *Chronographia* 1:5.29.1–5, ed. Reinsch, 95.
51 Ibid. 1:5.29.9–12, ed. Reinsch, 96.
52 Ibid. 1:5.29.12–13, ed. Reinsch, 96.

churches and monasteries, plundering the riches that had been unjustly hoarded there at the cost of the poor.[53]

Modern scholars who have been keen to buy into the literary image of the entire populace rising to defend the banished empress have tended to overlook or downplay these aspects of the revolt. For a considerable part of the mob, the main motive for their participation in social unrest was to plunder and, once they had achieved that, they were rather indifferent to the proclaimed goal of protecting the empress or deposing Michael V. All they were after was to secure as much booty as they could in order to make a profit. This is probably why the initial stage of the uprising seems to have caused no particular concern to the emperor, who obviously did not feel that his position was threatened by the actions of the mob. As Psellos relates,

> he sat in the palace, at first by no means alarmed at the course of events. His idea was to end the citizens' conflict without the shedding of blood, but when the rebellion was afoot beyond all doubt and the people adopted military formations, with quite a respectable battle-array, then he was fearfully troubled.[54]

This statement pinpoints the moment when the second and more important stage of the revolt, namely an organised assault on the palace, commenced. Psellos, an eyewitness of the events, speaks clearly of military formations and an organised battle array. This statement needs to be examined in relation to two of his previous statements, which seem to be interrelated. The first pertains to the preparation of the members of the guilds to commit acts of great daring; the second refers to the weapons which a part of the seditious people carried:

> Every man was armed; one clasped in his hands an axe, another brandished a heavy iron broadsword, another handled a bow, and another a spear, but the bulk of the mob, with some of the biggest stones in the folds of their clothing and holding others ready in their hands, ran in general disorder.[55]

These statements distinguish again between two groupings of people that participated in the unrest. The one was a disorderly mob that did not carry military equipment. Many of its members had little interest in the political cause of the revolt, taking advantage of the general unrest in order to commit deeds of plunder. The other was a well-organised group of men carrying proper weapons. The latter's main plan and goal was to depose the emperor. The military character of that group is confirmed by Attaleiates, who states that the final attack on the

---

53 Attaleiates, *History,* ed. Tsolakis, 12.19–23.
54 Psellos, *Chronographia* 1:5.30.2–6, ed. Reinsch, 96; trans. Sewter, *Michael Psellus,* 100.
55 Ibid. I:5.27.11–5, ed. Reinsch 94; trans. Sewter, *Michael Psellus,* 99.

palace was carried out by military men who assaulted the building sounding trumpets and bugles.[56]

The evidence from Psellos and Attaleiates regarding the nature of the group that attacked the palace deconstructs Skylitzes' impressionistic statement about a 'naked and unarmed' mob that was able to prevail over the emperor's soldiers only due to its higher numbers.[57] One needs to bear in mind that common people not only did not possess military equipment such as swords, bows, and spears, but even if they could get access to such weapons during the unrest, it is highly improbable that the majority of them would have been able to handle them properly because they lacked the necessary training and experience. Skylitzes, of course, contradicts himself when he presents members of the rebellious crowd as shooting with bows against the emperor in the hippodrome and then laying a tactically well-organised siege to the fortified palace of the lower terrace.[58] Such evidence hardly points to actions taken by a disorderly and unarmed group of civilians.

But who were the well-equipped men capable of laying proper siege to the palace – that is, able and determined to use popular unrest in the marketplace as a means to instigate a small-scale civil war in the city? Based on Psellos' information we may infer that the military group that laid siege to the palace consisted of foreign mercenaries and some members of the imperial guard that had defected to the rebels' party,[59] as well as of members of the guilds.[60] The military training of imperial guards and mercenaries goes without saying and makes them ideal participants in a rebellious force capable of handling military weapons and carrying out a well-organised siege of the palace. The city guilds, on the other hand, had many members with experience in military matters and the ability to efficiently handle proper weapons due to their role as defenders of the city walls.[61] These three groups made up a well-organised military force that had not come together spontaneously, but, rather, executed a carefully-devised plan

---

56 Attaleiates, *History*, ed. Tsolakis, 13.26–28.
57 Skylitzes, *Synopsis Historiarum*, ed. Thurn, 419.60–65.
58 Skylitzes, *Synopsis Historiarum*, ed. Thurn, 419.47 and 419.57–60. For the use of bows by the rebels c.f. Zonaras, *Chronicle*, ed. Büttner-Wobst, 610.19–611.1.
59 Psellos, *Chronographia* 1:5.25,18–19 and 30.10–12, ed. Reinsch, 94 and 96. The reference to men bearing axes points to members of the Varangian guard. The accounts of the sagas on Harald Hardrada's presence in Constantinople at that time claim that he and a part of the Varangian guard had been in disfavour and had lost their position as the emperor's body-guards under Michael V. If so, they had a good reason to support the rebels; see Blöndal, *The Varangians of Byzantium*, 77–94.
60 Psellos, *Chronographia* 1:5.25.15–16, ed. Reinsch, 94.
61 Haldon, Strategies of Defence, 146 and 149.

for the deposition of Michael V through the force of arms.[62] Therefore, the obvious next question is: who was behind the organisation of such a military force?

The social group which pulled the strings of a military revolt in the city is revealed when we take a closer look at the events that unravelled after Michael V's decision to satisfy the alleged principal demand of the rebellious populace; namely, to bring Zoe back to the palace. Psellos states that Michael made Zoe show herself on a balcony to cunningly quench the fire of the people's anger when they saw that the empress had been recalled from exile.[63] Once that had taken place,

> the rebels were afraid lest the combined efforts of Michael and Zoe might yet prove their undoing. Most of their supporters might be persuaded by her and give up the struggle. So a new policy was adopted, a policy which of itself was a complete answer to Michael's scheming.[64]

These are interesting statements in many ways. To begin with, the author divides those who continued to participate in the revolt into two groups: one group seems to have consisted of people who were not determined to depose Michael V and, therefore, would be susceptible to abandoning the unrest as soon as the initial pretext for their uprising, namely Zoe's banishment, was no longer valid. The other group evidently consisted of those who had carefully organised and set in motion a military rebellion aimed at deposing the emperor. The second group could be identified with that group which Attaleiates presented as determined to depose Michael V right from the very start of the riot in the marketplace.[65]

Those that made the decisions and guided the actions of this group now recognised the need for a new plan in order to respond to what Psellos presents as Michael's scheming, namely Zoe's return to the palace. Their intentions marked the turning point of the revolt, which is also reflected in the change of strategy regarding its legitimisation. Michael's response in bringing Zoe back to the palace represented, in fact, nothing other than a public act conceding to the main demand of the rioters which, according to Psellos, had motivated the whole city to become indignant and revolt in the first place.[66] Besides the author's attempt to

---

62 Psellos, *Chronographia* 1:5.26.16–18, ed. Reinsch, 94, speaks of battle positions and a phalanx which the whole city followed; Attaleiates, *History*, ed. Tsolakis, 13.26–27, explicitly calls those who attacked the palace *stratiotikoi andres* (military men).

63 Psellos, *Chronographia* 1:5.32.11–12, ed. Reinsch, 97.

64 Psellos, *Chronographia* 1:5.33, ed. Reinsch, 98; trans. Sewter, *Michael Psellus*, 102.

65 See note 47 above.

66 Psellos, *Chronographia* 1:5.31.13–14, ed. Reinsch, 97, admits as much when he states that the emperor and the nobellisimus decided to recall the empress from exile because it was because of her that the mob had broken out in revolt and the war was being fought on her behalf.

delegitimise the emperor's actions as mere scheming,[67] his discourse about the rebels' concern to find a new pretext to legitimise their actions reveals one more inherent contradiction in the literary narrative of the revolt. As soon as the initial legitimising cause for the uprising, the protection of Zoe's dynastic rights and her restoration in the palace, had evaporated due to the emperor's response, this cause not only became obsolete for those pulling the strings of the military revolt but also an obstacle to their true cause, namely the deposition of an emperor who threatened the privileges of certain factions of the elite. In this context, Zoe's function is subtly transformed in Psellos' account from that of the main victim of Michael V to that of potential accomplice, even if unwillingly; someone who could help the emperor bring the revolt to an end.

For that reason, the new policy of the rebels was to downplay Zoe's image as a symbol of dynastic legitimacy and bring her sister Theodora into the picture. According to Psellos, an attendant of her father who was 'of high-born ancestry and inspired respect' became the leader of a military column that was sent to take her from the monastery of Petrion and escort her to the Hagia Sophia.[68] Attaleiates confirms the organised, military nature of the group that was sent to escort Theodora to the Great Church.[69] At this point, the central role of members of the senatorial elite as the leading elements of an armed coup d'état against Michael V becomes explicit in the sources. The fact that Theodora was taken to the Hagia Sophia, where she was acclaimed in the middle of the night,[70] points to the Great Church as the headquarters of those making the decisions and pulling the strings behind the actions of the militarily-organised section of the rebels.

Two sources, Skylitzes and the Muslim historian ibn al-Athir, indicate that the patriarch Alexios Studites had a personal interest in pursuing the deposition of Michael V, because he feared that the emperor intended to remove him from his office or even murder him.[71] The patriarch's motive explains the role of the Great Church as the headquarters of the rebels and leaves little doubt about his leading role in the conspiracy against the emperor from its very beginning. Alexios

---

67 In this context, Psellos, *Chronographia* 1:5.32.6–15, ed. Reinsch, 97, claims that the empress was presented to the people wearing her monastic habit. In this, his is followed by Zonaras, *Chronicle*, ed. Büttner-Wobst, 611.5–9, who claims that her appearance fuelled the anger of the people even more. Skylitzes, *Synopsis Historiarum*, ed. Thurn, 419.42–43, however, contradicts these reports, stating that she was stripped of the monastic habit and clothed with imperial robes before appearing to the people. One cannot help noticing that presenting the empress in a nun's habit would have been a rather naïve and self-defeating move on Michael's part, which – if true – hardly corresponds with Psellos' argument that the emperor wanted to deceive the people regarding his true intentions.

68 Psellos, *Chronographia* I:5.36.7–37.5, ed. Reinsch, 99.

69 Attaleiates, *History*, ed. Tsolakis, 13.13–15.

70 Ibid. 13.18–25.

71 Skylitzes, *Synopsis Historiarum*, ed. Thurn, 418.12–15 and 418.33–55.; Ibn al-Athīr, *Al-Kāmil fī'l-ta'rīkh*, 9:341; c.f. Lounghis, Χρονικόν, 80 and Cheynet, Patriarches et empereurs, 3–4.

Studites was not forced by the 'spontaneous' reaction of the mob to participate in the revolt, as Attaleiates claimed, but rather acted together with those members of the senatorial elite who also had a distinct political interest in organising the deposition of Michael V. The decision to bring Theodora into the picture once Zoe could no longer serve the rebels' cause was not taken spontaneously by an anthropomorphised rebellious mob through some unspecified, mysterious process of popular decision making. It was a well-thought-out move by those leading elements of the revolt who were executing a well-organised plan.

With Theodora's acclamation, the leading forces behind the uprising officially sealed the transformation of the nature of the revolt from a popular riot in the marketplace into a military rebellion of usurpation. These events preceded the final attack against the palace, which took place very early in the morning of the following day, as explicitly stated by Attaleiates.[72] Skylitzes' account demonstrates that the final attack was carried out in a tactically well-prepared manner, with the rebellious forces approaching and laying siege to the fortified lower terrace palace by land from all sides.[73]

In the concluding phase of the revolt, during the arrest of Michael V and his uncle Constantine at the monastery of Stoudios, the literary image of the commoners is evidently changed in Psellos' account. The author no longer depicts them as a leading force acting in an irrational manner, which no one was able to constrain from undertaking acts of violence. They appear to be restrained in their actions towards the fugitives and do not let themselves be carried away by their violent instincts. They were ready to obey the orders of an official who was sent by Theodora to conclude the fugitives' arrest, and it was only at his command that they laid hands on them and dragged them out of the church in order to be blinded under the supervision of a person who had been sent to carry out the task.[74] The literary image of the imprudent and fickle nature of the mob had served its purpose in the narrative and could now give way to an image of restraint and obedience.

People and power in 1042: concluding remarks

If we are to believe the figures provided by John Skylitzes, at the end of the revolt against Michael V more than 3000 people had been killed in the streets of Constantinople.[75] Of course, such information should be addressed with caution

---

72 Attaleiates, *History*, ed. Tsolakis, 13.26.
73 Skylitzes, *Synopsis Historiarum*, ed. Thurn, 419.57–60. On the fortification of the Boukoleon palace in the time of Nikephoros Phokas, see Mango, The Palace of the Boukoleon.
74 Psellos, *Chronographia* 1:5.39–47, ed. Reinsch, 100–104.
75 Skylitzes, *Synopsis Historiarum*, ed. Thurn, 419.62–64.

considering the general tendency of medieval authors to inflate numbers. Still, there is good reason to surmise that the death toll of that small-scale civil war within the city was not insignificant, given that parts of an unarmed and militarily-inexperienced mob became involved in a conflict between two rival parties which were well-organised and equipped in military terms. This is one more indication that, beyond the literary image of 'city vs. emperor' in a conflict whose outcome elite authors present as teleologically predetermined with the benefit of hindsight, things on the ground looked different and had little to do with such a simplistic dichotomy.

The emperor was certainly not alone in that struggle. He had the support of certain factions of the elite and of armed forces that put up a fight on his behalf. The palace was defended by those parts of the imperial guard that remained loyal to Michael V, by the retinue of the emperor's uncle, the nobilissimus Constantine, who came to the emperor's aid, and by the general Kekaumenos, who had just arrived from Italy with his own men.[76] This is what forced the rebels to regroup after their first unsuccessful assault on the palace during the first day of the revolt, and conduct a second assault through a tactically well-organised siege the following morning. Therefore, even though the conflict lasted roughly a day and a half, the fighting was intense and considerable casualties unavoidable, given that the rebels attacked a well defended fortified structure twice.

In light of this, the answer as to why the emperor lost the conflict, and with it his throne, is not because this was God's will, as expressed through the unitary action of the whole populace, according to the literary image of the revolt of 1042. As we have seen, a considerable number of the commoners who got involved in the general unrest were rather indifferent to the cause of dethroning the emperor, whereas others were very much willing to abandon the riot once the initial pretext for it, the banishment of the empress, had been reversed. The main reason for Michael V's defeat was that the leaders of the revolt had taken particular care to put together a proper military force that was able and determined to pursue to the end their main goal of deposing the emperor. This force was evidently strong enough to defeat the forces that defended the fortified lower palace. Michael and his uncle decided to flee the palace once they had realised that, despite their determination to hold their ground and fight, their forces had been overwhelmed by those of the rebels.[77]

Here, it is worth drawing a comparison of the revolt of 1042 with another major revolt in which the city populace played a central role in an attempt to

---

76 Psellos, *Chronographia* 1:5.31.1–11, ed. Reinsch, 96–97; Skylitzes, *Synopsis Historiarum*, ed. Thurn, 419.49–55.
77 Skylitzes, *Synopsis Historiarum*, ed. Thurn, 419.60–68; Attaleiates, *History*, ed. Tsolakis, 13.26–30.

depose an emperor, the *Nika* riot.[78] One of the main differences between these two iconic revolts pertains to their outcome. Justinian I succeeded where Michael V failed, namely in maintaining himself on the throne, despite the fact that parts of the city populace led by the circus factions appeared determined to dethrone him. One needs to consider that the circus factions also participated in the defence of the city walls in Late Antique Constantinople (similar to the guilds in the eleventh century).[79] Therefore, they represented a rebellious force able to put up a fight against the emperor's soldiers. However, Justinian succeeded in prevailing in the conflict because he was able to maintain control over superior military power, bringing in additional forces from Thrace and thus overwhelming the forces of the rebels, who were massacred in the hippodrome.

In this regard, the key for understanding the different outcome of the revolt of 1042 lies in the ability of those who organised the coup d'état against Michael V to overpower him in military terms. The rebellious force that defeated the emperor's forces did not come together spontaneously and by chance. It was a combined result of organisation, economic capacity, and networking ability. As we have seen, money was the main means through which elite factions could secure the support of mercenaries residing in the city as well as of thugs in the marketplace. Moreover, the leaders of the revolt disposed of the necessary network to reach out to and win over members of the imperial guard, the demes and, most importantly, of the city guilds. The latter's role in turning the odds in favour of the rebellious forces was central and poses one important question: why did the guilds see it as in their interest to side with the senatorial elite and support a revolt that would depose an emperor whose policies favoured the people of the market?

To answer that, one should look at the political developments in Constantinople in the immediate aftermath of the revolt. The emperor who replaced Michael V at Zoe's side was Constantine Monomachos, a member of the senatorial elite whose privileges had been threatened by Michael V. Constantine IX is known for his policy of making lower senatorial titles broadly accessible to tradesmen during his reign.[80] This means that the member of the senatorial elite who succeeded Michael V enacted a policy that enabled wealthy and prominent members of the guilds to add the social privileges of status to their advanced economic situation. Based on that, it seems plausible to argue that the guilds' central role in the revolt of 1042 may have been the result of a trade-off between their leading elements and factions of the senatorial elite. If the guilds were willing to turn against an emperor whose policy favoured them – that is, against their social interest as a group – they did so not out of some abstract belief in

---

78 For a comprehensive modern account of the revolt, see Greatrex, Nika Riot.
79 Haldon, Strategies of Defence, 146.
80 Dagron, Urban Economy, 2:415.

'constitutional norms' or ideological adherence to 'dynastic legitimacy'. They chose the rebellious side in the conflict because their leading elements were promised social advancement. And this is what they got in the aftermath of the revolt.

The revolt of 1042 has often been highlighted as an exemplary event demonstrating the political power of the city populace when acting in unity. However, a closer look at the authorial agendas that shaped the historiographical image of the uprising, alongside a careful analysis of the microstructures of socio-political action, reveals that there was no such thing as 'the people' acting as a unitary political body and pursuing a common political cause against Michael V. The image of the 'whole city' rising in order to punish an emperor who violated dynastic legitimacy is a literary construct that did not exist beyond the historiographical context in which it came into being. Moreover, that literary construct was by no means intended to promote – explicitly or implicitly – the notion that the people formed *de facto* a sovereign political body entitled to depose a bad emperor. In the symbolic universe of elite authors, the 'whole populace' could be minded against an emperor, but the initiative for the unlawful attempt to violently depose him was attributed to a part of the whole, the 'imprudent' mob; the part that was excluded from political decision making and whose participation in politics could take place mainly through 'irrationally' violent behaviour when the order of the city had broken down.

The commoners' violent activity in the context of public unrest and political controversy in high medieval Constantinople had little to do with organised action informed by their own distinct political agenda. Still, such popular activity was inherently political. The readiness of members of those social strata that enjoyed a lower economic and social status to exploit every chance they got to participate in unrest and commit acts of destruction and plunder seems to have been interconnected with their class position and their lived experience within a structurally-oppressive social order. Popular violence may not have been the main determinant of the success of coups d'état and revolts against the emperor, the contingent outcome of which depended on multiple factors. Nonetheless, it was certainly a factor which various powerbrokers could take advantage of, and which no emperor could afford to ignore.

Acknowledgements

The research for the current study was conducted during my time as a post-doctoral research associate at the FWF P-Z288-G25 Wittgenstein Prize Project 'Moving Byzantium: Mobility, Microstructures and Personal Agency'. The project was directed by Prof. Claudia Rapp and was hosted at the Department of

Byzantine and Modern Greek Studies of the University of Vienna and the Division of Byzantine Research/IMAFO of the Austrian Academy of Sciences. I would like to thank the participants of the 'Late Antique Lunches' at the Classics department of the University of Edinburgh for discussing the final draft of this paper with me and providing useful feedback.

Bibliography

Primary Sources

Attaleiates, Michael, *History*, ed. Eudoxos Tsolakis, *Michaelis Attaliatae Historia*, CFHB 50 (Athens, 2011). English translation: Anthony Kaldellis and Dimitris Krallis, *Michael Attaleiates, The History* (Cambridge, Mass., 2012).

Choniates, Niketas, *Historia*, ed. Johannes van Dieten, *Nicetae Choniatae historia, pars prior*, CFHB 11.1 (Berlin, 1975). English translation: Harry Magoulias, *O City of Byzantium, Annals of Niketas Choniates* (Detroit, 1984).

Eustathios of Thessaloniki, *On the Capture of Thessaloniki*, ed. S. Kyriakidis, *Eustazio di Tessalonica. La espugnazione di Tessalonica* (Palermo, 1961).

Ibn al-Athīr, *Al-Kāmil fī'l-ta'rīkh*, 13 vols. (Beirut, 1965–67).

Leo the Deacon, *Historia*, ed. Charles-Benoît Hase, *Leonis diaconi Caloënsis historiae libri decem*, CSHB (Bonn, 1828). English translation: Alice-Mary Talbot and Dennis F. Sullivan, *The* History *of Leo the Deacon: Byzantine Military Expansion in the Tenth Century*, Dumbarton Oaks Studies 41 (Washington, D.C., 2005).

Psellos, *Chronographia*, ed. Dieter Roderich Reinsch, *Michaelis Pselli Chronographia*, Band 1: Einleitung und Text, Millennium Studies, 51 (Berlin/Boston 2014). English translation: E.R.A Sewter, *Michael Psellus: Chronographia* (New Haven, 1953).

Skylitzes, John, *Synopsis Historiarum*, ed. Hans Thurn, *Ioannis Scylitzae Synopsis Historiarum*, CFHB 5 (Berlin, 1973).

Zonaras, *Chronicle*, ed. Theodor Büttner-Wobst, *Ioannis Zonarae epitomae historiarum libri xviii*, vol. 3, CSHB (Bonn, 1897).

Secondary Literature

Agamben, Giorgio, *Means without End. Notes on Politics*, trans. Vincenzo Binetti and Cesare Casarino (Mineapolis/London, 2000).

Bell, Peter, *Social Conflict in the Age of Justinian: Its Nature, Management, and Mediation* (Oxford, 2013).

Blöndal, Sigfús, *The Varangians of Byzantium*. An aspect of Byzantine military history translated, revised and rewritten by Benedikt S. Benediks (Cambridge, 1978 – reprinted 1981).

Cameron, Alan, *Circus Factions: Blues and Greens at Rome and Byzantium* (Oxford, 1976).

Cheynet, Jean-Claude, La colère du peuple à Byzance (Xe–XIIe siècle), *Société française d'histoire urbaine* 3 (2001) 25–38.

Cheynet, Jean-Claude, Patriarches et empereurs: de l'opposition à la révolte ouverte, in: Michael Grünbart, Lutz Rickelt, and Matin Marko Vučetić (eds.), *Zwei Sonnen am Goldenen Horn ? Kaiserliche und patriarchale Macht im byzantinischen Mittelalter*, vol. II (Berlin, 2013) 1–18.

Croke, Brian, Uncovering Byzantium's Historiographical Audience, in: Ruth Macrides (ed.), *History as Literature in Byzantium, Papers from the Fortieth Spring Symposium of Byzantine Studies, University of Birmingham, April 2007* (Farnham, 2010) 25–53.

Dagron, Gilbert, The Urban Economy, Seventh-Twelfth Centuries, in: Angeliki Laiou (ed.), *The Economic History of Byzantium: From the Seventh through the Fifteenth Century*, Dumbarton Oaks Studies 39 (Washington, D.C., 2002) 438–44.

Fögen, Marie Theres, Das politische Denken der Byzantiner, in: *Pipers Handbuch der politischen Ideen, vol 2: Mittelalter* (Munich, 1993), 41–85.

Garland, Lynda, Political Power and the Populace in Byzantium Prior to the Fourth Crusade, *Byzantinoslavica* 53 (1992) 17–52.

Greatrex, Geoffrey, The Nika Riot: A Reappraisal, *The Journal of Hellenic Studies* 117 (1997) 60–86.

Haldon, John, Strategies of Defence, Problems of Security: the Garrisons of Constantinople in the Middle Byzantine Period, in: Cyril Mango and Gilbert Dagron (eds.), *Constantinople and its Hinterland. Papers from the Twenty-seventh Spring Symposium of Byzantine Studies, Oxford, April 1993* (Aldershot, 1995) 143–155.

Kaldellis, Anthony, *The Byzantine Republic. People and Power in New Rome* (Cambridge, Mass., 2015).

Karayannopoulos, Ioannis, *Ιστορία του Βυζαντινού Κράτους*, τόμος Β' (Thessaloniki, 1981)

Kiapidou, Eirini Sophia, *Η Σύνοψις Ιστοριών του Ιωάννη Σκυλίτζη και οι πηγές της (811–1057). Συμβολή στη βυζαντινή ιστοριογραφία κατά τον ΙΑ΄ αιώνα* (Athens, 2010).

Kontogiannopoulou, Anastasia, The Notion of Δῆμος and its Role in Byzantium During the Last Centuries (13th-15th C.), *Byzantina Symmeikta* 22 (2012) 101–124.

Lounghis, Telemachos, *Χρονικόν περί της αναιρέσεως του Αποβασιλέως Κύρου Μιχαήλ του Καλαφάτου, του Γεγονότος Καίσαρος, και των κατ' αυτήν συμβάντων, Byzantiaka* 18 (1998) 73–104.

Malešević, Siniša, *The Sociology of War and Violence* (Cambridge, 2010).

Markopoulos, Athanasios, Le public des textes historiographiques à l'époque macédonienne, *Parekbolai* 5 (2015) 53–74.

Mango, Cyril, The Palace of the Boukoleon, *Cahiers archéologiques. Fin de l'antiquité et Moyen Âge* 45 (1997) 41–50.

Mpourdara, Kalliopi, *Καθοσίωσις και Τυραννίς κατά τους Μέσους Βυζαντινούς Χρόνους. Μακεδονική Δυναστεία (867–1056)* (Athens/Komotene, 1981).

Schlumberger, Gustave, Une revolution de palais en l'An 1042 à Byzance, *Revue des Deux Mondes* 23/2 (1904), 417–445.

Simpson, Alicia, *Niketas Choniates: A Historiographical Study* (Oxford, 2013).

Stouraitis, Yannis, Civil War in the Christian Empire, in: Yannis Stouraitis (ed.), *A Companion to the Byzantine Culture of War, ca 300–1204* (Leiden, 2018) 92–123.

Stouraitis, Yannis, Is Byzantinism an Orientalism? Reflections on Byzantium's Con-
    structed Identities and Debated Ideologies, in: Y. Stouraitis (ed.), *Identities and
    Ideologies in the Medieval East Roman World* (Edinburgh, 2022) 17–47.

Vryonis, Speros, Jr., Byzantine ΔHMOKPATIA and the Guilds in the Eleventh Century,
    DOP 17 (1963) 287–314.

Whitby, Michael, The Violence of the Circus Factions, in: Keith Hopwood (ed.), *Organised
    Crime in Antiquity* (London, 1999) 229–53.

Ekaterini Mitsiou

Mobile Criminals: Crime and Punishment in Thirteenth-Century Byzantine Epirus

The period after the conquest of Constantinople by the Crusaders in 1204[1] in the Byzantine sphere is marked by the (social) mobility of individuals and groups in search of security in an insecure world. Many of them found shelter in the three Greek states formed on the periphery of the former Byzantine Empire (Nicaea, Epirus, and Trebizond).[2] However, the presence of newcomers created a new – often negative – dynamic inside the primarily rural local communities. Several murder cases attested in the first half of the thirteenth century in the region of Epirus may be an indication, but by no means proof of a higher level of criminality.[3]

In Medieval Studies, murder and crimes of violence have been studied from legal, anthropological, and socio-cultural perspectives.[4] Nevertheless, further explanatory models, ideas, and methods deriving from criminology can be applied in order to better understand violent behaviours – the aggressive expression of personal agency.

The murder cases registered in thirteenth-century Epirus (western Greece) have already been analysed by scholars such as Ruth Macrides. However, we will approach them from a criminological perspective.[5] Additionally, emphasis will be placed on the mobility of victims and culprits. Finally, we will focus on the offenders, the motives and execution of crime, the victims, and the types of crimes committed. In this way, we will calibrate our lenses to focus on the persons involved and their space.

---

1 The literature on the Fourth Crusade is immense, see indicatively: Laiou, *Urbs capta.*
2 Angold, *Byzantine Government in Exile*; Stauridou-Zaphraka, Νίκαια και Ήπειρος τον 13ο αιώνα.
3 Prinzing, In Search of Diasporas.
4 Indicatively see: Dietl and Knäpper (eds.), *Rules and Violence*; Wahl, *15000 Jahre Mord und Totschlag*; Reuter and Schiavone, *Gefährliches Pflaster*; Classen and Scarborough, *Crime and Punishment in the Middle Ages and Early Modern Age*; Dean, *Crime in Medieval Europe*; Butler, Getting Medieval on Steven Pinker: Violence and Medieval England.
5 A thorough study on 'Murder in Byzantium' is being prepared by the author and will be published by Palgrave.

Methodological framework

Criminality in the modern era, especially since the industrial revolution, has been the focus of research, facilitated by the birth of scientific criminology and forensic medicine.[6] Over time, various books have made their appearance focusing on murder cases from Antiquity and the Middle Ages.[7] The term 'criminology' emerged at the end of the nineteenth century 'because a group of theorists laid claim to systematic knowledge as to the nature of criminal behaviour, its causes and solutions.'[8]

Before continuing, it is important to define some of these terms. According to Dölling, Hermann, and Laue, 'criminology analyses the extent, structure, and development of crime. In addition, the manifestations of the individual offences (criminal phenomenology) are worked out and the spatial distribution of crime is analysed (criminal geography). In addition to the crimes, criminology examines the people who stand on 'both sides of the crime': the perpetrators and the victims. The part of criminology that deals with the crime victims is called victimology. In addition to describing the crime, criminology is concerned with determining the causes of crime (criminal etiology)' (my translation).[9]

But can we apply criminological ideas in Byzantium? I will argue, yes. Criminology accepts that 'writing about crime can be found from the earliest times. Sometimes they were in form of novels and on other occasions, they were accounts, such as the consequences of deprivation in slums and the evils of drink. Yet, such writers did not think of themselves as criminologists. They wrote from a variety of perspectives: religion, medicine and in particular, a growing concern about the governance of the country that arose from increasing urbanisation.'[10]

Texts from Antiquity and the Middle Ages therefore also include narrative descriptions of crimes which took place and raised the interest of the authors and their audience. Another point is that these authors did not perceive themselves as criminologists, but had other identities such as those of theologians, ecclesiastics, civil servants etc. As we are about to see, we possess some interesting descriptions from ecclesiastical circles in late Byzantium.

---

6 Emsley, *Crime, Police, and Penal Policy*; Watson, *Forensic Medicine in Western Society*.
7 Krause, *Kriminalgeschichte der Antike*; Hartz, *Tatort Antike: berühmte Kriminalfälle des Altertums*; Heidemann and Schäfer, *Tatort Mittelalter: berühmte Kriminalfälle*; Spierenburg, *A History of Murder*; Bednarski, *A Poisoned Past: The Life and Times of Margarida de Portu*; Zarinebaf, *Crime and Punishment in Istanbul.*
8 Jones, *Criminology*, 1. On Criminology see also Walklate, *Criminology. The Basics*; Neubacher, *Kriminologie*; Dölling *et al.*, *Kriminologie*.
9 Dölling *et al.*, *Kriminologie*, 4.
10 Jones, *Criminology*, 1.

Moreover, criminology acknowledges that 'in the pre-Enlightenment Europe [and this refers also to Byzantium] it was generally believed that crime was the consequence of evil. In some cases, it was assumed that the Devil or demons had taken over individuals and directed them to perform wicked acts. Alternatively, people whose faith in God was insufficiently strong might have yielded to temptation and made a pact with the Devil. Humans were seen as being both controlled by external forces and creators of their own destiny – a dichotomy which has remained central to explanations of crime up to the present day'.[11] Such a belief could indeed lead to various reactions towards weak persons who, under devil's influence, had committed a crime such as theft.

Part of the analysis of criminal behaviour and actions is based on forensic work. In the history of forensic science, one finds few contributions to this field from the Middle Ages. One prominent case is the story of Sung Tzu and the bloody sickle (1235), which was used to commit a murder. To find the murder weapon, the villagers had to present all their sickles in the sun. The culprit was caught when flies gathered on his sickle. From medieval China the book *His Duan Yu* (The Washing Away of Wrongs, 1248)[12] describes a detailed examination of the crime scene and the victim. The book even includes a chapter dedicated to the distinction between drowning and strangulation. In medieval Bologna, an autopsy of a nobleman was performed in 1302 by Bartolomeo da Varignana[13] because of suspicion of murder.

The most prominent example of the connection between forensics and the European Middle Ages is a fictional one and it comes from the novel – later a film – 'The Name of the Rose' by Umberto Eco. Despite the immense success of the novel and the movie, it did not initiate an extensive use of criminology in the analysis of behaviours and actions of medieval individuals,[14] despite the fact that at the centre of the story were a series of murders and a form of police investigation aimed at finding the person(s) behind it. The role of the investigator was played by a former member of the Inquisition, William of Baskerville. This is not surprising, because criminological history regards the Inquisition as an institution which tried to base any convictions not only on testimonies but also on physical evidence.[15]

As we have mentioned, mobility is a crucial parameter for the analysis of every criminal act. The paradigm of mobilities[16] is closely related to the spatial turn in

---

11 Jones, *Criminology*, 73–74.
12 *The Washing Away of Wrongs: Sung Tz'u*, trans. McKnight.
13 Siraisi, Taddeo Alderotti and Bartolomeo da Varignana.
14 An exception is the book by Tracy, *Medieval and Early Modern Murder.*
15 One other publication related to the topic, but covering a case from the nineteenth century (July 1859), is that of Wolf, *Die Nonnen von Sant' Ambrogio.*
16 Urry, *Mobilities.*

human sciences. 'Mobilities' encompasses the movement of people, objects, and ideas, while at the same time societies and systems are also regarded as being on the move. However, our focus is criminal and legal mobility.

Justice and murder in thirteenth-century Epirus

For Christianity, the beginning of murderous behaviour is to be found in the Old Testament, in the murder of Abel by his brother Cain. Speaking about the murder of Abel, Theodoret of Cyrus argues that Cain did something illegal (παράνομος) according to the law of nature. Cain used deceit to commit his act: he took his victim away from the parents who could have protected him.[17] From a criminological point of view, it is interesting that the offender's motives were anger and jealousy, while deceit is generally a significant element in committing a crime.

In Byzantium, research into murder has focused primarily on the murders of emperors, such as the very prominent murders of Michael III (23/24 September 867) and Nikephoros Phokas (11 December 969).[18] However, less interest has been shown in crimes committed by and against common people, although the sources necessary for an analysis of murder on the microlevel are available. For the thirteenth century we possess the decisions of the Archbishop of Ohrid, Demetrios Chomatenos (1216/17–1236),[19] and the Metropolitan of Naupaktos, John Apokaukos (1199/1200–1232).[20] Although the Church officials were more interested in penitential aspects, the narration of the events enables the crimes committed to be reconstructed to a certain extent in criminological terms. At the same time, these narratives offer us a fascinating glimpse into the motives, actions, and ways of thinking of the murderers; all of which form a cluster of topics addressed by criminologists.

Before delving into the murder cases, we will briefly present the justice system in early thirteenth century. It certainly lacked the complexity of the previous period, as the high courts of Constantinople such as *tou prokathemenou tōn*

---

17 Theodoret of Cyrus, *Quaestiones in Octateuchum*, ed. Marcos and Sáenz-Badillos, 54: Τῇ φύσει τοὺς ἀναγκαίους ἐντέθεικε νόμους ὁ ποιητής. οὕτω τὸν Κάϊν κατέκρινεν ἐπειδήπερ αὐτὸν ἡ φύσις ἐδίδασκεν, ὡς ὁ φόνος παράνομος· αὐτίκα γοῦν δόλῳ χρησάμενος συνεργῷ, πόρρω τῶν γεγεννηκότων ἀπαγαγών, ἀνεῖλε τὸν ἀδελφὸν καὶ τοῦ Θεοῦ πυνθανομένου'.

18 See indicatively Markopoulos, Αἷμα στο παλάτι, which deals with further cases of political murder in Byzantium.

19 Chomatenos, *Ponemata*, ed. Prinzing.

20 Bees, Unedierte Schriftstücke; Bee-Sepherle, Προσθῆκαι καὶ παρατηρήσεις; Apokaukos, Ἐπιστολαί, πράξεις συνοδικαὶ καὶ ἔμμετρα, ed. Papadopoulos-Kerameus; Apokaukos, *Letters and Other Writings*, ed. Pétridès. All Apokaukos' documents and letters were collected by Delemares in Apokaukos, Ἅπαντα Ἰωάννου Ἀποκαύκου.

demosiōn dikastēriōn ceased to exist. A phenomenon which comes into being in this period is the involvement of ecclesiastical courts also in civil cases, and not only in those related to canon and marriage law.[21] The sources from Epirus, indeed, depict the activity of the two synodical courts in Ohrid and Naupaktos, although civil courts also sat. The theme governor (*dux*) had judicial duties and could assemble courts of law, sometimes including church officials. In addition, elected judges could decide upon lesser cases of property disputes related to *pronoiai*. As in the period before 1204, any plaintiff could present his or her case in front of the emperor and receive a ruling. The imperial court could either discuss the case or delegate it to other authorised judges.

In general, the justice system after 1204 became inefficient as the decisions could not be easily implemented, cases were overruled, and they had to be heard twice or three times. Such outcomes were also related to the neglect of the principles relating to the jurisdiction of the lawcourts. According to the *Ecloga Basilicorum* (twelfth century), serious crimes such as murder could not be decided by elected judges.[22] Consequently, the only courts with legal competence to judge these crimes were the court of the Epirote rulers, the courts of the thematic officials, and the ecclesiastical courts. A decision by a court without legal competence to judge the case could be dismissed as invalid. Other criteria which generally determined which court of law was legally competent to judge a case was that the defendant was to be judged by a court in his or her own region. Finally, the identity of an individual determined the right court for his case: priests and monks were to be judged by the bishop or the patriarch, senators by the emperor, soldiers by a military court, and guild members by the eparch of the city.[23] The existence of both civil and ecclesiastical courts did not mean that people could simply turn to the synodical ones, because they would impose penances, rather than the harsher judgment of civil courts. The synodical courts did not replace the civil ones. Indeed, some of the cases dealt by Chomatenos and Apokaukos had been passed on to them following imperial or ducal delegation.[24]

---

21 Gkoutzioukostas, *Η απονομή δικαιοσύνης*, 296–297 with all the relevant bibliography on the matter.

22 *Ecloga Basilicorum*, ed. Burgmann (32, 6) B.7.2.32.6= D.4.8.32.6, 244, l. 18–25: 'Κωλύεται ὁ αἱρετὸς δικαστὴς ψηφίζεσθαι ἐπὶ ἀτιμοποιῷ ἐξ ἁμαρτήματος ἀγωγῇ ἢ δημοσίῳ ἐγκλήματι· κἂν ψηφίσηται, οὐχ ἁρμόζει ἀπαίτησις.' Αἱρετὸν δικαστήριον ὁ νόμος οὐ παραχωρεῖ συνίστασθαι ἐπὶ ἐγκλήματι μεγάλῳ, οἷον ἐπὶ μοιχείᾳ ἢ φόνῳ ἢ ἱεροσυλίᾳ, οὔτε ἐπὶ πριβάτῳ ἤτοι ἰδιωτικῷ, οἷον περὶ κλοπῆς ἢ περὶ ὕβρεως· ταῦτα γὰρ παρ' ἐκείνων τηροῦνται τῶν ἐχόντων δικαιοδοσίαν καὶ κράτος ἤτοι ἀρχὴν μεγάλην, οἷον τοῦ δρουγγαρίου, τοῦ δικαιοδότου καὶ ἁπλῶς τῶν ὀφφικιαλίων ἤτοι τῶν ἐχόντων ἀρχὰς καὶ προκαθημένων δικαστηρίου.

23 Gkoutzioukostas, *Η απονομή δικαιοσύνης*, 251–256, with the relevant source references.

24 Papagianni, Legislation and Legal Practice, 208, 210; c.f. also Troianos, *Οι πηγές του βυζαντινού δικαίου*, 279; Gkoutzioukostas, *Η απονομή δικαιοσύνης*, 295–298; Simon, Provinzialjustiz, 453–477, esp. 316.

With regard to the murder cases, we can perhaps assume that some may have been judged by the ecclesiastical authorities because the defendants had sought asylum. This forbade any involvement of the civil court and fiscal officials in the punishment procedure.[25]

Nine murder cases judged by of Apokaukos and nine by Chomatenos provide personal information on the actors (mostly young men), the victims (mostly young men of poor social and economic background) the crime scenes (such as workplaces, family homes, streets, forests, and vineyards), the motivation (mostly anger, but also long disputes and unhappiness), the method of killing (such as attacks with a sharp object and poisoning) and the weapons (stones, knives, arrows, swords, piece of wood, etc.).The court charters cover a range of verdicts, from innocent to guilty of premeditated or non-premeditated murder.[26] The criminogenic circumstances are restricted to a non-urban environment; the decisions are urban. The accused persons travelled long distances to present their case in front of Apokaukos or Chomatenos. On the other hand, some murders were enabled by the movement of the defendants, mostly in areas of their everyday activities.[27]

In what follows we present two types of murder based on criminological categories: situational, and murders related to domestic violence. All cases are analysed criminologically.

Situational murders

In the first case, a certain Xenos from Arta travelled to Naupaktos (see map) and confessed to the metropolitan Apokaukos that he had attacked and killed a young man. The crime had happened while both were supervising the harvesting of grapes in the vineyards of their lords; one of these lords was George Petomenos. The killing can be dated to around the end of August and beginning of September. Due to the high demand for labour, men and women were involved in

---

25 *Novels of Manuel I Komnenos*, ed. Macrides, 99–204, here 156–167.

26 The legal framework relating to murder in Byzantium included various regulations. For reasons of convenience, we mention here the most significant: *Ecloga* 17.45–49, ed. Burgmann, 242; *Eisagoge* 40.85–92, ed. Zepos, 229–368; *Procheiros Nomos*, XXXIX, 79–86, ed. Zepos, 226–227; *Basilica*, ed. Scheltema *et al.*, 39, 3 and 51.15; novels 10 and 11 of Constantine VII (d. 945–959), *Novels of Constantine VII*, ed. Zepos, and Zepos, 214–239. From the perspective of canon law, of paramount importance are canons 8 and 11 of Basil the Great, ed. Courtonne, letter 188, ch. 8 and 11. See also Tourtoglou, *Το φονικόν και η αποζημίωσις του παθόντος*; c.f. also Troianos, *Ο «Ποινάλιος» του Εκλογαδίου*; Troianos, *Εισηγήσεις Βυζαντινού δικαίου*, 198–200.

27 For a thorough legal analysis of the cases, see Macrides, *Killing*; and eadem, *Kinship and justice*, no. X.

the harvesting, which implies a crowded crime scene; at the same time, it introduces us to the upcoming events.[28] Xenos made the following statement:

> The young man in the service of Petomenos, either because he was licentious, being young, or because he took pleasure in pranks and delighted in jesting with women, was harassing the women as they came and went along the path of the vineyard I was supervising, and he was coming into contact with them unnecessarily, not allowing them to come and go unimpeded. He did this often and I forbade him as many times but since I did not dissuade him, I took a stick into my hands, eager to strike him on the body and I brought it down on him but he turned this way and that to avoid the blow of the stick and twisted his head, so that he received the blow there and died two days later.

The young man was victimised by the older supervisor who in return presents him as a perpetrator. Xenos argued that it was the inappropriate behaviour of the victim towards his female workers that led to the deadly event. After repeatedly insisting that his future victim should stop, Xenos became angry and hit him. It is unclear whether he wanted to defend these women or was simply keen to finish the harvesting. The latter was probably the case.

The version of the murder provided is unreliable. Xenos argues that he intended to strike the young man on the body, but the victim moved around, taking the blow on the head. He speaks of an unlucky strike. However, the description does not reflect how those under attack would defend themselves. The victim would have tried either to cover his head with his hands or to completely avoid the blow. There was probably more than one blow which led to the death of the victim (from internal bleeding?) two days later. No further witness was called to support or contradict this story, not even from the side of the victim. The general impression is that Xenos often applied violence to subdue his workers and his opponents; this was certainly not the first incident. Apokaukos declared it a premeditated murder, ordering the necessary penances (*epitimia*). Finally, he forbade the *praktores* (fiscal officials) to confiscate Xenos' property under the threat of excommunication.[29]

Although the exact location of the crime scene is not given, the vineyard may have been located on the slopes of Athamanika (or Tzoumerka mountains) near Arta, where many wineries exist even today. Regarding the mobility involved,

---

28 Apokaukos, *Lettres and Other Documents*, ed. Pétridès, Document no. 14, 86–87 (=Apo-
kaukos, Ἅπαντα Ἰωάννου Ἀποκαύκου, ed. Delemares, 434–436): Ἄνθρωπός τις ἐξ Ἄρτης, ὄνομα
Ξένος, ἐλθὼν εἰς ἡμᾶς τὴν σήμερον ἐξηγήσατο, ὅτι κατὰ τὴν ἐνεστῶσαν τρύγην ἐφεστὼς ἦν τῷ
ἀμπελῶνι τοῦ κυρίου αὐτοῦ· ἐχόμενος δὲ κατὰ τὸν αὐτὸν στίχον καὶ ἕτερος ὑπὸ χεῖρα τοῦ Πετομένου
κυροῦ Γεωργίου τοὺς τρυγητὰς τοῦ ἀμπελῶνος αὐτοῦ ἐπετρόπευεν· οἷα δέ, φησί, φιλεῖ ἐν ταῖς
πολυχειρίας δεομέναις ὑπηρεσίαις, καὶ γυναῖκες καὶ ἄνδρες τὸν τρυγητὸν ἐποιοῦντο; trans. Macrides, *Killing*, 521. For this document, see Lampropoulos, Ἰωάννης Ἀπόκαυκος, no. 31, 292.
29 Confiscation was not an independent punishment but an ancillary penalty to go with the
condemnation of the murder either by corporal punishment or exile, see Troianos, Εἰσηγήσεις
Βυζαντινοῦ δικαίου, 199–200.

Xenos covered the distance from Arta to Naupaktos (c. 145 km) for his case to be heard (see map),[30] while for the crime he moved from Arta to the crime scene (vineyard on the mountain slopes?) and from the vineyard to the house of his lord (in Arta?).

The second case brings into the discussion movement as a criminogenic circumstance, especially when transhumant populations are involved. A heated exchange escalated into a physical attack resulting in the death of one individual after twelve days:

> Theodore Vodinopoulos, from Mikra Vagenitia,[31] the village of Vrestianes, came to us and explained that as the present winter was setting in, as is the custom of his region, he was transporting meal to the lower parts which border on the theme of Nikopolis,[32] where he intended to spend the winter with the flocks which belonged to him, [taking the precaution] lest the river Reachova[33] flood and prevent them from crossing over from there with the meal. He and one of his servants, Mavros by name, having done this, were returning home. As they had some acquaintance in the intermediate villages, they were given hospitality by him (and were invited) to eat. And Theodore had reclined and was eating. Mavros led the beast of burden, on which Theodore rode, to pasturage and was following it. When Theodore had eaten, he went to the horse and its herdsman Mavros and rebuked Mavros most reproachfully, as he had not also joined their host to eat. He said that Mavros, who had a wild character and an uncontrolled tongue, hurled abuses at those who had invited them and set the food before them. The host were indignant at Mavros's words and said to Theodore, 'It is not good that we should be unjustly insulted by your servant'. Theodore, wanting to vindicate the hosts, took a staff in his hand and ran to hit Mavros about the feet. Mavros, he said, seeing the staff descending, inclined shoulders and head towards his feet to deflect the blows, but he failed, protecting his feet but receiving the blow on his head.[34]

The crime was committed by Vodinopoulos while returning to the southern parts of Mikra Vagenitia bordering the theme Nikopolis. For an unknown reason, his servant Mavros did not want to eat together with their hosts. Insulted by his attitude, Vodinopoulos hit his servant in the name of retribution. His claim that he tried to hit his victim, but Mavros used his shoulders to protect his feet, can be considered as a typical reaction of a person trying to defend themselves.

---

30 On the probable route of this journey, based on the road system of the region, see Soustal and Koder, *Nikopolis und Kephallēnia*, 94.
31 Soustal and Koder, *Nikopolis und Kephallēnia*, 119–120. Mikra Vagenitia was the area between c. Chimara and Bouthroton (Butrint); see also Komatina, ОБЛАСТ ВАГЕНИТИЈА, 83–100.
32 Soustal and Koder, *Nikopolis und Kephallēnia*, 213–214 and 53f.
33 Soustal and Koder, *Nikopolis und Kephallēnia*, 249.
34 Apokaukos, *Letters and Other Documents,* ed. Pétridès, Document 6, 75–76 (=Apokaukos, Ἅπαντα Ἰωάννου Ἀποκαύκου, ed. Delemares, 427–429); trans. Macrides, *Killing,* 522; Lampropoulos, Ἰωάννης Ἀπόκαυκος, no. 27, 289.

Vodinopoulos travelled during the autumn for a specific distance together with his future victim, c. 100 km from Vrestianes to the river Reachova (perhaps mod. Kalamas in Thesprotia) and then to the unnamed village which became the crime scene. The final movement mentioned in this document was the one from Vrestianes to Naupaktos – that is, c. 350 km (see map).[35] The Vodinopoulos case demonstrates the difficulties people on the move faced, even when they travelled regularly. They had to take into consideration all possible weather conditions and difficulties, such as a flooded river, and to be thankful for any possibilities for accommodation they could find while on the move.

The unpredicted behaviour of the victim could be related to previous negative experiences with their hosts. As transhumant (probably Vlachs),[36] they would have been in conflict with the peasants whenever their animals grazed on the lands of the sedentary population. Vlachs are frequently mentioned in Byzantine sources in instances where the insubordinate character of a Vlach is brought up as a reason for the escalation of a conflict resulting in violence. For example (case no. 3), in 1228 a pronoia-holder in a village in Vlachia[37] asked villagers in his pronoia to prepare a reception for George Choniates, the *protovestiarites* of the despot Manuel Doukas.[38] When he realised that they had not prepared anything for the special guest, a quarrel started, in which a Vlach said (in demotic Greek): ᾿Σὺ πολλὰ τσαμπουνίζεις καὶ πρόσεχε καλά" ('You prate on much. Take care!).[39] The relevant 'semeioma on murder' by Apokaukos includes extraordinary details about the cause of death. The accused described the murder as follows:

> I turned round to him and taking hold of him by the hair, twisted his head and threw him onto the ground, warning him not to behave impudently to me in the future or belch forth his rough talk. The man lay on the ground from that moment, neither speaking nor moving. I thought he was pretending to be motionless and he seemed to me to lie still and remain so like one under the influence of wine. But he was really and truly dead in an instant, and there was neither breath nor voice in him, except that his face was tinged a deep black, like the dye of cloth.[40]

---

35 The map includes only the land route, although sea travel is also plausible. As starting point I took Chimara, since Vrestianes is not located. The route is based on the land road system of the region, see Soustal and Koder, *Nikopolis und Kephallēnia*, 88–89, 90–93 and 94–96.

36 On the Vlachs in Byzantium see indicatively: *ODB*, 2183–2184; Nasturel, Les Valaques balkaniques aux Xe–XIIIe siècles; Curta, *Southeastern Europe in the Middle Ages*, 280–281; idem, *Eastern Europe in the Middle Ages*, 672–674; Winnifrith, *The Vlachs*.

37 On pronoia in Byzantium see Bartusis, *Land and Privilege*, and particularly on this case 229–232. In this case, Vlachia designates the mountains area between Epirus and Thessaly on Pindus Mountains.

38 Puech, *Aristocratie*, I, 75.

39 Translation: Bartusis, *Land and Privilege*, 230.

40 Apokaukos, Σημείωμα φόνου, ed. Papadopoulos-Kerameus, no. 4. 379–382 (=Apokaukos, Ἅπαντα Ἰωάννου Ἀποκαύκου, ed. Delemares, 406–409); trans. Macrides, *Killing*, 521; Lampropoulos, Ἰωάννης Ἀπόκαυκος, no. 21, 281–282.

The metropolitan declared it a non-premeditated murder and attributed it to the anger (πάθος) of the defendant which he was unable to control. Apokaukos offers an almost forensic description of the *modus operandi* of the culprit: he grabbed the victim's hair and violently twisted his head, breaking the spinal cord which led to an immediate death. This could be deduced by the victim's face turning blue, a clear sign of the lack of oxygen.

The pronoia-holder had moved to the crime scene together with George Choniates, but the original point is not mentioned. After the crime, he travelled from his pronoia village in Vlachia to Naupaktos (c. 250 km, taking into consideration the rough landscape) (see map). If he covered c. 30 km per day, then he must have reached his destination in about nine days.

Many murders in the documents of the thirteenth century are the immediate result of trespassing and illegal use of one's land, forests, or grazing areas. In the fourth example, the defendant Konstantinos Melachrenos[41] was the steward of the μεγαλοδοξότατος Constantine Tzirithnos.[42] His victim died in the following way:

> Therefore, out of necessity I seized a staff from one of those collecting the acorns, named Vratonas, and first tried to scare him from collecting, but I forgot to strike Vratonas on the fingers with the staff. Bearing down very severely on the entrails and belly, I hoped to halt his inclination toward the acorns. At that very moment, contrary to my expectations, he let out a gasp and was beheld among the dead, given neither an hour nor a half-hour by the wound. The blow of the staff burst his entrails at once, and at once it drove the soul of the man out from there.[43]

This was not an exceptional violent act for Melachrenos. The expression 'I forgot to strike Vratonas on the fingers with the staff' indicates a habitual use of violence as a means of problem solving. In this case, however, the blow must have caused a haemorrhage of the internal organs (probably liver or spleen), which led to a quick death (οὐδ' ὥραν οὐδ' ἡμιώριον τῇ πληγῇ ἐπαρκέσας). The murder weapon was a staff used for the collection of acorns.[44] The murder was declared premeditated and Melachrenos had to receive spiritual penances (this part is missing in the document).

---

41 Due to a lacuna in the manuscript, the name is not certain. It may be completed as Μελαγχρηνός, Μελαχρηνός, Μελαχρινός, or Μελαχηλός (see *PLP*, nos. 17626–68). On this case see Macrides, Killing, 524; Maniati-Kokkini, Μαρτυρία, 298–299, 297–306.

42 According to Maniati-Kokkini, Μαρτυρία, 298, note 14 it was a copy error instead of 'Tzirithon' (Τζιρίθων). On the Tzirithon family, whose members are also attested in Asia Minor, see Puech, *Aristocratie*, I, 206–207.

43 Apokaukos, *Letters and Other Documents*, ed. Pétridès, Document no. 15, 87–88 (Apokaukos, Ἄπαντα Ἰωάννου Ἀποκαύκου, ed. Delemares, 436–438); Translation: Bartusis, *Land and Privilege*, 228. On the document see Lampropoulos, Ἰωάννης Ἀπόκαυκος, no. 32, 292–293; on the case see Bartusis, *Land and Privilege*, 228–229.

44 Germanidou, Μια μορφή «περιβαλλοντικού» πολέμου στο Βυζάντιο.

There is only one geographical reference point in the document, the village Hermenea (Ἑρμηνέα), whose peasants tried to exploit Tzirithon's properties. Unfortunately, Hermenea is unattested in other sources and its exact location remains unknown.[45] However, based on the textual description we can assume that the crime scene – close to the land property of Tzirithnos – was an area some metres above sea level, as the oaks mentioned coexist with arable land. The oaks found in the area may have been of the genus *Quercus ithaburensis* subsp. *Macrolepis,* which reaches 30 metres in height and thrives in a warm and dry environment. This genus of oaks is found in the Eastern Mediterranean regions in lowland areas, as well as in the foothills of mountains.[46] We could assume that it took place around Vonitsa, where another similar incident related to acorns occurred; however, this would only be speculation.[47]

In a fifth document, dated c. 1225–c. 1236, we see again the aggressive behaviour of the victims cited as the trigger for murder. The victims were representatives of the state (tax collectors) in the Acheloos theme, and they were annoying some of the peasants of stratiotes Theodoros Demnites.[48] The latter took a sword in his possession and went to confront them. At the sight of the angry Demnites, the tax collectors took stones in their hands to defend themselves. In the ensuing confrontation, Demnites hit a certain Sgouros on the head with a sword and half of his head/face was instantly paralysed. Because of the (severity of) the wound, death followed immediately.[49] Since Demnites used a sword (a sharp object), his case fell into the category of premeditated murder and he received the relevant penances.

Demnites did not have to cover a long distance to travel to Naupaktos as the Acheloos theme denoted the area around Angelokastron, north of Anatoliko and Katoche[50](see map); he probably made the journey on horseback or on foot in order to demonstrate his repentance.

---

45 There is no entry for Hermenea in the TIB volume.
46 Oaks, pines, firs, and cypresses grew on higher ground than fruit trees. As timber they could be used as construction material and as firewood. Acorns were important as pig food, see Mitsiou, *Wirtschaft und Ideologie,* 78, with source references.
47 Bees, Unedierte Schriftstücke, no 18, 78–79.
48 Puech, *Aristocratie,* I, 81.
49 Chomatenos, *Ponemata,* no. 118, l. 30–32, ed. Prinzing 383–384: παραλύσας εὐθὺς αὐτῆς τὸ ἡμίκρανον. Καὶ ἐπειδὴ τοιαύτη γέγονεν ἡ πληγή, εὐθυωρὸν ταύτην ὁ θάνατος διεδέξατο; Macrides, Killing, 522; Bartusis, *Land and Privilege,* 233.
50 Soustal and Koder, *Nikopolis und Kephallēnia,* 101–102.

Domestic violence/abuse

Some of the cases were the outcome of domestic abuse or aggression. A fight between a bride and her mother-in-law in Leukas ended in violence between her husband and his father. In 1217, Basileios Kaliges killed his son in a moment of anger in the following way:

> From the exchange of words the father was moved to anger against his son, as a father is, and supposedly to chasten him and check his opposition, he took a stone as large as his hand could hold and aimed it against his own son. This struck him on the temple, killing him immediately.[51] (Translation: R. Macrides)

Apokaukos declared it a premeditated murder and ordered several spiritual punishments for a period of five years. The murder was the result of long-lasting tensions between the young couple and the man's parents, who lived in a multiple family household. Because they shared the same house, a de-escalation of the aggression became difficult. The animosity between the daughter- and mother-in-law created a tense group dynamic between the two sides: the older and the younger couple. The two males tried to defend their female partners, ending in a lethal confrontation.

Kaliges travelled from Leukas to Naupaktos, probably by sea. The distance is c. 58 nautical miles; in favourable sailing conditions it could be covered in approximately 10 hours, and in difficult conditions in around 30 hours. A land journey (c. 175 km) would have been a less likely option as it would have taken at least 5 days (if Kaliges had crossed over the Ambracian Gulf, reached Amphilochia, and then followed a route such as the one in the first case) (see map).

Domestic violence motivated an attempted murder-suicide by poison.[52] Chryse, the niece of Georgios Spathas, tried to kill her husband, Manuel. The unidentified poison was handed to him in a cup. But her plan was well-thought-out: 'She therefore determined to part from him and to this end poured the potion of death for herself as well as him, so that if the cup should pass him by, it might be effective in her'. The motive behind her actions was the 'πολλὰ πάσχουσα

---

51 Bees, Unedierte Schriftstücke, no 14, 75–76, here 75 (=Apokaukos, Ἅπαντα Ἰωάννου Ἀποκαύκου, ed. Delemares, no. 2, 353–355): καὶ ἐκ τούτων τῶν λόγων καὶ ἐξ ἐκείνων τῶν ἀντιλόγων
εἰς θυμὸν κατὰ τοῦ υἱοῦ ὁ πατὴρ ἐκινήθη, οἷα πατήρ· καὶ σωφρονίζων δῆθεν αὐτὸν καὶ ἀναστέλλων
τοῦ τῷ πατρὶ αὐτῷ ἀντιφέρεσθαι, λίθον ἄρας ὅσον ἐχώρει ἡ χείρ, τοῦ ἰδίου υἱοῦ κατηκόντισε· καὶ
τυχὼν αὐτοῦ περὶ τὸν μήνιγγα εὐθύωρον ἀνεῖλεν αὐτόν; Macrides, Killing, 523; Lampropoulos,
Ἰωάννης Ἀπόκαυκος, no. 2, 262–263.
52 Chomatenos, Ponemata, no. 121 (Περὶ γυναικὸς ἐπιβουλευσαμένης τὸν ἑαυτῆς ἄνδρα διὰ
δηλητηρίου φαρμάκου·καὶ διαζύγιον πρὸς ταῦτα γεγονός), ed. Prinzing, 389 and 238*; Angelomatis-Tsougarakis, Women in the Society of the Despotate of Epiros, 479; Kiousopoulou, Ο
θεσμός της οικογένειας στην Ήπειρο, 62, 110, 125, n. 70; Macrides, Killing, 523, 532; Leontaritou,
Ἐκ γυναικὸς ἐρρύη τὰ φαῦλα (emphasis on law and punishment of female criminality). On
gender representations of women who kill see Seal, Women, Murder and Femininity.

παρὰ τοῦ τοιούτου ἀνδρὸς τὰ ἀνήκεστα (=she suffered much incurable harm at the hands of this man)',[53] but the charter does not provide any further details about the nature and the duration of the abuse. Chomatenos decided that the couple, who were present in Ohrid, should divorce, and Chryse should enter the nunnery of the Holy Apostles, as part of her punishment.[54] The emphasis on the ineffectiveness of the poison, which is mentioned three times, is worth noting. However, we hear nothing about the crime scene, probably their residence, nor about the distance they covered to attend the court. Criminologically, the case can be listed under the category of spousal/consortial murder-suicides, with domestic violence as a major characteristic.[55] Usually, this type of crime is committed by male perpetrators when they feel that their partners will abandon them. However, the case reflects the smaller percentage of cases where the perpetrator is female. It shows the desperation of Chryse, who felt socially tied and unable to leave an abusive relationship.[56] The attempted murder, an expression of personal agency, allowed her plea to be heard, even in a tragic way.

Another interesting case, also in relation to a Byzantine household, is offered by the murder case presented by Zoe, the daughter of the late Nikolaos Petzikopoulos, from the *thema* of Koloneia (today Kolonja, south of Korça).[57] She knelt in front of the archbishop and confessed in tears that six years earlier she had caused the death of her servant who had repeatedly stolen things and threatened her in her bed with a knife. Other servants caught him and cut both his hands. The wounds were left untreated, and the servant died.[58] Zoe felt responsible for his death; she repented, and cried. For her punishment, Chomatenos took into consideration female weakness, the difficult living space, and her repentance: Ἐδέξατο δὲ καὶ ἐπιτίμια εἰς ἔκτισιν τοῦ πλημμελήματος ἀνάλογον τῇ τε γυναικείᾳ τῇ κατ' αὐτὴν ἀσθενείᾳ, τῷ τε ἀπαραμυθήτῳ τοῦ τόπου, ὡς μανθάνομεν, ἐν ᾧ κατοικεῖ, καὶ τῇ κατανύξει αὐτῇ. However, he imposed various penances such as fasting, genuflexions, exclusion from the Eucharist, and donations to charitable causes, for five years.[59] Zoe covered the distance Kolonja-Ohrid (c. 189 km) on

---

53 Macrides, *Killing*, 523. Spousal violence was also condemned by John Chrysostom, who showed an interest on the phenomenon, c.f. Schroeder, John Chrysostom's Critique of Spousal Violence.

54 The location of the convent of the Holy Apostles is uncertain. Regarding the entrance to a nunnery by women who committed crimes such as murder see Troianos, Εἰσηγήσεις Βυζαντινοῦ δικαίου, 174–175 with the relevant sources.

55 Eliason, Murder-Suicide: A Review of the Recent Literature, 375.

56 On women and Byzantine law see Buckler, Women in Byzantine Law; Beaucamp, La situation juridique de la femme à Byzance; eadem, *Le statut de la femme à Byzance*; Laiou, *Gender, Society and Economic Life in Byzantium*; eadem, *Mariage, amour et parenté à Byzance*.

57 Soustal and Koder, *Nikopolis und Kephallēnia*, 40 and 55.

58 Chomatenos, *Ponemata*, no. 129, ed. Prinzing, 400–402.

59 Chomatenos, *Ponemata*, no. 129, ed. Prinzing, 401; c.f. p. 246*-248*.

foot in six days. On this basis we can deduce that she walked c. 31.5 km per day (see map). Taking into consideration the rough terrain of the region, however, it seems unrealistic that she could have completed the journey in only six days.

From a criminological point of view, the case contains unclear points. For example, the document provides no information on the reasons of her appearance at the synodical court six years after the incident. In the first instance, she visited her spiritual father, who prohibited her from receiving the Holy Communion, which put social pressure on her since she could be regarded as a sinner/killer. However, no other civil or ecclesiastical punishment is mentioned. The death of the victim – probably from heavy bleeding or infection – can be attributed to a neglect by his mistress. We should, however, mention that such punishment of a servant was not in complete agreement with civil legislation.[60] It is presented, however, as the victim having triggered the harsh decision of his lady (victim blaming).

Conclusion

The murderers and murders presented above demonstrate the importance of the geographical aspects of any criminal act as well as movement in a specific space, especially in the case of the transhumant individuals where the killing resulted because one of them wanted to maintain a good relationship with the sedentary population. On the other hand, most of the murderers do not reveal all their movements after the criminal act. The only certain movement is towards an ecclesiastical authority to avoid (?) punishment. This journey could cover many kilometres (from 100 to 350) in western Greece. The movement is from north to south (as in the first case) or from west to east (see the case of Leukas). To a certain degree, a difficult journey to the synodical court worked in favour of the defendants (such as in the case of Zoe).

A surprising aspect is the ease by which some testimonies were taken at face value. Of course, there were no modern methods of criminal investigation; but Byzantine law could identify premeditated and non-premeditated murder by the weapon used: whenever a sword or poison came into play, the murder was declared premeditated and the punishment was harsher.

Finally, some murder cases in thirteenth-century Epirus provide valuable information on another aspect of the Wittgenstein Prize Project 'Moving Byzantium: Mobility, Microstructures and Personal Agency': microstructures. Some cases offer some glimpses into the tensions between peasants and their lords, who could easily turn to violence to subordinate the peasants. The content

---

60 Troianos, *Εισηγήσεις Βυζαντινού δικαίου*, 216–217.

of these cases should not be disregarded as literary expressions. In fact, juridical texts are often closer to reality than other written testimonies of the past and their accuracy can be proved by attestations from other regions. As an example, one could mention the violent attacks by peasants against the Lembos monastery in Smyrna; these speak of social tensions and suppressed anger which could unexpectedly erupt and result in death.[61]

Acknowledgements

The present study was written as part of the FWF P-Z288-G25 Wittgenstein Prize Project: 'Moving Byzantium: Mobility, Microstructures and Personal Agency' directed by Professor Claudia Rapp (Department of Byzantine and Modern Greek Studies, University of Vienna and Department of Byzantine Research/ IMAFO, Austrian Academy of Sciences).

It was finalised as part of the ENCHANT-Project: 'Entangled Charters of Anatolia', FWF P 36403-G, directed by Johannes Preiser-Kapeller) (Department of Byzantine Research/IMAFO, Austrian Academy of Sciences, and Department of Byzantine and Modern Greek Studies, University of Vienna)

Bibliography

Primary Sources

Apokaukos, John, Σημείωμα φόνου, ed. Athanasios Papadopoulos-Kerameus, Ἰωάννης Ἀπόκαυκος καὶ Νικήτας Χωνιάτης, in: Τεσσαρακονταετηρὶς τῆς καθηγεσίας Κ. Σ. Κόντου (1909) 375–382.
Apokaukos, John, Ἅπαντα Ἰωάννου Ἀποκαύκου, ed. Ioannes Delemares, Πατέρες τῆς Ἐκκλησίας καὶ ἐκκλησιαστικοὶ συγγραφεῖς τῆς Δυτικῆς Ἑλλάδος, 1 (Naupaktos, 2000).
Apokaukos, John, Ἐπιστολαί, πράξεις συνοδικαὶ καὶ ἔμμετρα, ed. Athanasios Papadopoulos-Kerameus, Ἰωάννου Ἀποκαύχου Μητροπολίτου Ναυπάκτου Ἐπιστολαί, πράξεις συνοδικαὶ καὶ ἔμμετρα (St. Petersburg, 1913; reprint Leipzig, 1976) 249–294.
Apokaukos, John, Letters and Other Documents, ed. S. Pétridès, Jean Apokaukos. Lettres et autres documents inédits, Izvestija Russkago Archeologiceskago Instituta v Konstantinopole 14 (1909) 69–100.
Basil the Great, ed. Yves Courtonne, Saint Basile. Lettres, vol. 2 (Paris, 1961).
Basilica, ed. H.J. Scheltema, D. Holwerda, and N. van der Wal, Basilicorum Libri LX (Gröningen, 1945–1988).

---

61 Miklosich and Müller, *Acta et diplomata*, IV, no. 163 (d. 1303 or 1307) 257–258.

Bees, Nikolaos A., Unedierte Schriftstücke aus der Kanzlei des Johannes Apokaukos, des Metropoliten von Naupaktos (in Aetolien), *BNJ* 21 (1976) 57–160.

Bee-Sepherle, E., Προσθῆκαι καὶ παρατηρήσεις, *BNJ* 21 (1971–1976) 161– 247.

Chomatenos, Demetrios, *Ponemata*, ed. Günter Prinzing, *Demetrii Chomateni ponemata diaphora*, CFHB 38 (Berlin, 2002).

Ecloga, ed. Ludwig Burgmann, *Ecloga. Das Gesetzbuch Leons III. und Konstantinos V.*, Forschungen zur Byzantinischen Rechtsgeschichte 10 (Frankfurt am Main, 1983).

Ecloga Basilicorum, ed. Ludwig Burgmann, *Ecloga Basilicorum*, Forschungen zur Byzantinischen Rechtsgeschichte 15 (Frankfurt am Main, 1988).

Eisagoge, ed. Panagiotis Zepos, *Leges Imperatorum Isaurorum et Macedonum*, Jus Graecoromanum 2 (Athens, 1931).

Novels of Manuel I Komnenos, ed. Ruth J. Macrides, *Justice under Manuel I Komnenos. Four Novels on Court Business and Murder*, Fontes minores 6 (1984) 99–204 = eadem, *Kinship and Justice in Byzantium, 11th-15th Centuries* (Aldershot/ Brookfield, Vt., 1999), IX.

Novels of Constantine VII, ed. Ioannis Zepos and Panagiotis Zepos, *Leges Imperatorum Isaurorum et Macedonum*, Jus Graecoromanum 1 (Aalen, 1962).

Procheiros Nomos, in: Panagiotis Zepos (ed.), *Leges Imperatorum Isaurorum et Macedonum*, Jus Graecoromanum 2 (Athens, 1931; reprint Aalen, 1962).

The Washing Away of Wrongs: Sung Tz'u, trans. Brian E. Mc Knight (Ann Arbor, 1981).

Theodoret of Cyrus, *Quaestiones in Octateuchum*, ed. Natalio Fernández Marcos and Agnel Sáenz-Badillos, *Theodoreti Cyrensis quaestiones in Octateuchum* (Madrid, 1979).

Secondary Literature

Angelomatis-Tsougarakis, Hélène N., Women in the Society of the Despotate of Epiros, *JÖB* 32/2 (1982) 437–479.

Angold, Michael, *A Byzantine Government in Exile. Government and Society under the Laskarids of Nicaea 1204–1261* (Oxford, 1975).

Bartusis, Mark C., *Land and Privilege in Byzantium: The Institution of Pronoia* (Cambridge, 2012).

Beaucamp, Joëlle, La situation juridique de la femme à Byzance, *Cahiers de Civilisation Médiévale* 20 (1977) 145–176.

Beaucamp, Joëlle, *Le statut de la femme à Byzance (4e–7e siècle)*, 2 vols. (Paris, 1990–1992).

Bednarski, Steven, *A Poisoned Past: The Life and Times of Margarida de Portu, a Fourteenth-Century Accused Poisoner* (Toronto, 2014).

Buckler, Georgina, Women in Byzantine Law about 1100 A.D.. *Byz.* 11 (1936) 391–416.

Butler, Sara M., Getting Medieval on Steven Pinker: Violence and Medieval England, in: Philip Dwyer and Mark Stephen Micale (eds.), *On Violence in History* (New York/ Oxford, 2020), 29–40.

Classen, Albrecht and Connie Scarborough (eds.), *Crime and Punishment in the Middle Ages and Early Modern Age: Mental-Historical Investigations of Basic Human Problems and Social Responses* (Berlin/Boston, 2012).

Curta, Florin, *Eastern Europe in the Middle Ages (500–1300)*, 2 vols. (Leiden/Boston, 201.

Curta, Florin, *Southeastern Europe in the Middle Ages, 500–1250* (New York, 2006).

Dean, Trevor, *Crime in Medieval Europe: 1200–1550* (Harlow, 2001).

Dietl, Cora and Titus Knäpper (eds.), *Rules and Violence. On the Cultural History of Collective Violence from Late Antiquity to the Confessional Age* (Berlin, 2014).

Dölling, Dieter, Dieter Hermann, and Christian Laue, *Kriminologie: Ein Grundriss* (Berlin/Heidelberg, 2022).

Eliason, Scott, Murder-Suicide: A Review of the Recent Literature, *Journal of the American Academy of Psychiatry and the Law* (Online) 37/3 (2009) 371–376.

Emsley, Clive, *Crime, Police, and Penal Policy: European Experiences 1750–1940* (Oxford, 2007; paperback edition, 2013).

Germanidou, Sophia, Μια μορφή «περιβαλλοντικού» πολέμου στο Βυζάντιο: Γεωργικές δολιοφθορές και αγροτικά εργαλεία ως φονικά όπλα, *Byzantina Symmeikta* 27 (2017) 145–172.

Gkoutzioukostas, Andreas E., *Η απονομή δικαιοσύνης στο Βυζάντιο (9ος–12ος αιώνες). Τα κοσμικά δικαιοδοτικά όργανα και δικαστήρια της πρωτεύουσας*, Βυζαντινά Κείμενα και Μελέται 37 (Thessaloniki, 2004).

Hartz, Cornelius, *Tatort Antike: berühmte Kriminalfälle des Altertums* (Darmstadt, 2012).

Heidemann, Malte and Schäfer, Franziska, *Tatort Mittelalter: berühmte Kriminalfälle* (Darmstadt, 2013).

Jones, Stephen, *Criminology*, fifth edition (Oxford, 2013).

Kiousopoulou, Antonia, *Ο θεσμός της οικογένειας στην Ήπειρο κατά τον 13ο αιώνα* (Athens, 1990).

Komatina, Predrag, ОБЛАСТ ВАГЕНИТИЈА И ЕПИСКОПИЈА СВ. КЛИМЕНТА (=The region of Vagenitia and the bishopric of St. Clement), *Zbornik radova Vizantološkog instituta* 53 (2016) 83–100 (doi:10.2298/ZRVI1653083K).

Krause, Jens-Uwe, *Kriminalgeschichte der Antike* (München, 2004).

Laiou, Angeliki E., *Gender, Society and Economic Life in Byzantium* (Aldershot,1992).

Laiou, Angeliki E., *Mariage, amour et parenté à Byzance aux XIe–XIIIe siècles* (Paris, 1992).

Laiou, Angeliki (ed.), *Urbs capta. The Fourth Crusade and its Consequences* (Paris, 2005).

Lampropoulos, Kosmas, *Ιωάννης Απόκαυκος. Συμβολή στην έρευνα του βίου και του συγγραφικού έργου του* (Athens, 1988).

Leontaritou, Vassiliki, Ἐκ γυναικὸς ἐρρύη τὰ φαῦλα: Η γυναικεία εγκληματικότητα στο Βυζάντιο, in: Spyros Troianos (ed.), Ἔγκλημα καὶ τιμωρία στο Βυζάντιο (Athens, 1997), 203–233.

Macrides, Ruth J., Killing, Asylum and the Law in Byzantium. *Speculum* 63/3 (1988) 509–538 (repr.: Macrides, *Kinship and Justice*, no. X).

Macrides, Ruth J., *Kinship and Justice in Byzantium, 11th-15th Centuries* (Aldershot/Brookfield, Vt., 1999).

Maniati-Kokkini, Triantafyllitsa, Μαρτυρία Ἰωάννου τοῦ Ἀποκαύκου γιὰ τὴν κοινωνία τοῦ ιγ΄αἰώνα. Δύο ὑποθέσεις φόνου, in: *Πρακτικά του Α΄ Ἀρχαιολογικού και Ιστορικού Συνεδρίου Αιτωλοακαρνανίας* (Agrinion, 1991), 297–306.

Markopoulos, Athanasios, Αίμα στο παλάτι. Ανταγωνισμοί για τον βυζαντινό θρόνο, in: Troianos, Spyros (ed.), Ἔγκλημα και τιμωρία στο Βυζάντιο (Athens, 1997), 257–272.

Mitsiou, Ekaterini, *Untersuchungen zu Wirtschaft und Ideologie im "Nizänischen" Reich*, Unpubl. Dissertation (Vienna, 2006) (online access: https://utheses.univie.ac.at/detail/58879/).

Našturel, Petre Şerban, Les Valaques balkaniques aux Xe–XIIIe siècles (mouvements de population et colonisation dans la Romanie grecque et latine), *ByzF* 7 (1979) 89–112.

Neubacher, Frank, *Kriminologie* (Cologne, [3]2017).

Papagianni, Eleftheria, Legislation and Legal Practice, in: *Brill's New Pauly* (Supplements 10), ed. Falko Daim and John Noël Dillon, trans. Duncan Alexander Smart (Leiden/ Boston, 2019), 190–213.

Prinzing, Günter, In Search of Diasporas in the Byzantine 'Successor State' of Epirus (c. 1210–1267), in: Georg Christ *et al.*, *Union in separation. Diasporic groups and identities in the Eastern Mediterranean (1100–1800)* (Rome, 2015), 123–136.

Puech, Vincent T, *L' aristocratie et le pouvoir à Byzance au XIIIe siècle (1204–1310)*, 2 vols. (Université de Versailles-Saint-Quentin-en-Yvelines, 2000).

Reuter, Marcus and Romina Schiavone, *Gefährliches Pflaster. Kriminalität im Römischen Reich* (Mainz, 2011; 2nd edition 2013).

Schroeder, Joy A, John Chrysostom's Critique of Spousal Violence, *Journal of Early Christian Studies* 12 (2004) 413–442.

Seal, Lizzie, *Women, Murder and Femininity. Gender representations of Women who kill*, Cultural Criminology series (Basingstoke, 2010).

Simon, Dieter, Byzantinische Provinzialjustiz, *Byzantinische Zeitschrift* 79 (1986) 453–477.

Siraisi, Nancy G., Taddeo Alderotti and Bartolomeo da Varignana on the Nature of Medical Learning, *Isis* 68/1 (1977) 27–39.

Soustal, Peter and Johannes Koder, *Nikopolis und Kephallēnia*, TIB 3 (Vienna, 1981).

Spierenburg, Pieter, *A History of Murder: Personal Violence in Europe from the Middle Ages to the Present* (Cambridge, 2008).

Stauridou-Zaphraka, Alkmene, *Νίκαια και Ήπειρος τον 13° αιώνα* (Thessaloniki, 1990).

Tourtoglou, Menelaos A., *Το φονικόν και η αποζημίωσις του παθόντος: Βυζάντιον – Τουρκοκρατία – μετεπαναστατικοί χρόνοι μέχρι και του Καποδιστρίου* (Athens, 1960).

Tracy, Larissa, *Medieval and Early Modern Murder: Legal, Literary and Historical Contexts* (Woodbridge, 2018).

Troianos, Spyros N., *Εισηγήσεις Βυζαντινού δικαίου* (Athens, 2014), 198–200.

Troianos, Spyros N., *Ο «Ποινάλιος» του Εκλογαδίου συμβολή εις την ιστορίαν της εξελίξεως του ποινικού δικαίου από του Corpus Iuris Civilis μέχρι των Βασιλικών* (Frankfurt am Main, 1980).

Troianos, Spyros N., *Οι πηγές του Βυζαντινού δικαίου*, 3rd ed. (Athens, 2011).

Urry, John, *Mobilities* (Cambridge, 2007).

Wahl, Joachim, *15000 Jahre Mord und Totschlag: Anthropologen auf der Spur spektakulärer Verbrechen* (Stuttgart, 2012).

Walklate, Sandra, *Criminology. The Basics* (London/New York, [3]2017).

Watson, Katherine D., *Forensic Medicine in Western Society A History* (Abingdon/New York, 2011).

Winnifrith, Tom J., *The Vlachs. The History of a Balkan People* (London, 1987).

Wolf, Hubert, *Die Nonnen von Sant' Ambrogio* (Munich, 2013).

Zarinebaf, Fariba, *Crime and Punishment in Istanbul, 1700–1800* (Berkeley/Los Angeles/ London, 2010).

Map

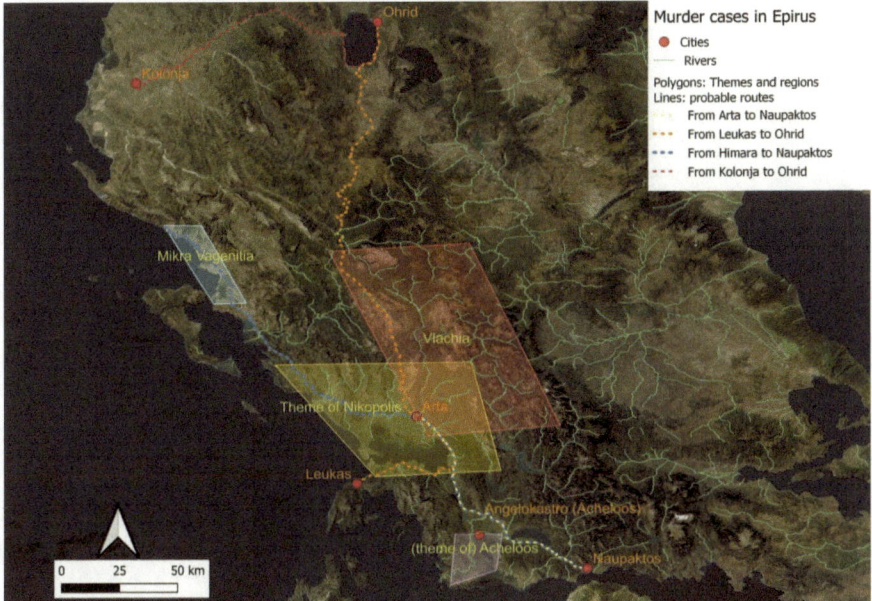

Murder cases in Epirus (© Ekaterini Mitsiou) (created with Google Maps and QGIS. Note: the routes and the limits of themes and regions are given only approximately).

Christos Malatras

Towards the Upper Echelon: Patronage, Agency, and Social Ascent in Late Byzantium

Social inequality is observed in all complex societies in human history, from the Neothilic Age to our Post-Industrial World. Every society has created a set of resources that it defines as important, the unequal distribution of which creates the social stratification. These resources may range from human (e. g. physical power, magic skills, literacy), political (e. g. possession of an office), economic (e. g. means of production, income) to social (e. g. possession of social networks, friends, supporters etc.) and cultural (birth, lifestyle etc.).

Late Byzantine society, too, was unequal. Most of the valued resources were held/enjoyed by a small segment of society, the elite. The most important criteria determining social status in Late Byzantium were the possession of wealth, honours, ancestry, and education.[1] It should be made clear that for the Byzantine elite, wealth was a means to generate a specific cultural lifestyle: clothing, elegant food, religious and artistic patronage, followings of servants and supporters, and so on. The Late Byzantine government still controlled a huge share of the financial resources, distributing the greater part of them, through the institution of *oikonomia* or *pronoia*, in order to maintain its supporters and an army. A great part, if not the greatest, of the properties of the Late Byzantine elite derived from imperial grants. These grants were principally lifetime grants and the government retained the right to revoke them at any time. Even the practice of granting patrimonial rights to a piece of *oikonomia/pronoia* (γονικεύω), widespread in the Early Palaiologan period, was a privilege granted to individuals directly from the emperor and could also be revoked.[2] In fact, the government regularly im-

---

1 Kazhdan and Ronchey, *Aristocrazia bizantina*, 91–93, recognises four elements, the combination of which determined membership of the Middle Byzantine aristocracy: origins, wealth, function, and merit. It is best to avoid the term aristocracy, unless we mean that section of the elite whose membership of the upper strata we suppose was continuous over generations and claimed ancestry/nobility.

2 For the institution of *pronoia* see now Bartusis, *Land and Privilege*. During the period under examination here, *oikonomia* and *pronoia* are synonymous, although earlier, in the twelfth century, *pronoia* was mostly used in conjunction with the military form of the institution of

plemented confiscations or exchanges of land properties affecting all strata of society.[3] Since land ownership status was thus fluid and as there were no lordship rights in Byzantium – excluding here the appanage-type of lordships created in the last century, mostly for the members of the imperial family, such as Mystras, Ainos, and Thessaloniki –, land meant nothing more than one source of income amongst others for the elite, rather than a source of economic (in the sense of owning the means of production) or political power.[4]

Honours in Late Byzantium were translated into the honorific epithets and designations that ranged from those used to denote exalted status (such as κύρ, αὐθέντης, εὐγενέστατος, ἐντιμώτατος), to the court titles (some of which retained a function), and to the offices. Although the first of these were purely a source of social prestige, the titles and the offices, both attributed by the emperor, were also a source of political power. In a provincial administrative context, the holder could be a governor or an army official, influencing decisions at a local level. In the context of central administration, the holder could be the head of financial departments or a member of the senate influencing the decisions of the government, as well as the distribution of the state's resources and positions to specific individuals. The Byzantine bureaucratic system was not based on objective criteria of office possession, such as on merit, certainly not in respect to the upper levels, but on selection, which itself heavily depended on patronage (including inter-family) or other external factors, such as the balance of power or even the purchase of an office/title. Besides, both titles and offices normally implied an income either through the attribution of an *oikonomia* or through the granting of special taxes and privileges (for example, the *kephalatikion* for a provincial governor).[5] As such their possession was indispensable for the preservation of a family among the elite.

oikonomia. For *gonikon* see Patlagean, 'Γονικόν', although she considers *gonikon* similarly a conditional landholding, returning to the old theory that the concept of private property was absent in Byzantium. For the role of the state in the economic and social establishment of the Early Palaiologan elite see Kyritses, *Byzantine Aristocracy*, 165–183 and Ragia, Agrarian policy.

3 Smyrlis, State, Land and Private Property, 58–87. Confiscations of lay properties were equally common. Nevertheless, there are pieces of property that were held for successive generations by a family, such as for example the estate of Prinarion in Southern Macedonia, held by the family of Tzamplakones for more than a century, until it was donated in different stages to the monastery of Vatopedi: *Actes de Vatopedi II*, ed. Lefort *et al.*, nos. 105, 107, 135.

4 Malatras, *Social Stratification*, 98.

5 Oikonomides, Title and Income, 210–213. Kantakouzenos also mentions this policy when he says that Sphrantzes Palaiologos was awarded the title of *megas stratopedarches* and the *corresponding* annual revenues: Kantakouzenos, *Historiae*, ed. Schopen, I, 457. For the rights of Late Byzantine governors see: Matschke, Late Byzantine kephalai.

Ancestry was a quality that had been becoming increasingly important since the tenth century.[6] Although in Komnenian Byzantium nobility was inextricably connected to the imperial family, in the Palaiologan period nobility had been diffused outside the imperial family and was no longer controlled by it. Noble status was effectively controlled by the few families of the higher aristocracy, but in a provincial context and in reference to people of much lesser social strata, certain persons belonging to the local elite could also be regarded as of exalted ancestry.[7]

Education was another important source of status and power. An educated person (not necessarily an intellectual) would normally have a position in the state, the civic, or the ecclesiastical hierarchy, something that would place them socially above the average. Intellectuals, on the other hand, can only be placed among the elite of society. They produced public discourse and actively participated in decision-making, or at least were in a position to influence the decisions of important people. One might also place on the same level religious figures, such as ascetics and spiritual teachers, who, in the period under discussion, would also be educated, although not necessarily in classical *paideia*. It should be stressed, however, that it was necessary to be of at least average financial means in order to be able to invest in education. Therefore, although education was occasionally used as a means to achieve social ascent, in practice the right to it was a privilege of the elite.[8]

The functional division of a society can be encountered in many pre-modern societies; in its strictest version it can take the form of a caste society, like in India, where a person's profession and social position are ascribed at birth, are hereditary and immutable, and social groups are sanctioned with certain legal rights and restrictions. In less rigid functional social stratification systems this can take the form of estates or orders; this is known, for example, from medieval western Europe (i.e., the soldiers, the priests, and the peasants).

Late Byzantine society, however, was not a society of estates. Ideas of the functional division of society had little impact in Late Byzantium. Although heritability of a profession was widespread for practical reasons (as it used to be until quite recently in our modern world), in no way was this made compulsory. Social groups, with the exception of marginal slavery, were not governed by specific legal regulations. This was true as much for the dependent peasants, the *paroikoi*, whose status was neither personal nor inherited and was connected to

---

6 Kazhdan and Ronchey, *Aristocrazia bizantina*, 76–152; Magdalino, Byzantine Snobbery, 64–67.
7 See Kyritses, *Byzantine Aristocracy*, 251–254; Malatras, *Social Stratification*, 85–88.
8 For a sociological analysis of the Late Byzantine intellectuals see: Matschke and Tinnefeld, *Gesellschaft im späten Byzanz*, 221–346. On the importance of education for the Byzantine elite see: Grünbart, Byzantine (Urban) Aristocracy.

their tax obligations, as it was for the priests, who were socially fully integrated into society (they were subjects of the emperor, tax liable, dependent peasants, and commonly had another occupation etc.). Besides, Byzantium lacked social groups defined by their level of income/property, unlike to the ancient Greek and Roman societies, for example.[9]

Social ascent and the role of patronage

Since social groups were not legally static and rigidly defined in Byzantium, this means that to the modern eye Byzantine society was more 'open' than other medieval societies. In fact, Byzantine authors were prone to think that their society should be immutable and that everyone ought to remain in their allotted position.[10] Much of the financial (economic resources), political, and social (ancestry, lifestyle) capital was transmitted through the family. Marriages were meant to be concluded on the basis of equality of social status or alliance for social and political reasons. The family was important for yet another reason: networks. Each elite family had created a political and social network of relatives, friends, and supporters that would help perpetuate the acquisition of privileges, lands, and offices from the emperor and participation in state/civic councils and decision-making. Besides, the aforementioned criteria of social status were used in order to regulate and prevent any social mobility. Poverty and lack of education or of illustrious ancestry were considered as bad qualities.

Nevertheless, partly in order to preserve social harmony, partly for the elite to acquire political supporters, there was still room for social mobility. The most important way through which this was realised was patronage. There were two main categories of patronage. The first one is closer to the Roman Republican and Early Imperial *patronicium* (not the rural patronage of Late Antiquity), an association of friendship and political support, with the main difference lying in the fact that Byzantine patronage was not institutionalised, but was a free-will, unofficial, and sometimes temporary association between two persons who may or may not have had an equal social status.[11] The second type of patronage is closer to the so-called Mediterranean patronage, wherein a person of a higher social status accepts a person of a lesser social status into their service, providing

---

9 See Malatras, *Social Stratification*, 113–119.
10 For example, Alexios Makrembolites, *Dialogus inter divites et pauperes*, ed. Ševčenko, 206; Eustathios of Thessaloniki, *Oratio in magnam quadragesimam preparatoria*, ed. Tafel, 80–81; Kokkinos, *Against Gregoras*, ed. Kaimakes, 36.
11 Brunt, *Fall of the Roman Republic*, 382–442; Garnsey, Roman Patronage; Saller, *Personal Patronage*; Wallace-Hadrill, Patronage in Roman Society; Drummond, Early Roman clientes.

them with education, financial security, and possibly an office, but expecting social and political support.[12]

Since the emperor remained the main source for the distribution of the state's financial capital and of titles and offices (political capital), the ability to petition him or influence his decision was an important asset. This is how, for example, John Kalekas became patriarch (1334–1347). Kalekas allegedly did not come from an elite background, though he was well enough educated; a simple priest in the palace, married with children and in the service of the *megas domestikos* John Kantakouzenos. Kantakouzenos convinced Andronikos III (1328–1341) to support the election of Kalekas to the patriarchal throne. The Synod convened then in the presence of Kantakouzenos and opposed the proposal, claiming that it was because Kalekas was not yet a metropolitan; more plausibly, however, because the metropolitans preferred to elect someone from amongst themselves, rather than from the imperial clergy, which they did not control. Kantakouzenos persisted and reconvened the Synod, eventually forcing the metropolitans to accept the election of Kalekas.[13]

Even important officials often needed to petition the emperor through intermediaries. Constantine XI Palaiologos decided to award a higher title to one of his closest associates, George Sphrantzes, at that point *protobestiarites*, who had just concluded a favourable marriage for the emperor. Sphrantzes had already expressed his indignation at the fact that a title could be held by more than one person simultaneously. However, Constantine XI was unable to find a suitable high office, while Demetrios Palaiologos Metochites, a cousin of the emperor and governor of Constantinople at the time, with the title of *megas stratopedarches*, would have been aggrieved if Sphrantzes had been invested with the only available high title, that of *megas logothetes*, and thus been placed hierarchically above himself. Under the advice of the *mesazon* Loukas Notaras, the emperor proposed the title of *megas primmikerios*, which was already held, however, by another person. The offer was communicated to Sphrantzes by Notaras, who declined it and prepared to leave Constantinople completely for the Morea. But shortly afterwards, and before Sphrantzes departed, Notaras – who was, as the emperor's first minister, the most powerful official in the state at the time – used a certain priest, Antonios, as intermediary to propose to the emperor that his – Notaras' – own two sons should be granted the titles of *megas konostaulos* and *megas logothetes*. Eventually, the emperor, angered by Notaras' demands, granted Sphrantzes the title of *megas logothetes*.[14]

---

12 Blok, Variations in Patronage, 365–378; Eisenstadt and Roniger, Patron-Client Relations, 42–77; Gellner, *Patrons and Clients in Mediterranean Societies*; Johnson and Dandeker, Patronage: Relation and System.
13 Kantakouzenos, *Historiae*, ed. Schopen, I, 432–435.
14 Sphrantzes, *Chronicon*, ed. Maisano, 124–130.

Thus, the acquisition of an important and influential patron was a most important asset for someone to maintain or improve his financial and social status. Privileges were granted to a wide range of people after intercession by an influential person. The agency of the monk Kallinikos, an ambassador of the king Milutin of Serbia to Byzantium, resulted in the granting of several properties to the Athonite monastery of Chilandar, but also to individuals, such as the soldier Manuel Garianos.[15] A very desirable privilege for low-born scholars was the acquisition of a state salary for their professorial duties. One of them, Theodoros Hyrtakenos, several times asked the Andronikos II's *mesazon*, Theodoros Metochites, whose son was his student, to intercede with the emperor in order to acquire this privilege. We learn that a certain Hyaleas and a Chalkomatopoulos were able to secure a salary following the mediation of Theodoros Mouzalon and Nikephoros Choumnos respectively, the forerunners of Theodoros Metochites in the office of *mesazon*.[16] At the other end of the social spectrum, the letters of Patriarch Gregory of Cyprus (1283–1289) reveal a great number of petitions, often resolved after his petition for brokerage to his friend and *mesazon* Theodoros Mouzalon. The patriarch often petitioned for his 'own people', appealing more to his personal relationship with and trust of the petitioner and to his friendship with the intercessor than to justice.[17]

The patronage relationship was often reciprocal. When, in 1305, the tax assessor (*apographeus*) Kounales appropriated an estate of Symeon Madarites, the monastery of Prodromos in Serres intervened successfully in favour of Madarites. Then the grateful Madarites donated 200 *modioi* of land to the monastery and another 400 for two *adelphata* (annual pensions in kind). A few years later, he sold the remaining estate of 4000 *modioi* to the monastery for the very low price of 200 *nomismata*.[18]

Service and social ascent

Entry into the service of a powerful person, under the terms of the Mediterranean type of patronage mentioned above, was a more successful way to rise in the social hierarchy. In the narrative sources the protégé is referred to as *oiketes*, and in the documentary sources mostly as *anthropos*. The *oiketai* constitute part of the household; they can in fact be 'bequeathed'. Theodoros Sarantenos, a member of

---

15 *Actes de Chilandar I*, ed. Giros *et al.*, no. 37; *Actes de Chilandar*, ed. Petit, nos. 74–75.
16 Hyrtakenos, *Epistulae*, ed. Karpozilos and Fatouros, nos. 16, 17, 20, 21, 36, 65, 74 (the reference to the previous holders of the state salary), 90.
17 Laiou, *Gregorios Kyprios*, 99–108.
18 *Actes de Prodromou*, ed. Bénou, 55–61 (p. 56 remembering this donation; in l. 22: the correct reading is χ΄ not λ΄).

the provincial elite, had at least twelve named male servants and an unspecified number of female and child servants (*paidopoula*) at the time of his testament. He ordered that after his death they should be placed under the service of the monastery of St. John Prodromos, which he had personally founded, and under the orders of his brother Gerasimos, the abbot of the monastery. One of these servants, Ioannes Phoinikes, was assigned to serve Gerasimos 'materially and spiritually'. Nevertheless, Sarantenos took care to leave gifts to his servants in his testament, mostly consisting of horses, oxen, clothing, and cash. Notably, two of his servants (two brothers) bear the distinguishing epithet *kyr*.[19] The father of the chronicler George Sphrantzes was the educator (*tatas*) of the despot Thomas Palaiologos, and his uncle was the educator of the despot Constantine Palaiologos, the last emperor. Their sons were also considered 'companions, friends, and servants to them' ('*συνανάτροφοι καὶ φίλοι καὶ δοῦλοι*'). George Sphrantzes at sixteen was taken into the service of the emperor Manuel II, where he remained until the latter's death in 1425. By the testamentary wish of Manuel II, Sphrantzes was assigned to the new emperor, John VIII.[20] The servants did not necessarily stay at the house of their lord, at least not the most distinguished of them.[21]

In fact, there was a group of people in the palace, the emperor's *oiketai*, throughout the Palaiologan period, who served the emperor and expected thereafter a privileged position. There is a distinction between the *oikeioi* of the emperor, who are considered to include all the officials in the Palaiologan period, and the *oiketai* of the emperor, who include the servants of the emperor and are the successors to the eleventh- to thirteenth-century *bestiaritai*.[22] The latter emerged after the fall in significance of the court eunuchs in the second half of the eleventh century. The *paidopoula* (pages), likewise distinguished servants who grew up with the imperial princes, were often important personalities, such as Petros Doukopoulos, a large landowner in Thessaloniki; the ambassador John Laskaris Kalopheros; and George Sphrantzes.[23] In the fifteenth century, as Sphrantzes' account reveals, they were called *kelliotai* (a term equivalent to *oiketes* and *bestiarites*): they served in the chamber (*κελλίον*) of the emperor.

---

19 *Actes de Vatopedi I*, ed. Lefort *et al.*, 359. Horses and oxen were quite expensive at this time. A warhorse in this period could cost more than the price of 200 *modioi* of land, which would be enough to sustain around 3–4 peasant families. A normal horse would cost around a third of this price, still a considerable amount.

20 Sphrantzes, *Chronicon*, ed. Maisano, 12–14 and 30–36.

21 Kydones, *Epistulae*, ed. Loenertz, no. 330.

22 Unlike Verpeaux, Oikeioi, 89–92, who considered the *oiketai* and the *oikeioi* to be the same group of people. In all official documents of the Palaiologan period, all the state officials (apart from the relatives of the emperor) are always called *oikeioi* and themselves sign as *douloi* of the emperor.

23 *Actes de Lavra III*, ed. Lemerle *et al.*, 49; *Actes de Prodromou*, ed. Bénou, 387.

Therefore, families of a high social background chose to send some of their offspring to be distinguished imperial servants.

Being in the service of a powerful person was considered a social distinction. George Sphrantzes feels honoured through his submissiveness to his master. Similarly, Demetrios Kydones considered it a distinction that his father had served Kantakouzenos.[24] Although the family of Kydones was not completely undistinguished – it may have belonged to the upper middle stratum –, it came to the fore with Demetrios Kydones and his father.[25] The service of Demetrios' father to Kantakouzenos must have played an important role in this ascent, as well as the esteem for his person due to his high level of education. Demetrios Kydones became a *mesazon* for three successive emperors and dominated the politics of the empire for more than four decades.

This kind of patronage involved a personal moral code of loyalty and therefore a servant of this kind was considered reliable and was entrusted with important or confidential duties. Servants of the deceased emperor Andronikos III remained loyal to the regency during the second civil war and were entrusted with the governorship of important towns in Thrace.[26] Kantakouzenos entrusted the command of the fortress Platamon in Macedonia to his servant Theodoros Pepagomenos, whose affection for Kantakouzenos was so great that he preferred to die rather than to insult Kantakouzenos in public when he was arrested.[27] One of the servants of Alexios Apokaukos remained loyal to his master even after the latter's murder. Tzefrai-Geoffrey paid and armed the common people and especially the sailors in order to attack and massacre the 200 political prisoners who had rebelled and murdered Apokaukos in the summer of 1345.[28]

Michael Kabasilas entered the service of Joseph, metropolitan of Apros and *katholikos krites*. He had been raised and educated by the metropolitan, whose niece he later married. Thus, with time, one servant could rise socially to such a degree that he was considered equal to his patron, a rise that was confirmed by this marriage. Despite the deposition and exile of the metropolitan of Apros, along with two of the three other *katholikoi kritai*, after the bribery scandal of 1337, Kabasilas was able to acquire a high position in the patriarchal clergy: he became archdeacon and *sakelliou*.[29]

---

24 Kydones, *Epistulae*, ed. Loenertz, I, 2.
25 Kydones, *Apologia I*, ed. Mercati, 359. Demetrios Kydones informs us that his parents decided not to send him learn a manual labour occupation, but wanted him to receive education. However, this is an indication that artisanship was initially an obvious career option for Kydones.
26 Kantakouzenos, *Historiae*, ed. Schopen, II, 277, 394.
27 Kantakouzenos, *Historiae*, ed. Schopen, II, 382.
28 Kantakouzenos, *Historiae*, ed. Schopen, II, 544–545.
29 *Patriarchal Register 2*, ed. Hunger and Kresten, 286; 3, 176.

It is very difficult with the present state of our sources to observe similar cases of social ascent in a lesser milieu, that is from the lower to the middle stratum (for example from casual worker to owner of a business) or in a rural context (from dependent to independent or wealthier peasants) and the contribution of patronage to this mobility. Demetrios Kydones informs us, for example, that he had a servant of the same age to him, whose company he enjoyed. After several years of service, Kydones decided to care for the servant's future: he arranged a marriage for him and granted him a modest property, comprising at least one shop.[30] The institution of apprenticeship functioned in a similar way to patronage. In this system, the owner of a shop and craft took under his service a young boy, assuming the obligation for the boy's living costs and instruction, as well as often their future first professional steps, by providing raw material and tools and a cash gift or loan.[31]

Social agency and patronage: the case of Michael Gabras

The previous two sections analysed aspects of the normal operation of the patronage system. Society and patronage did not, however, function rigidly. Creating, expanding, protecting, and using social networks and new contacts was equally significant. The most successful people proved to be those who were able to secure not just a single sponsor, but multiple appropriate ones, moving from one to the other and using them according to each context. Michael Gabras, a scholar of the first half of the fourteenth century, is one such case. He petitioned several people with different requests. For example, he requested a horse from Demetrios Glykes, the *parakoimomenos of the koiton* Ioannes Choumnos, the *sakelliou* Manuel Koutales, the *domestikos of the eastern themata* Michael Atzymes, the *prokathemenos of the koiton* Michael Kallikrinites, and an unnamed monastery.[32] He was shrewd enough to demand appropriate things from people. For example, when he initiated correspondence with the Chrysoloras brothers, administrators of the imperial salt pans, he asked for salt.[33]

Gabras' most imperative concern was to obtain support from the emperor. For a petition potentially to succeed, it was necessary to ensure not only that it would reach the imperial hands and ears, but also that someone influential at court would endorse it. Gabras sought, then, to find people who had a proximity to the emperor, such as the *protostrator* Ioannes Philes, who had managed to defeat the

---

30 Kydones, *Epistulae*, ed. Loenertz, no. 268.
31 *Registro Vaticano*, ed. Ferrari della Spade, 264 and 266.
32 Gabras, *Epistulae*, ed. Fatouros, nos. 71, 76, 100, 152, 153, 214, 282, 357.
33 Gabras, *Epistulae*, ed. Fatouros, no. 454.

Turks who had been raiding Thrace for years;[34] the *megas domestikos* John Kantakouzenos, the closest associate of Andronikos III;[35] the appropriate official, that is the *epi tōn deêseōn* (i. e., in charge of the petitions to the emperor) George Chatzikes;[36] the *tatas tes aules* Michael Monomachos, who during the first civil war remained at the side of the elder emperor Andronikos, though he was later entrusted with the administration of the newly-conquered Thessaly and Epirus by Andronikos III;[37] a certain *kyr* Konstantinos Phokas;[38] Nikephoros Gregoras, an intellectual close to both the emperor and the literary circle of Theodoros Metochites;[39] Joseph the Philosopher, one of the most influential intellectuals of his time and teacher to Theodoros Metochites, Andronikos II's first minister;[40] as well as other unnamed 'friends' or 'powerful correspondents', among whom Theodoros Metochites should be counted.[41]

Michael Gabras tried to build up and maintain a network of patrons and supporters, whom he would use to gain access to networks or open channels to powerful people. He asked his brother Ioannes, who had an official position, to find two powerful men in high positions who would act as patrons (προστάτας) of Michael's and Ioannes' uncle.[42] He asked his friend Kaloeidas to intercede with a certain powerful man in favour of Gabras' nephew.[43] In his first contact with the *megas domestikos* John Kantakouzenos and Michael Glabas, he used as intermediaries Nikolaos Matarangos (later one of the first four *katholikoi kritai*) and Kyriotes respectively, in order to make sure that his letters would reach the recipients and would be positively received.[44] When a certain Philaretos physically and verbally insulted his uncle, Gabras wrote to his friend Philippos Logaras

---

34 Gabras, *Epistulae*, ed. Fatouros, no. 128.
35 Gabras, *Epistulae*, ed. Fatouros, no. 421.
36 Gabras, *Epistulae*, ed. Fatouros, no. 312.
37 Gabras, *Epistulae*, ed. Fatouros, nos. 104 and 105.
38 Gabras, *Epistulae*, ed. Fatouros, nos. 254 and 257.
39 Gabras, *Epistulae*, ed. Fatouros, no. 307.
40 Gabras, *Epistulae*, ed. Fatouros, no. 300.
41 Gabras, *Epistulae*, ed. Fatouros, nos. 14, 42, 84, 102, 132, 155, 156, 160, 460 ('*dynatos*'; letters no. 84 and 460 come from Theodoros Metochites, as the editor of Gabras' letters has shown); nos. 78, 302, 438 ('friends').
42 Gabras, *Epistulae*, ed. Fatouros, no. 59.
43 Gabras, *Epistulae*, ed. Fatouros, no. 159. The play on the words χρυσός and ζώνη in the last sentence of the letter may suggest that the name of this powerful man was Chrysoloras ('καὶ πεῖθε τοῦτον τὸν χρυσῷ συνεκκροτούμενον εἰς τὴν προσηγορίαν, προακούοντα ἀπὸ τῆς ζώνης'). The etymology of the name Χρυσολωράς comes from the compound χρυσός ('gold') and λώρος-λωρίς ('thong', 'belt', 'strip') whose close synonym is ζώνη. As we already mentioned, the brothers Chrysoloras were some of those whom Gabras asked for help.
44 Gabras, *Epistulae*, ed. Fatouros, nos. 351–354. In the above-mentioned bribery scandal of 1337, of the four *katholikoi kritai*, only Nikolaos Matarangos was not accused. Was this just a coincidence or perhaps the protective umbrella of the second most important person in government, i. e., his friend John Kantakouzenos?

asking him to send out some of his own men to intimidate this Philaretos, pretending that this punishment had been ordered by the emperor.[45] At some point during the first civil war, Gabras' brother was imprisoned, because he abandoned his position as a soldier during the war and plundered imperial property (perhaps an indication of change of sides?). Gabras then aimed to gain the support and intercession of Kantakouzenos, whom he petitioned more than once for this cause. Although he may have encountered obstacles – including from men such as his old friend Demetrios Kerameas, who had sent soldiers to threaten his brother, or from an unnamed 'familiar' who refused to help Gabras, and suffered a temporary disruption to his relations with Kantakouzenos – his brother, we learn, was pardoned.[46]

About 56 letters in Gabras' correspondence were deliberately left without the name of the recipient. As the author himself wrote in the margin of the edition of his letters, he had removed the name of the recipient of a letter who had not helped in the fulfilment of a petition in order to preserve his future reputation.[47] Theodoros Metochites, for some unknown reason, was possibly one of these hostile *dynatoi*. In a few of his letters, Gabras complains that the unnamed recipient acts against the author and demands that he change his attitude.[48] This complaint is repeated in a later letter addressed specifically to Theodoros Metochites, albeit in a less pronounced manner.[49] Perhaps Theodoros Metochites is the 'powerful enemy' to whom Michael Gabras alludes in a letter to Joseph the Philosopher – a teacher of Theodoros Metochites –, whose help he asks for as intermediary with this *dynatos*,[50] as well as in a letter to Michael Kaloeidas, though that mediation failed.[51] This identification with Theodoros Metochites is strengthened by a reference to the 'office of philosopher' possessed by the enemy of Gabras, mentioned in a letter addressed to the emperor, whose material aid and benevolence Gabras pleaded for in order to eliminate the malice of the enemy.[52]

He had more enemies than just Theodoros Metochites, about whom we learn quite early in his correspondence. In one of his letters he thanks a certain monk Gregorios for successfully interceding in favour of Gabras and advocating for him against his slanderers in front of the emperor.[53] A little later he tries to win over

---

45 Gabras, *Epistulae*, ed. Fatouros, no. 220.
46 Gabras, *Epistulae*, ed. Fatouros, nos. 368–373, 386–388, 396, 403.
47 Gabras, *Epistulae*, ed. Fatouros, 15.
48 Gabras, *Epistulae*, ed. Fatouros, nos. 268, 333.
49 Gabras, *Epistulae*, ed. Fatouros, no. 322, especially l.128 ff.
50 As above note 40.
51 Gabras, *Epistulae*, ed. Fatouros, nos. 296–297.
52 Gabras, *Epistulae*, ed. Fatouros, no. 346.
53 Gabras, *Epistulae*, ed. Fatouros, no. 9.

the support of his friend Ioannes Skleros and of the intellectuals Theodoros Moschabar, George Lekapenos, and Ioannes Zacharias. He also defends himself against perhaps the same slanderer in a letter sent to the literary circle of Ioannes Hebdomenos.[54] Unfortunately we do not learn the nature of the defamation or the identity of the slanderer, but he probably was not the same as the 'powerful' enemy, who could have been Theodoros Metochites, as has been claimed above. He was, though, a literary enemy, as can be envisaged by references to his 'lack of wisdom and education'. This enemy may have been the same as the 'barbarian' or the enemy 'with a barbarian name', whom we learn of later in letters sent to Theodoros Xanthopoulos, Demetrios Kerameas, and the monks Zagarommates and Maximos.[55] Another enemy was a priest, who was close to the emperor and against whom he asked for help from the *epi tōn deêseōn* George Chatzikes. This priest punched Gabras, who turned to Manuel Koutales, *chartophylax* of the patriarchate, asking him to rebuke the priest.[56]

Gabras himself also acted as a patron. He asked his friend Manuel Koutales, *sakelliou* of the patriarchate, to authorise a relative's marriage.[57] Demetrios Opsikianos was asked to release a man from prison after a plea from the latter's wife to Gabras.[58] In another case, a certain Andronikos had the desire to become a priest, but he lacked the necessary referees, and appealed to Gabras for aid. Gabras, on his part, wrote a letter – carried by Andronikos – to his familiar Gregorios, archbishop of Bulgaria, requesting him to provide a letter of reference for the man. When Gregorios provided the testimony, Gabras wrote to the *chartophylax* of the patriarchate Manuel Koutales, the official responsible for such procedures and also one of Gabras' familiars (fifteen letters in Gabras' correspondence are addressed to him), demanding that Andronikos should be granted the consecration, something that we learn was eventually accomplished.[59] In a similar case, a certain monk from Philadelpheia appealed to Gabras to ask Manuel Gabalas, the *protonotarios* of the metropolis of Philadelpheia, to act as middleman in his turn to Theoleptos, the metropolitan of Philadelpheia, so that the monk's children could be materially aided.[60]

The case of Gabras, thanks to the quantity and the nature of his correspondence – 462 letters, 60% of which are related to petitions – is the most

---

54 Gabras, *Epistulae*, ed. Fatouros, nos. 22, 24, 43 and 45.
55 Gabras, *Epistulae*, ed. Fatouros, nos. 92–95 and 111. References to the 'barbarian' origins of this enemy can be found in letters 95 (l. 11ff.) and 111 (throughout but especially at the beginning).
56 Gabras, *Epistulae*, ed. Fatouros, nos. 271 and 305.
57 Gabras, *Epistulae*, ed. Fatouros, no. 211.
58 Gabras, *Epistulae*, ed. Fatouros, no. 316.
59 Gabras, *Epistulae*, ed. Fatouros, nos. 362–364.
60 Gabras, *Epistulae*, ed. Fatouros, no. 72.

detailed source we have for how people, and especially intellectuals operating in literary circles and who by virtue of their education had a greater access to the powerful, could make use of networking and patronage in different and quite flexible ways in order to promote their interests and to better their social and financial status. His case is far from an exception. Theodoros Hyrtakenos, a contemporary of Gabras and professional teacher to several members of the elite, made use of his network in a similar way. When he failed, for example, in his attempt to petition the patriarch John Glykys, he contacted his old student Basileios, the son of the patriarch, whom he asked to intervene with his father, so that the patriarch in his turn speaks favourably of Hyrtakenos to the emperor.[61]

Social ascent and the independence of the protégé

The connection between a patron and his protégé, a person who entered the service of a more powerful household, normally lasted for a long time, if not for a lifetime, as we have seen. On some occasions, however, the protégé used this connection only for his first steps, until he had acquired the desired social ascent. Then he could become independent and wean himself from the patron.

Alexios Apokaukos has been presented by modern scholarly literature as a parvenu, who rose, thanks to his cunning, into the higher echelons of the government. This is how he is described by our two main narrative accounts, both from authors hostile to him, John Kantakouzenos and Nikephoros Gregoras.[62] Another account, however, friendly to Alexios Apokaukos, describes him as a man of high birth.[63] His immediate origins are a bit shadowy, but we know that he was born in Bithynia. In any case, the Apokaukoi had been an elite family since the late tenth century, when they served as generals.[64] Later on, they are still attested, for example Theodoros Apokaukos in the second half of the twelfth century, with the dignity *sebastos*, still an important dignity reserved for a few

---

61 Hyrtakenos, *Epistulae*, ed. Karpozilos and Fatouros, nos. 3–4 (the failed petition to the patriarch), 67, 87, 93 (the petitions to Basileios Glykys).

62 Kantakouzenos, *Historiae*, ed. Schopen, I, 25: 'ἄνδρα γένους ἀφανούς ὄντα'; Gregoras, *Historiae*, ed. Bekker and Schopen, II, 577 and 585: 'γένους γὰρ τῶν ἀδόξων ὑπάρχων ἐκ νέου καὶ πενίᾳ συντεθραμμένος νῦν μὲν τούτῳ νῦν δ' ἐκείνῳ μισθοῦ διακονούμενος διετέλει τὸν χρόνον' and 'εἰς γὰρ δόξαν καὶ περιφάνειαν ἐξ ἀσήμου γένους ἐληλυθώς'.

63 Magdalino, Byzantine Churches, 311: 'εἷς τῶν Ἀποκαύκων, καὶ κρείττων κατὰ γένος, ἀνὴρ πλούτῳ τε κομῶν καὶ δόξῃ'. The passage is part of a homily-encomium to saint Agathonikos. Towards the end of the homily the author praises all those who renovated the church, among them Apokaukos.

64 For example: Basileios Apokaukos, *protospatharios* and *strategos* of the Peloponnesos (ed. Davidson, *The Minor Objects*, no. 2764; Demetrios Apokaukos, *patrikios* and *archegetes* of the West (*Catalogue of Byzantine Seals 1*, ed. Nesbitt and Oikonomides, no. 1.3).

individuals just below the imperial clan.[65] John Apokaukos, metropolitan of Naupaktos in the thirteenth century, is well known, while in 1277 a certain Ioannes Apokaukos with the dignity of *sebastopanhypertatos* was considered worthy enough to sign a treaty with Venice and ranked hierarchically just below the *megas logothetes* and son-in-law of the emperor, George Akropolites, and above the *logothetes of the genikon* Theodoros Mouzalon, the *megas tzaousios* Nikephoros Arianites, and other unnamed 'nobles', all of them described by the emperor Michael VIII as 'magnificent men and lords of my empire'.[66] Therefore, although the family of Alexios Apokaukos did not belong to this small circle of a dozen of noble families, it was still part of the elite. His rise, however, as a leading official of the government, definitely represents a social and political ascent, and was viewed as such by the noble (and snob) Kantakouzenos.

Alexios Apokaukos had served in the household of Andronikos Asanes, a cousin of the emperor Andronikos II. Later he managed to enrich himself through the practice of tax farming. Just before the first civil war we meet him with the office of *domestikos* of the western *themata*, which in this period was a financial office connected to tax collection and registration, and had acquired the administration of the state salt pans (an important state monopoly in the Late Byzantine period). He was already in a position to receive petitions from people such as Michael Gabras and, most importantly, to be able to participate among the leading men of the faction of Andronikos III that led to the first civil war.[67] With this move Apokaukos earned a place in the higher elite of the empire and the prominent title of *parakoimomenos*. He acquired landed estates, built up a fortress for his protection in the vicinity of Constantinople, acquired servants of his own, became patron of churches. He married himself and his children to families of the higher aristocracy: already before the second civil war he had acquired as wife a niece of George Choumnos, an uncle of the emperor, and married one of his daughters to Andronikos Palaiologos, cousin of the emperor and grandson of a despot of Thessaly. After the latter's premature death, his daughter married the brother of the empress Eirene Kantakouzene, the *sebastokrator* Ioannes

---

65 Leontiades, Unpublished Seals, no. 1.
66 MM III, 96: 'παρόντων [...] τῶν μεγαλοπρεπῶν ἀνδρῶν καὶ ἀρχόντων τῆς βασιλείας ἡμῶν τοῦ τε γαμβροῦ τῆς βασιλείας ἡμῶν τοῦ μεγάλου λογοθέτου κῦρ Γεωργίου τοῦ Ἀκροπολίτου, τοῦ σεβαστοπανυπερτάτου κῦρ Ἰωάννου τοῦ Ἀποκαύχου, τοῦ πανσεβάστου λογοθέτου τοῦ γενικοῦ κῦρ Θεοδώρου τοῦ Μουζάλωνος καὶ τοῦ πανσεβάστου μεγάλου τζακίου [sic! lege τζαουσίου] Νικηφόρου τοῦ Ἀριανίτου καὶ ἑτέρων πολλῶν εὐγενῶν τῆς βασιλείας ἡμῶν'. Considering, first, the Byzantine naming tradition going from the grandfather to the child and, second, that the first son of Alexios Apokaukos was named Ioannes, one could hypothesise that this Ioannes Apokaukos was the father of Alexios Apokaukos.
67 Gabras, *Epistulae*, ed. Fatouros, nos. 193–195; Gregoras, *Historiae*, ed. Bekker and Schopen I, 301; Kantakouzenos, *Historiae*, ed. Schopen, I, 25.

Asanes.[68] These marriages marked his acceptance into the higher aristocracy and his effective social ascent from the lesser elite, as Kantakouzenos himself has to admit.[69] When Apokaukos was preparing the plot against Kantakouzenos which led to the second civil war, he approached Andronikos Asanes, whom he reminded of his old service and that, despite his current eminent status, he remained a trustworthy servant. He convinced Asanes that the latter would in fact be the leader of the plot and the state after the removal of Kantakouzenos. Nonetheless, the reality was different by this point. Apokaukos had created a strong basis of power and was effectively the leading man of the regency; less than two years later, Andronikos Asanes was imprisoned by Apokaukos.[70]

In another case, the later emperor John Kantakouzenos VI (r. 1341–1354) had a servant called Apelmene, whom he had raised since the latter's childhood, providing him with military and literary education and wealth. Kantakouzenos made him 'glorious from humble beginnings and the most eminent among his servants'. After the proclamation of Kantakouzenos as emperor, Apelmene expected a distinguished treatment and that he would be assigned important offices and take part in significant decisions. But Kantakouzenos reserved these for his relatives and the nobility. Apelmene felt disappointed, and abandoned him by joining the regency, the only servant of Kantakouzenos who acted in this way.[71] Apelmene was probably not as low socially as Kantakouzenos presents him. Members of this family are attested in the civil service as fiscal or church officials.[72] This incident shows the expectations that a member of the lesser elite may have had when he entered the service of a higher aristocrat, but also the limitations for social ascent. Patronage is a controlled mechanism for social ascent and Kantakouzenos was someone who was aware of and wanted to perpetuate the social differences. Equating Apelmene with his relatives and the nobility was absurd for Kantakouzenos.

---

68 Kantakouzenos, *Historiae*, ed. Schopen, II, 70–71 (on the fortress and the desire of Apokaukos to acquire more land and governorship of towns), 102 (on the retinue); Gregoras, *Historiae*, ed. Bekker and Schopen II, 797 (on the landed properties in Traïanoupolis and the second marriage of Apokaukos' daughter); Eyice, Alexis Apocauque, 77–124.
69 Kantakouzenos, *Historiae*, ed. Schopen, II, 120 and 218.
70 Kantakouzenos, *Historiae*, ed. Schopen, II, 421.
71 Kantakouzenos, *Historiae*, ed. Schopen, II, 247–248.
72 PLP, nos. 1154–1158.

Concluding remarks

Were there any chances of social ascent without the aid of patronage? There were always financial resources that were almost completely outside imperial control, such as resources generated by banking and trade activities. It has generally been believed in recent decades that, during the last century of its existence, the Byzantine aristocracy, having lost its traditional sources of income due to foreign conquests, turned to the domain of trade and capital.[73] This historiographical axiom has been questioned recently with regard to the extent of the supposed change. It now seems that the Byzantine elite was already involved in trade activities well before the late fourteenth century.[74] This should not, in any case, obscure the fact that the era of the great privileges and immense wealth of the elite in the Early Palaiologan period was gone, and that trade and banking activities may have contributed to a greater degree than before to the composition of the income of much of the elite. Yet there was still scope for the distribution of privileges and lands from the remaining state resources, for profit to be made from holding an office, and for all other benefits connected with the proximity to the emperor.

In the same period some new elite families make their appearance, the most illustrious examples being those of Goudeles and Notaras. The first known Goudeles was the cup-bearer (οἰνοχόος) of the empress Anne of Savoy, and was entrusted with the governorship of Polystylon in Thrace during the second civil war, as soon as the regency had managed to occupy the town by driving out the forces that were loyal to Kantakouzenos. He has been identified as the ancestor of the illustrious family of Goudeles that rose in the late fourteenth century with George Goudeles. George Goudeles became *mesazon* in 1386 and married himself and his family to other families of the higher aristocracy. His banking and trade activities predate his nomination to the office of *mesazon*. His appointment was probably the result of his previous enrichment and proximity to the Genoese, but his own marriage to a certain Raoulaina (one of the higher aristocratic families) took place in the mid-1360s, long before we learn of any trade and banking activities.[75] Therefore, although George Goudeles with his financial enterprises

---

73 Oikonomides, *Hommes d'affaires*.
74 Gerolymatou, Aristocratie et le commerce; Jacoby, Byzantine Elite and Market Economy, 67–86; Matschke, *Gesellschaft im späten Byzanz*, 160–175.
75 Ganchou, Géôrgios Goudélès, 277–358. The problem with the identification of the father of George Goudeles, Manuel, with the *oinochoos* of the empress is that, at least in the eleventh to thirteenth centuries, Goudeles could be used as a first name: Goudeles Beridares (seal in the Dumbarton Oaks collection BZS 1947.2.1165), Goudeles, brother of Nikolaos Zoros and a *paroikos* of the monastery of Iviron (*Actes d'Iviron II*, ed. Lefort *et al.*, 258), Goudeles Tzykandeles (Laurent, *Orghidan*, nos. 478–179), Goudeles Tyrannos (most probably two individuals: Akropolites, *Historiae*, ed. Heisenberg, 90 in 1253 and MM IV, 285–287 in 1294).

was responsible for the subsequent illustrious fortunes of the family, his first steps may have been assisted by his father's service to the empress Anne who secured a prominent marriage for the son.

In sum, Late Byzantine society was highly unequal. In the absence of rigidly-defined social groups and orders, it had created a number of parameters that would serve as boundaries between the upper and the lower strata, thus preventing social mobility. Most of the political, social, and economic capital was possessed by an elite, and this possession was perpetuated in successive generations through patrimony. Nevertheless, the distribution of a great proportion of this capital was directly or indirectly controlled by the government. The method of distribution was by no means objective, although for reasons of political harmony, several already-acquired privileges were transferred to heirs. This allowed the rise of mechanisms with more personal character, whereby a more powerful person would act on behalf of the less privileged or people with fewer connections, representing their interests to the government. This type of patronage usually allowed the preservation of the social position of an individual or a family, or a small social ascent through the acquisition of a higher office/title or substantially more financial resources. Patronage acquired a character of protection when it took the form of attachment to a powerful household through informal voluntary service. This type of patronage allowed a safer means to maintain social harmony through regulating social ascent, at the same time establishing political and social support.

Despite the restrictions to social mobility, patronage gave Byzantine society considerable flexibility, due to the need to create and maintain social networks and establish social bonds with powerful people. These social networks and affiliations were not themselves static. Adept petitioners were able to move through different social networks, defend their own against outsiders, and locate suitable patrons in order to acquire or preserve their share of the valued resources. Protégés of a household were also in a position to rise socially, sometimes as substantially as their patron. Even if they were normally expected to remain loyal to their patrons, they could prove flexible enough, once they had risen socially, to distance themselves from this protection and even betray their old masters. Despite the desire of the upper strata to present Byzantine society as immutable and limit social ascent, the reality was different: social mobility was undoubtedly present.

Bibliography

Primary sources

Actes de Chilandar, première partie, ed. Louis Petit, Actes de l'Athos 5:I (St. Petersburg, 1911) (repr. Amsterdam 1975).

Actes de Chilandar I, ed. Charalampos Giros, Vasiliki Kravari, and Mirjana Živojinović, Actes de Chilandar tome I: des origines à 1319, Archives de l'Athos 20 (Paris, 1998).

Actes d'Iviron II, ed. Jacques Lefort, Nikos Oikonomides, Denise Papachryssanthou, Vasiliki Kravari, and Hélène Métrévéli, Actes d'Iviron tome II: du milieu de XIe siècle à 1204, Archives de l'Athos 16 (Paris, 1990).

Actes de Lavra III, ed. Paul Lemerle, André Guillou, Nicolas Svoronos, and Denise Papachryssanthou, tome III: de 1329 à 1500, Archives de l'Athos 10 (Paris, 1979).

Actes de Prodromou, ed. Lisa Bénou, Le Codex B du monastère Saint-Jean-Prodrome Serrès, XIIIe–XVe siècles (Paris, 1998).

Actes de Vatopedi I, ed. Jacques Bompaire, Christophe Giros, Vasiliki Kravari, and Jacques Lefort, Actes de Vatopedi tome I: des origines à 1329, Archives de l'Athos 21 (Paris, 2001).

Actes de Vatopedi II, ed. Jacques Lefort, Vasiliki Kravari, Christophe Giros, and Kostis Smyrlis, Actes de Vatopedi tome II: de 1330 à 1376, Archives de l'Athos 22 (Paris, 2001).

Akropolites, George, Historiae, ed. Augustus Heisenberg, Georgii Acropolitae opera (Leipzig, 1903) 1:3–189.

Davidson, Gladys, The Minor Objects, Corinth XII (Princeton, 1952).

Eustathios of Thessaloniki, Oratio in magnam quadragesimam preparatoria, ed. Gottlieb Lucas Friedrich Tafel, Eustathii metropolitae Thessalonicensis opuscula accedunt Trapezuntinae historiae scriptores Panaretus et Eugenicus (Amsterdam, 1964) 76–88.

Gregoras, Nikephoros, Historiae, ed. Immanuel Bekker and Ludovicus Schopen, CSHB 25–27 (Bonn, 1829–1855).

Hyrtakenos, Theodoros, Epistulae, ed. Apostolos Karpozilos and Georgios Fatouros, The letters of Theodoros Hyrtakenos (Greek text, English translation and commentary) (Athens, 2017).

Kantakouzenos, John, Historiae, ed. Ludovicus Schopen, CSHB 5–7 (Bonn, 1828).

Kokkinos, Philotheos, Against Gregoras, ed. Dimitrios Kaimakes, Φιλοθέου Κοκκίνου δογματικά έργα, volume 1 (Thessaloniki, 1983) 19–515.

Kydones, Demetrios, Apologia I, ed. Giovanni Mercati, Notizie di Procoro e Demetrio Cidone, Manuele Caleca e Teodoro Meliteniota ed altri appunti per la storia della teologia e della letteratura bizantina del secolo XIV, Studi e Testi 56 (Vatican City, 1931), 359–437.

Kydones, Demetrios, Epistulae, ed. Raymond-Joseph Loenertz, Démétrius Cydonès correspondance (Vatican City, 1956–1960).

Laurent, Vitalien, Documents de sigillographie Byzantine: la collection C. Orghidan (Paris, 1952).

Leontiades, Ioannes, Unpublished Lead Seals with Family Names, in: Christos Stavrakos (ed.), Hypermachos. Studien zur Byzantinistik, Armenologie und Georgistik. Festschrift für Werner Seibt zum 65. Geburtstag (Mainz, 2008).

Makrembolites, Alexios, *Dialogus inter divites et pauperes*, ed. Ihor Ševčenko, Alexios Makrembolites and his 'Dialogue between the Rich and the Poor', *ZRVI* 6 (1960) 203–215.

Catalogue of Byzantine Seals 1, ed. John Nesbitt and Nikos Oikonomides, *Catalogue of Byzantine Seals at Dumbarton Oaks and in the Fogg Museum of Art, vol. 1: Italy, North of the Balkans, North of the Black Sea* (Washington, D.C., 1991).

Patriarchal Register II, ed. Herbert Hunger and Otto Kresten, *Das Register des Patriarchats von Konstantinopel. Edition und Übersetzung der Urkunden aus den Jahren 1337–1350, Teil 2*, CFHB 19.2 (Vienna, 1995).

Patriarchal Register III, ed. Johannes Koder, Martin Hinterberger, and Otto Kresten, *Das Register des Patriarchats von Konstantinopel. Edition und Übersetzung der Urkunden aus den Jahren 1350–1363, Teil 3*, CFHB 19.3 (Vienna, 2001).

Registro Vaticano, ed. Giannino Ferrari dalle Spade, *Studi Bizantini e Neoellenici* 4 (1935) 249–267.

Sphrantzes, George, *Chronicon*, ed. Riccardo Maisano, CFHB 29 (Rome, 1990).

Secondary Literature

Bartusis, Mark, *Land and Privilege in Byzantium: The Institution of Pronoia* (Cambridge, 2012).

Blok, Anton, Variations in Patronage, *Soziologische Gids* 16 (1969), 365–378.

Brunt, Peter A., *The Fall of the Roman Republic and Related Essays* (Oxford, 1988).

Drummond, Andrew, Early Roman clientes, in: Andrew Wallace-Hadrill (ed.), *Patronage in Ancient Society* (London/New York, 1989), 89–115.

Eisenstadt, Shmuel and Louis Roniger, Patron-Client Relations as a Model of Structuring Social Exchange, *Comparative Studies in Society and History* 22 (1980) 42–77.

Eyice, Semavi, Alexis Apocauque et l'église de Sélymbria, *Byzantion* 34 (1964) 77–104.

Ganchou, Thierry, L'ultime testament de Géôrgios Goudélès, homme d'affaires, mésazôn de Jean V et ktètôr (Constantinople, 4 mars 1421), *TM* 16 (2010) 277–358.

Garnsey, Peter, Roman Patronage, in: Michael Peachin (ed.), *The Oxford Handbook of Social Relations in the Roman World* (Oxford, 2011) 33–54.

Gellner, Ernest, *Patrons and Clients in Mediterranean Societies* (London/New York, 1977).

Gerolymatou, Maria, L'aristocratie et le commerce (IXe–XIIe siècles), *Symmeikta* 15 (2002) 77–89.

Grünbart, Michael, 'Byzantine (Urban) Aristocracy and its Attitudes towards Literacy', in Georges Declercq, Marco Mostert, Walter Ysebaert, and Anna Adamska (eds.), *New Approaches to Medieval Urban Literacy* (Brussels, 2013) 53–60.

Jacoby, David, The Byzantine Social Elite and the Market Economy, Eleventh to Mid-Fifteenth Century, in: Alison Frazier and Patrick Nold (eds.), *Essays in Renaissance Thought and Letters: in Honor of John Monfasani* (Leiden/Boston, 2015) 67–86.

Johnson, Terry and Christopher Dandeker, Patronage: Reality and System, in: Andrew Wallace-Hadrill (ed.), *Patronage in Ancient Society* (London/New York, 1989) 219–242.

Kazhdan, Alexander Petrovich and Silvia Ronchey, *L'aristocrazia bizantina dal principio dell' XI alla fine del XII secolo* (Palermo, 1997).

Kyritses, Demetrios, *The Byzantine Aristocracy in the Thirteenth and Early Fourteenth Centuries*. Unpublished PhD thesis (Harvard University, 1997).

Laiou, Angeliki, The Correspondence of Gregorios Kyprios as a Source for the History of Social and Political Behaviour in Byzantium or, on Government by Rhetoric, in: Werner Seibt (ed.), *Geschichte und Kultur der Palaiologenzeit. Referate des Internationaler Symposions zu Ehren von Herbert Hunger (Wien 30. November bis 3. Dezember 1994)* (Vienna, 1996) 91–108.

Magdalino, Paul, Byzantine Churches of Selymbria, *DOP* 32 (1978) 309–318.

Magdalino, Paul, Byzantine Snobbery, in: Michael Angold (ed.), *The Byzantine Aristocracy, IX to XIII Centuries* (Oxford, 1984) 58–78.

Malatras, Christos, *Social Stratification in Late Byzantium* (Edinburgh, 2023).

Matschke, Klaus-Peter, Notes on the Economic Establishment and Social Order of the Late Byzantine kephalai, *ByzF* 19 (1993) 139–143.

Matschke, Klaus-Peter and Franz Tinnefeld, *Die Gesellschaft im späten Byzanz: Gruppen, Strukturen und Lebensformen* (Cologne/Weimar/Vienna, 2001).

Oikonomides, Nikos, Title and Income at the Byzantine Court, in: Henry Maguire (ed.), *Byzantine Court Culture: From 829 to 1204* (Washington, DC, 1997) 199–215.

Patlagean, Évelyne, 'Γονικόν. Note sur la propriété allodiale à Byzance', in Anna Avramea, Angeliki Laiou, and Evangelos Chrysos (eds.), *Byzantium: State and Society; In Memory of Nikos Oikonomides* (Athens, 2003) 423–434.

Ragia, Efi, Agrarian policy in the early Palaeologan period, ca. 1259–1300 from the archives of Mt. Athos and West Asia Minor, in Marie-Hélène Blanchet and Raúl Estangüi Gómez (eds.), *Le monde byzantin du XIIIe au XVe siècle anciennes ou nouvelles formes d'impérialité*, Travaux et Memoires 25.1 (2021), 503–562.

Saller, Richard Paul, *Personal Patronage in the Roman Empire* (Cambridge, 1984).

Smyrlis, Konstantinos, The State, the Land, and Private Property: Confiscating Monastic and Church Properties in the Palaiologan Period, in: Dimiter Angelov (ed.), *Church and Society in Late Byzantium* (Kalamazoo, 2009) 58–87.

Verpeaux, Jean, Les oikeioi. Notes d'histoire institutionnelle et sociale, *REB* 23 (1965) 89–99.

Wallace-Hadrill, Andrew, Patronage in Roman Society: From Republic to Empire, in: Andrew Wallace-Hadrill (ed.), *Patronage in Ancient Society* (London/New York, 1989), 68–87.

Florence Liard

Pottery Traditions as Indicators of Interactions, Connectivity, and Microstructures in Byzantium

The study of pottery traditions in the Late Medieval Mediterranean is a relatively new area of research that has been supported by significant findings in Greece and in the adjacent regions. These discoveries allows us to take a fresh look into peoples' lifestyles, tastes, and networks of communication at a time when written records mostly concerned sacred, religious, political, and administrative matters. Following an historiographical tradition that is particularly attentive to cities as centres of political power and economic growth, the focus has mostly been on pottery unearthed in urban contexts.[1] Systematic and rescue excavations of medieval domestic settlements and their associated dumping pits, industrial areas, ecclesiastical buildings, and other types of public structures have revealed a large range of pottery types and styles that allow us to clarify each site's character and its role in the broader networks of commerce and communication. These findings have also contributed to the reconstruction of local production outputs as well as traditions of pottery use including culinary and dining habits, storage purposes, and waste management.[2] More recently, the analysis of surface pottery remains collected during regional archaeological prospection has completed this picture by offering glimpses into the daily life in hamlets and villages and the relationship of these settlements to urban centres.[3] Macroregional and global approaches to trade contacts have been developed by incorporating pottery evidence from diverse sites distributed across the Mediterranean into mapping systems and network analysis.[4]

In parallel with these discoveries, there has been a growing interest in archaeological remains of workshop structures, kilns, and unfinished wares, tripod

---

1 See, for example: François and Spieser, Pottery and Glass.
2 See, for example: Sanders, Frankish Pottery; Armstrong, Byzantine Thebes; MacKay, Pottery of the Frankish Period; Kondyli et al., Thebes at the Time of the Catalans.
3 Armstrong, Eastern Phocis; Vroom, After Antiquity; Vionis, Thespiai.
4 Yangaki, Trade Networks, Mapping, Network Analysis.

stilts, and kiln wasters.[5] Elemental analyses have been performed on these ceramic materials and reference groups of pottery provenance have been created on this basis.[6] In a smaller number of cases, ceramic petrography has been used to connect a specific fabric mineralogy to a particular geological setting.[7] This line of multidisciplinary research has offered a fresh look into the origin of the pottery that was found in consumption sites and for which the provenance remained unclear on archaeological and stylistic grounds. From there, it has become possible to reconstruct pottery supply strategies, commercial networks, workshop production outputs and their connection with the local consumers' demands, fashions, and aesthetic tastes.

Archaeometrists also focus on the decoration techniques of the so-called 'Sgraffito Wares,' a series of pottery dishes, bowls, chalices, and jugs in red fabrics that were covered with a white slip and a transparent lead-rich glaze, and that adorned peoples' tables and church walls throughout and beyond the Byzantine world.[8] A greater awareness has emerged as to the technological knowledge that lies behind the execution of this decoration. Potters had to choose slipping materials that would provide a white background before the application of the glaze; they needed to master the preparation of suitable lead oxide compounds and mixtures; they had to know which colourants were most convenient for specific stylistic effects. Production and decoration techniques shared between different locations provide new grounds for investigating the possibility of craftsmen mobility,[9] because technical learning between artisans is often facilitated by regular contacts and a shared language.[10] With the fierce economic competition, and the quickly-transforming geopolitics of the Late Medieval Mediterranean, identifying phenomena of stylistic imitation and appropriation is also worthy of attention. Imitation of foreign pottery types and styles may be indicative of a concurrence between markets, with local workshops sustaining

---

5 For instance, see: François, Ateliers de Nicée/Iznik; Armstrong and Günsenin, Ganos; Papanikola-Bakirtzi, *Art of Sgraffito*, 222–248 (Serres, Mikro Pisto); Girgin, Sirkeci (Constantinople); Antonaras, Artisanal Production in Byzantine Thessaloniki.

6 For instance, see: Waksman *et al.*, 'Middle Byzantine Production' (Chalkida).

7 For instance, see: Vogt and Bouquillon, Plaques murales (Balkans); Kuleff *et al.*, Provenance of Sgraffito Ceramics (Balkans); White, *Byzantine Glazed Pottery from Corinth* (Greece); Kırmızı, Zeuxippus from Kusadasi (Anatolia). Petrography has been more routinely applied to lead-glazed pottery found in Italy: Lazzarini, Nuovi dati; Mignucci, Venetian Ceramic production; Capelli, Analisi petrografiche.

8 For instance, see: Armstrong *et al.*, Byzantine Glazing Technology; Capelli and Cabella, White Slips; Kırmızı *et al.*, Colouring Agents (Anaia); Palamara *et al.*, Technology Issues (Corinth); Davis and Stocker, Palace of Nestor (Eglianos); Raškovska *et al.*, Characterization of Pottery; Charalambous *et al.*, Cypriot Byzantine Glazed Pottery.

9 On this topic, see: Lis *et al.*, Mobility.

10 On this topic, see: Gosselain, *Poteries du Cameroun méridional*, 131–138; also Gosselain, D'une histoire à l'autre.

and adapting their production and distribution in an attempt to respond to the market demand.[11] Likewise, there is plentiful anthropological, art historical, and archaeological evidence for political control through the appropriation of artistic heritage in colonial contexts,[12] and the question remains to what extent northern Italian trading powers may have used this as a means to reach out to the local communities in their possessions overseas.

A new way of examining microstructures in Byzantium

Because they can highlight new patterns of interactions between individuals, scientific developments in pottery analysis offer a great potential to help us further our knowledge of social boundaries and microstructures in the Byzantine world. Indeed, the negotiation of collective identities is mainly operated through the sharing of various cultural vectors between individuals such as languages, faith, and beliefs, as well as aesthetic tastes and fashions. Likewise, a nation state organisation can be perceived as a combination of such individual interactions, with group dynamics aiming to ensure access to resources, internal security, and social cohesion and prosperity.[13] But there are also patterns of human contacts, or 'invisible boundaries',[14] that do not necessarily fit into wider hierarchical organisational schemes, even though they still contribute to the creation of significant connections within and between communities, and therefore also participate in the making of a society. In the Late Byzantine society, political frontiers, social norms, and cultural references were constantly in flux, and our picture of people's daily lives has been drawn from a few written sources that are often imprecise and patchy. In such conditions, the study of individual interactions, which can be achieved through the multidisciplinary analysis of pottery production and decoration, opens new avenues for examining the structure of a society and the way in which collective representations were preserved and transformed through time.

This article revisits some social and cultural boundaries in Byzantium and the wider medieval world during the years 1100–1450, using archaeometric analysis

---

11 On this topic, see: Oka *et al.*, 'Imitation' Industries and Imperial Restrictions.

12 On this topic, see: Thomas, Colonial Power; Georgopoulou, Late Medieval Crete and Venice; Flexner, Historical Archaeology. See also Silliman's efforts to draw a distinction between evidence for 'culture contact' and for 'colonialism': Silliman, Culture Contact.

13 For instance, see: Gounaris and Frangopoulos, Nation grecque moderne; Ratti *et al.*, Drawing Boundaries.

14 On this concept applied to medieval and post-medieval realities, see the recent essays in honour of Paul Freedman's work on hidden frontiers or changing perceptions of social boundaries within history and the historical discipline (Barton *et al.*, *Boundaries in the Medieval World*).

of pottery fragments. These three centuries are marked by widespread geo-
political changes across Greece that relate, first, to the diplomatic actions and
economic expansion of various Latin groups in the East and to the new networks
of alliances that resulted from it; and, second, to the growing Ottoman threat in
the southern Balkans up to the conquest of mainland Greece in 1458.

This research is based on a multidisciplinary analysis of pottery provenance[15] and decoration[16] applied to a selection of 183 items of lead-glazed
ceramic tableware that were found in urban and rural contexts in mainland
Greece. First, 43 samples were selected from excavations at the city of Thebes in
Boeotia (Figure 1). Twelve of these samples come from a twelfth- to thirteenth-
century domestic habitation on the slopes of Ismenion Hill, a residential area
with remains of artisanal activity that was located directly outside the walled
city centre.[17] The other 31 samples come from a 'bothros' assemblage that
testifies to domestic waste management on Ismenion Hill at the time of the
establishment of a Frankish Duchy by the dynasty de la Roche,[18] a minor
Burgundian knight of the Fourth Crusade.[19] This discarding pit might also
include some lead-glazed pottery items from the early days of the domination
of the city by the mercenaries of the Grand Catalan Company (1311–1388).[20]

---

15 Pottery provenance was researched using thin section petrography assisted by elemental
analysis (using Wavelength Dispersive X-ray Fluorescence, WD-XRF) of a selection of samples from each petrographic group. In this way, the compositional characteristics of the
ceramic fabrics were linked with both geological settings and pottery of known provenance.
The petrographic analyses were carried out by the author at the Fitch Laboratory of the British
School at Athens and at Archéosciences Bordeaux. The WD-XRF analyses were undertaken
by Noémi Muller at the Fitch Laboratory of the British School at Athens.

16 The composition, texture, and microstructure of the slips and glazes were examined by the
author and Ayed Ben Amara (Université Bordeaux-Montaigne) using Scanning Electron
Microscopy coupled with Energy Dispersive Spectroscopy (SEM-EDS) at Archéosciences
Bordeaux. The presence of pigments in the glaze was explored by Bernard Gratuze (Université
d'Orléans) using LA-ICP-MS at the Centre Ernest Babelon on a selection of samples at the
Université d'Orléans. In addition, Raman Spectroscopy was performed by the author at
Archéosciences Bordeaux.

17 This site was excavated under the auspices of the Ephorate of Boeotia in the early 2000s. More
information on this archaeological context, including the coarse pottery finds, is provided in
Liard et al., Household Pottery in Crusader Greece.

18 This archaeological context was excavated in July 2011 under the auspices of the Thebes
Synergasia Excavation Project, a Greek and American collaboration between the Ephorate of
Antiquities of Boeotia and Kevin Daly and Stephanie Larson of Bucknell University. On the
archaeological study of the bothros assemblage and the discussion of the pottery, coins, and
small objects found in this discarding pit deposit, see Kondyli et al., Thebes at the Time of the
Catalans.

19 Armstrong, Byzantine Thebes, 296; Louvi-Kizi, Thebes, 632; Kondyli et al., Thebes at the Time
of the Catalans.

20 On the Catalan domination of central Greece, see Dourou-Eliopoulou, Catalan Duchy of
Athens; Jacoby, Catalan Company.

Second, a set of 42 pottery fragments comes from the Mazi plain, a fertile plain that was strategically located in the hinterland of Thebes[21] and with archaeological evidence for a flourishing craft activity.[22] These pottery samples come from surface findings collected during a regional archaeological prospection that was carried out under the auspices of the Ephorate of Antiquities of West Attica, Pireus, and Islands and the Swiss School of Archaeology at Athens. The selected pottery spans the twelfth to the fifteenth centuries: this period encompasses the final years of Byzantine domination of central Greece, the conquest of central Greece by several Latin groups between 1204 and 1456, and the first years of Ottoman rule over the Aegean.[23]

Third, at Corinth, a commercial city of the north-eastern Peloponnese that was also home to one of the main lead-glazed pottery industries in Byzantine Greece, 98 lead-glazed pottery fragments were selected from various archaeological contexts in the so-called 'Frankish area' of the lower city, that was excavated by the American School of Classical studies at Athens. Some pottery fragments may be contemporaneous with Frankish rule over the city (from 1204),[24] but most of them are attributable to the Florentine administration of Corinth (from 1376 to the Ottoman conquest of 1458).[25]

These results revealed pottery production techniques and consumption choices which, when considered within the wider framework of archaeological and historical data so far published, provide further insights into connections between individuals and communities. Special attention is drawn to the question of craftsmen mobility and the underpinning processes of technological transfer, artistic appropriation, and innovation. Indeed, craftsmen mobility accelerated the transmission of practices, customs, tastes, and references in the long run, from generation to generation, at short to long distances. In this context, the diffusion of pottery types and styles contributed to the creation of new networks of sharing sociocultural practices that had the potential to make a difference to the way some groups of people behaved, interacted, and perceived themselves within a larger complexity. Such connections between peoples and ideas contributed to shape Byzantine society; they also had an impact on the Byzantine legacy in the Late Medieval and Renaissance cultures across Europe.

---

21 On the environmental setting and historical landmarks of the Mazi plain, and on the archaeological prospection undertaken in this area in recent years, see Fachard *et al.*, Mazi Archaeological Project, and the following yearly reports published in *Antike Kunst*.
22 Gerstel *et al.*, Late Medieval Panakton, 148.
23 Including the foundation of new Ottoman villages in the vicinity of the Mazi plain in the sixteenth century; see Tsevas, Ἱστορία τῶν Θηβῶν.
24 MacKay, Pottery of the Frankish Period, 401–403.
25 Williams and Zervos, Frankish Corinth, 177, n. 39.

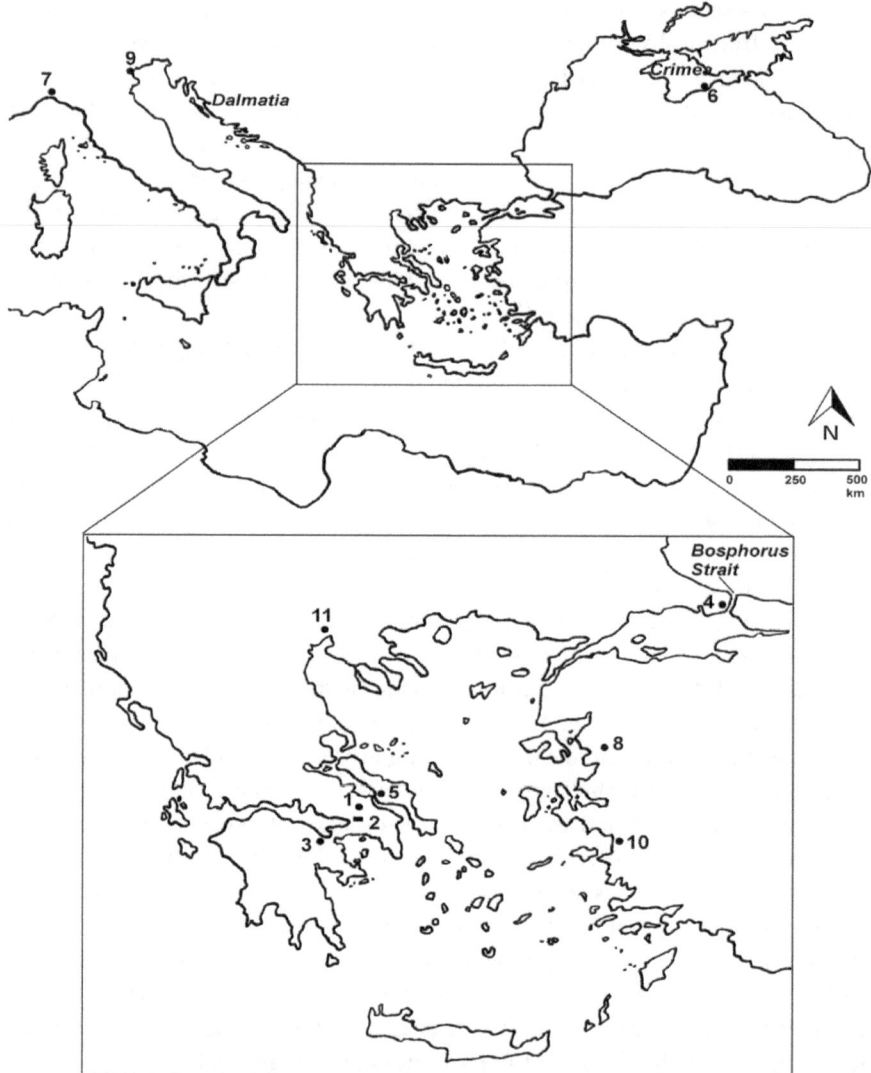

Fig. 1: Map of Greece, the central and eastern Mediterranean, with indication of the main sites mentioned in the text: 1. Thebes; 2. Mazi Plain; 3. Corinth; 4. Constantinople; 5. Chalkida; 6. Caffa; 7. Genoa; 8. Pergamon; 9. Venice; 10. Anaia; 11. Thessaloniki.

This article focuses on patterns of production and use of two iconic types of glazed tablewares in the Late Byzantine world: Glazed White Wares and Sgraffito Wares.

Glazed White Wares

Glazed White Wares were produced in the Byzantine world from the seventh century until at least the thirteenth century. Scholarly interest has mostly focused on early types of Byzantine Glazed White Wares spanning from the seventh to the eleventh centuries; that is, Glazed White Wares types I and II. Such pottery vessels were excavated in large quantities in Constantinople, while also being attested in major and minor sites across the Empire.[26] The stylistic as well as compositional homogeneity of this pottery is outstanding.[27] More particularly, the elemental analysis of fragments of Glazed White Ware types I and II revealed a match with clayey sediment resources from the site of Arnavatkoy on the Bosphorus Strait in modern Istanbul.[28] As a result, the name 'Constantinopolitan White Wares' has been commonly used: it was the general consensus that these wares were produced at Constantinople until around the beginning of the Komnenian era, before a new tradition of Sgraffito Ware in red fabrics started in provincial centres.[29] This scholarly assumption has thrived despite the scarcity of archaeological evidence for a centralised production of these early types of Glazed White Wares in Constantinople.[30] Therefore, little progress has been made in defining the analytical fabric fingerprint of the Constantinopolitan Glazed White Wares based on unfinished wares found in archaeological contexts at Istanbul and thus of obviously local origin.[31]

The commonly accepted assertion of a strictly Constantinopolitan origin of these early types of Byzantine Glazed White Wares is at odds with scientific results obtained from more ancient types of lead-glazed pottery with a green glaze and white kaolinitic fabric, from which the Byzantine Glazed White Wares may derive, and which were produced in western regions of the Roman world, notably in northern Italy and the Balkans, between the fifth and the seventh centuries AD.[32] Likewise, scientific analysis indicates that the later types of Byzantine Glazed White Wares from the twelfth and thirteenth centuries were not

---

26 For instance, see: Hayes, *Excavations at Saraçhane*; Armstrong *et al.*, Byzantine Glazing Technology, 225.

27 Waksman *et al.*, Byzantine Glazed White Wares, 130–132.

28 Megaw and Jones, Byzantine and Allied Pottery, 256–258. Some more recent compositional data pertaining to Byzantine Glazed White Wares is given in Waksman *et al.*, Byzantine Glazed White Wares, and in Bouquillon, Analyses chimiques.

29 For a recent account on this topic, see: Raptis, Firing Glazed Wares.

30 Hayes, *Excavations at Saraçhane*, 12.

31 So far, one fragment of unfinished Glazed White Ware II has been reported at the excavations of Sirkeci at Istanbul, and the elemental composition of its fabric is different from the main reference group thus far defined for this type of ware: see Waksman and Girgin, Fouilles de Sirkeci, 465–467.

32 Waksman *et al.*, Premières 'Byzantine Glazed White Wares'; Waksman *et al.*, 'The First Byzantine Glazed White Wares'.

produced exclusively at Constantinople or its immediate region, as originally suspected on a strictly archaeological basis. At Corinth, several dozen fragments of sturdy open vessels with a smooth finish display a distinctively pale brown fabric; they are covered with a greenish-to-ochre brown lead-rich glaze, with engraved decoration on the rim and upper body (Figure 2).[33] Such vessels were tentatively described as 'Olive-Brown Ware' by MacKay[34] and 'green-glazed ware' by Sanders,[35] but their provenance remained unknown. In line with the more recent developments in Byzantine ceramic studies, these vessels can now be attributed to Glazed White Ware V from the twelfth and thirteenth centuries[36] This variant was first defined by John Hayes based on findings from the excavations at Saraçhane in Istanbul.[37] Occasional discoveries have been made at other sites,[38] but in general Glazed White Ware V seems to receive less scholarly interest than its earlier counterparts, types I and II.

Fig. 2: Fragment of bowl in Glazed White Ware V found in the Frankish Area at Corinth, during excavations by the American School of Classical Studies at Athens.

Hayes assumed that this late variant of Byzantine Glazed White Wares was manufactured in smaller pottery centres around Constantinople, rather than in

---

33 Liard *et al.*, Late Medieval Corinth.
34 MacKay, Byzantine and Frankish Pottery, 256, pl. 63, fig. 1, cat. 17–18.
35 Sanders, Frankish Pottery, 177.
36 These vessels combine the green glaze that is characteristic of Glazed White Ware II with the thin wash (or wet smoothing) of the gritty fabric that is typical of Glazed White Ware IV (Hayes, *Excavations at Saraçhane*, 21, 31, 33). Glazed White Ware was presumably produced in the twelfth and thirteenth centuries.
37 Hayes, *Excavations at Saraçhane*, 12.
38 François, *Vaisselle de terre à Byzance*, 57–58, 184, cat. 67–68; this ware is also mentioned in Vroom, Pottery from Kaman-Kalehöyük, 168.

Constantinople itself.[39] However, the provenance analysis of eighteen fragments of thirteenth-century Glazed White Ware V from Corinth provides strikingly different results.[40] Five other provenances are suggested, and while these regions had been Byzantine possessions or protectorates prior to 1204, they were located outside the frontiers of the Empire after the Fourth Crusade. Three fragments were identified as local products from the Latin-controlled city of Corinth. Four other fragments turned out to be imports from the southern shores of Crimea in the area of Caffa; this region belonged to the Byzantines until the eleventh century and it was granted to the Genoese by the Byzantine emperor Michael VIII Palaiologos in 1261 in exchange for their help in the Byzantine reconquest of Constantinople.[41] One sample originated from western Anatolia. Two fragments came from the Veneto and eight others from the Dalmatian coastline (modern Croatia), where the Venetians had extended their maritime power since the tenth century; the following centuries were marked by disputes over the sovereignty of the Dalmatian coastline between the Byzantines, the Venetians, and the Hungarians, until the Venetians consolidated their control over the region in the early fifteenth century.[42]

The examination of the Corinthian assemblage features a critical decentralisation in the production of Byzantine Glazed White Wares in the twelfth and thirteenth centuries. It also indicates that some formerly Byzantine territories that had an old tradition of lead-glazed pottery production in buff fabrics that went back to the Roman period (such as northern Italy and the Balkans area) and passed under Latin control in 1204, played an important role as suppliers of Glazed White Ware V in the Aegean region in the twelfth and thirteenth centuries. This is notably the case at Corinth, even though this city hosted one of the main lead-glazed ceramic tableware industries of the Byzantine world between the late eleventh and thirteenth centuries.[43]

It is also interesting that beyond the shared use of a pale brown fabric and an olive-green to ochre-brown lead-rich glaze, the techniques of production and decoration of these wares were not the same in each identified workshop. The fabrics are low- to medium-calcareous in composition and their mineralogical

---

39 Hayes, *Excavations at Saraçhane*, 30.
40 The full petrographic results are published in Liard *et al.,* Late Medieval Corinth.
41 On the historical context of this region, see Balard, *Les Latins en Orient*, 241.
42 On this historical context, see Wolff, Venice and the Slavs, 428–9, 436. It should be noted that north-eastern Italy and the Danube area (Roman Province of Pannonia) hosted lead-glazed pottery workshops in Late Antiquity, and that the development of the Byzantine Glazed White Ware I may derive from this tradition (Waksman *et al.,* Byzantine Glazed White Wares). Moreover, some findings of early types of Byzantine Glazed White Wares are reported in the south-eastern Adriatic basin (modern Albania), and they are considered as Constantinopolitan imports (Vroom, From One Coast to Another, 356).
43 White, *Byzantine Glazed Pottery from Corinth*, ii.

fingerprint and their aluminum and silica contents[44] rule out the use of kaolinitic clays that were regularly used in earlier types of Byzantine Glazed White Wares. Moreover, for most vessels, a thin clay wash was laid on the ceramic surface before the application of the glaze, but in some cases this clay wash was applied in thick layers in a fashion that resembles the practice of white slipping (typical of the red-firing Sgraffito Wares, see below), but certainly not early types of Byzantine Glazed White Wares. It thus appears that beyond the willingness to continue the tradition of Byzantine Glazed White Ware, the potters' communities were not familiar with all the technological aspects of this production.

This trend observed in the production of Glazed White Wares over time provides the grounds for understanding the adaptations and diversification in the types, styles, and technological aspects (mostly firing techniques) of Sgraffito Ware in Late Byzantine territories between the thirteenth and fifteenth centuries. These changes are attributable to an increase in the local demand and in the production rates of glazed tablewares after the period of Latin occupation; with new social groups willing to consume affordable and waterproof decorated tableware.[45] Similar developments occurred in various Latin-controlled territories. In Lusignan Cyprus, Late Byzantine Sgraffito Ware production started with the establishment of Frankish rule in the thirteenth century; it continued elsewhere on the island throughout the medieval period, 'using technical practices that were evidently different and (...) were set up to serve the new, local demands deriving from an intensification of commercial activities on the island'[46]. Likewise, the above results indicate that, the new Latin settlers may have fostered the manufacture of (affordable) pottery in Byzantine styles, notably in cities with a long history of trade and a strong Byzantine legacy (such as Corinth). This procedure may have been used as a way to create new channels for the dissemination of these objects among local communities, and to reinforce the collective conception of their sovereignty upon these communities. In this respect, the appropriation of ostentatious cultural symbols of Byzantine origin by the Republic of Venice after 1204 is a widely-acknowledged phenomenon, and the major role of this practice in shaping Venice's political identity is obvious in her commercial ventures and diplomatic activities in the East. According to Maria Georgopoulou, 'the Venetian colonies may be seen as providing grounds for the manipulation of Byzantine traditions by the Venetians [...]. Instead of imposing their hegemony in the colonies violently, the Venetians appropriated certain Byzantine traditions

---

44 Indeed, the combined aluminum and silica content of these fabrics does not exceed 80 wt%. By contrast, early types of Byzantine Glazed White Wares, as well as the productions from Italy and the Balkans from which these may derive (see above), were all manufactured using kaolinites: Waksman *et al.*, Byzantine Glazed White Wares, 130.

45 Raptis, Firing Glazed Wares, 102–103.

46 Ting *et al.*, Cypriot Glazed Ware.

to secure a smooth transition from Byzantine to Venetian rule.'[47] Nonetheless, this process has so far been approached through the appropriation of luxury goods, crafts, relics, and artistic symbols; our results indicate that this process may also have embrassed much more modest objects such as lead-glazed pottery. Therefore, this new result provides further insights into the willingness of the Venetians to reach out to people in their daily lives, and not only in the public and elite areas of interaction.

Sgraffito Wares

Middle Byzantine Styles and the Chalkida/Negroponte workshops

The beginning of the second millennium AD initiated a change in the production and consumption of lead-glazed pottery in the Byzantine world. In parallel to the continued tradition of Glazed White Wares, several sites across the Empire began to produce Sgraffito Wares in red-bodied fabrics, covered with a layer of clayey buff slip and decorated with incised patterns. This production is believed to have started under the Komnenoi.[48] The advent of this new type of lead-glazed pottery thus broadly corresponded in time with the Empire's maximal extension in the eleventh century. While this period saw increased economic and cultural contacts with the Latin West before the Fourth Crusade, the Empire also faced internal problems fostered by its rapid expansion.[49]

From the early days of their production, Sgraffito Wares were consumed in urban centres as well as in rural settlements of the Byzantine Empire; their consumption outside Constantinople outscored considerably that of the Glazed White Wares.[50] Each workshop usually produced a series of different types and styles with incised decoration which have been gathered under the name 'Middle Byzantine production.'[51] This cohesive stylistic tradition includes Slip-Painted, Green and Brown Painted, Fine Sgraffito, Painted Sgraffito, Incised Sgraffito, Plain Glazed, Aegean, and Champlevé Wares. This tradition is considered to have been lasted from the twelfth to mid- to late-thirteenth century,[52] with no significant break at the time of the Fourth Crusade.

Nonetheless, the application of archaeometric analyses of provenance has started to challenge this model. Chalkida in Euboea, which served as an im-

---

47 Georgopoulou, Late Medieval Crete and Venice, 480.
48 Armstrong *et al.*, Byzantine Glazing Technology; François, *Vaisselle de terre à Byzance*, 57.
49 On this topic, see: Mango, *Oxford History of Byzantium*, 182.
50 Armstrong *et al.*, Byzantine Glazing Technology, 225.
51 Waksman *et al.*, 'Middle Byzantine Production', 379.
52 Sanders, Recent Developments in Byzantine Pottery.

portant centre of administration and trade and as the commercial harbour of the city of Thebes under Byzantine rule,[53] has emerged as one of the main centres of production and distribution of Middle Byzantine Pottery.[54] Archaeometric investigations carried out on post-1204 material also suggest that the Sgraffito pottery workshops remained active in the city after the Venetian conquest of the island of Euboea. Thebes also imported Chalkidan Sgraffito wares, even after a local workshop began in this Frankish-controlled city.[55] The Latin-controlled city of Corinth imported Late Byzantine Sgraffito Wares from Chalkida in the late thirteenth and throughout the fourteenth century,[56] around the time when the local lead-glazed pottery industry, which was flourishing under the Byzantines, suddenly declined.[57] The distribution of these wares was not limited to urban settlements; it also reached the rural hinterland, as shown by the occurrence of Chalkidan imports in the Middle Byzantine Styles among the twelfth-century pottery collected in the Mazi Plain.[58]

The existence of a pottery workshop of such importance on the periphery of Byzantium is noteworthy at a time when Sgraffito Ware production at Constantinople itself remains scanty[59]. It suggests the decentralisation of a major craft industry at a time when intense social change and economic development were taking place across the Empire and fostered a cultural and artistic revival, referred to by some as the 'Byzantine Renaissance.'[60] It also reveals the perpetuation of Byzantine craft traditions after the Venetian conquest of Euboea, and the maintenance of some ceramic workshops as crucial actors in the long-distance trade of lead glazed pottery in the Latin-controlled territories of the Aegean region.

Several technological aspects of the Chalkidan Sgraffito Ware industry under Venetian rule should be highlighted. First, a pendent cone is a recurring feature on the internal side of the ring-foot of these vessels, and it is also encountered among Venetian lead-glazed pottery from the Late Medieval period.[61] Second, Chalkida is one Sgraffito Ware industry in mainland Greece that continued the

---

53 Kontogiannis, Euripos-Negroponte-Egriboz.
54 Waksman *et al.*, 'Middle Byzantine Production', 414–415.
55 Kondyli *et al.*, Thebes at the Time of the Catalans.
56 Liard *et al.*, Late Medieval Corinth.
57 MacKay, Pottery of the Frankish Period, 419–420.
58 On-going research by the author.
59 See François, *Vaisselle de terre à Byzance*. For instance, the Sirkeçi workshops in Istanbul have produced unfinished Sgraffito Wares and kiln wasters from the thirteenth and fourteenth centuries; some rare fragments of misfired Glazed White Ware II are broadly dated to the ninth to twelfth centuries (Waksman and Girgin, Vestiges de Sirkeci); but there is so far no clear archaeological evidence for the production of Sgraffito Wares in Istanbul during the twelfth century.
60 Magdalino, *Empire of Manuel I Komnenos*.
61 MacKay, Byzantine and Frankish Pottery, 254–5, fig. 1.11.

Byzantine tradition of slip-painting, notably for the decoration of the vessels' rims, after the Fourth Crusade.[62] The same decoration characterises one Venetian import from the thirteenth or fourteenth century at Corinth.[63] Third, small quantities of a synthetic yellow opacifier – that is, the lead antimonate or 'Naples Yellow' pigment – have been detected by archaeometry in lead glazes from the Trade Republic of Venice and from the Venetian colony of Chalkida.[64]

The presence of lead antimonate in Byzantine Sgraffito glazes had until then scarcely been reported: the only proven occurrence concerned some Late Byzantine pottery from the city of Anaia in western Anatolia, aside from some isolated occurrences in fourteenth-century glazed pottery from Greece.[65] For a long time scholars assumed that by the fourth century, glassmakers abandoned the long-lasting tradition of using lead-antimonate yellow pigments to colour glass in the Roman East, and started using tin-based yellow pigments to colour glass instead.[66] Since then, patchy occurrences of Naples Yellow have been reported in medieval glass objects and ceramic glazes from diverse cultural contexts across the Mediterranean,[67] but the pigment was not used again on a regular basis until the late fourteenth century, when it emerged as one of the main colourants in Venetian glass, in Italian majolicas, and in Italian Renaissance painting.[68] The recipe for this pigment has been considered by some as being

---

62 This is exemplified by bowls and plates from the thirteenth and early-fourteenth-century bothros on Ismenion Hill at Thebes, some of which were assigned petrographically to the area of Chalkida. See Kondyli et al., Thebes at the Time of the Catalans.

63 On this topic, see Liard et al., Late Medieval Corinth.

64 This pigment was identified using a combination of four different archaeometric techniques. The presence of traces of antimony in the glazes was identified by LA-ICP-MS; SEM imagery combined with EDS analysis allowed for the identification of concentration of these elements in the form of cubic to tabular crystals within the glaze; Raman Spectrometry allowed for the most probable identification of these crystals as a lead antimonate (Naples Yellow) pigment. The results of these analyses are explained in Liard et al., Late Medieval Corinth.

65 Kırmızı et al., Colouring Agents. One should note that traces of Naples Yellow were also identified archaeometrically by other scholars on fourteenth-century lead-glazed pottery found at Corinth (Palamara et al., Technology Issues, 143) and at Englianos (Davis and Stocker, Palace of Nestor) but the provenance of these sherds has not been investigated by archaeometric techniques and thus remains uncertain.

66 Tite et al., Tin-Based Opacifiers, 79.

67 For instance, see: Tite et al., Tin-Opacified Islamic Glazes, 89–90 (occurrences detected in late ninth- and tenth-century lead glazes from Egypt and Tunisia). It should be noted, however, that scientific analyses of natron glasses from Late Antique and Early Medieval contexts in northern Italy have demonstrated the occurrence of a small quantity of antimony- and tin-based opacifiers that most probably come from processes of glass-recycling, rather than being the result of an intentional addition of pigments (Uboldi and Verità, Glasses from Northern Italy). A similar situation is encountered in the case of thirteenth-century Sgraffito Ware from Cyprus (Ting et al., Cypriot Glazed Ware, 35).

68 Molina et al., Lead Antimonate Yellow Glass, 171, with references.

transferred from the Late Byzantine world to Venice via the migration of glass artists following the fall of Constantinople to the Ottomans in 1453.[69]

The crystalline form of the pigment affects the translucency of the glaze and it is thus responsible for a less shiny surface on the finished product. This might seem to be at odds with the glossy aspect of the glaze that was generally seen as the result that was sought for in the use of high-lead glazes. However, recent research demonstrates that by using this pigment, the potters could achieve other aesthetic effects; namely, a distinctive mustard or lemon yellow colour of the glaze and a stronger contrast with the incised decoration, which might have been in line with a diversity of tastes and demands among consumers.[70] These considerations draw our awareness to the diversity of aesthetic tastes for glazed pottery and raise new questions about the identity of the consumers of these wares in the Latin-controlled territories of the Aegean region.

Furthermore, the preparation of Naples Yellow necessitated access to a specific recipe[71] and to raw materials such as antimony that were not always available locally. It is interesting that lead antimonate was used in some glazed pottery workshops of the Byzantine Empire which came under Venetian control after the Fourth Crusade (this is the case, for instance, at Chalkida).[72] In parallel, this pigment occurs among Venetian pottery imports at Corinth that are dated to the thirteenth and fourteenth centuries.[73] These results raise new questions about the (Byzantine, Venetian, or other) cultural background of the people who were involved in lead-glazed pottery production and decoration at Venice and at Chalkida. Moreover, the question remains as to whether the potters travelled long distances to purposely share their technical knowledge or learn new pottery-making skills. Were these potters Byzantines or Latins, in view of the continued aesthetic traditions that characterise pottery-making in the thirteenth century? The 1200s saw an increase in the circulation of people, goods, and commodities between the western and eastern Mediterranean which also implied a greater mobility of craftsmen and techniques. There is written evidence for long-distance mobility of craftsmen in the framework of the (albeit more luxurious) glass production industry, and the role of Venice seems to have been substantial in these processes of knowledge exchange. Indeed, while there is so far little ar-

---

69 Dik *et al.*, Early Production Recipes.
70 Liard and Kondyli, Between Tradition and Experimentation.
71 Dik *et al.* Early Production Recipes.
72 The Naples Yellow pigment was detected in Chalkidan lead glazes found at the Late Byzantine settlement on Ismenion Hill. This pottery is preliminarily dated to the twelfth to early-thirteenth century. The results of this on-going research will be published separately. In addition, the same pigment was identified in Corinthian products from the thirteenth and fourteenth centuries: Liard *et al.*, Late Medieval Corinth.
73 More research remains to be done on medieval Venetian craftsmanship in order to identify when Naples Yellow started to be used on a regular, and not only experimental, basis.

chaeological evidence for glass workshops across the territories of the Late Byzantine Empire, the Venetian archives do report glass production on Crete, as well as the activity of Cretan and Venetian glassworkers both in Venice and in Crete during the fourteenth and fifteenth centuries.[74] In the fifteenth century, young people from the Byzantine Peloponnese were sent to Italy to learn, amongst other things, the craft of glasswork, as stated in a letter of Cardinal Bessarion to the Despot of Morea and later Emperor Constantine XI Palaiologos.[75] In this context, the role of the interaction between people in the diffusion of the Naples Yellow pigment deserves further research.

The so-called 'Thessaloniki Ware'

Aside from the production of pottery in the Middle Byzantine styles, some regional aesthetic traditions emerged across the Byzantine Empire, in some cases as early as the twelfth century.[76] As explained above, these stylistic traditions were further established in the thirteenth century, under favourable economic conditions in the Byzantine Empire and in parallel to an increased importance of urban centres located on the periphery of Constantinople.[77] They were continued in the fourteenth century, despite a dramatic decrease in the number of lead-glazed pottery factories in the Aegean region.[78] Some flourishing provincial workshops even produced Late Byzantine Sgraffito Wares in the regions that formerly belonged to the Byzantine Empire and had been conquered by the Franks and the Venetians in the early thirteenth century.[79]

Thessaloniki Ware is one of these Late Byzantine products that was contemporaneous with the Palaiologan dynasty. It is characterized by slip-painted "tongues" on the exterior, horizontal lines around the interior rim, and a variety of geometric or stylized designs on the vessel's floor. It has for a long time been attributed exclusively to the eponymous city, despite its presence in many sites in the Aegean region. Thessaloniki was the first place of discovery of unfinished fragments and wasters in association with other archaeological evidence for a local pottery workshop, thereby giving the ware its name.[80] This interpretation fits in well with the position of Thessaloniki as one of the most important cities

---

74 Antonaras, Glass Vessels, 408, n. 150.
75 Antonaras, Glass Vessels, 408, with references.
76 For instance, Measles Ware is deemed to be a twelfth-century Peloponnesian production.
77 Papanikola-Bakirtzi, Art of Sgraffito, 21.
78 François, Vaisselle de terre à Byzance, 78.
79 For instance, Chalkida and Thebes: Waksman et al., 'Middle Byzantine Production'; Kondyli et al., Thebes at the Time of the Catalans.
80 Papanikola-Bakirtzi, Art of Sgraffito, 21.

remaining to the Byzantine state in the years following the recovery of Constantinople from the Latin conquest in 1261; it enjoyed a thriving local industry and a wide-ranging trade network.[81]

More recently, however, some unfinished fragments exhibiting a similar repertoire of incised patterns have been discovered in Istanbul, and their compositional fingerprint is different from the Thessaloniki production.[82] Likewise, some fragments in the same style were discovered at Pergamon, and identified as local products on archaeological and archaeometric grounds.[83] At Corinth, two fragments of this ware were attributed to the northern Aegean region based on the compositional fingerprint of their fabric.[84] Such developments in pottery provenance studies demonstrate that Late Byzantine styles were shared by various workshops dispersed across the Empire, despite a general atmosphere of political and social unrest.

The debated 'Zeuxippus Ware'[85]

Zeuxippus Ware is probably one of the most meticulously-decorated and eye-catching types of Sgraffito Ware among the Late Byzantine pottery production. Within this ware family, vessels in Zeuxippus Ware class I are decorated with carefully-incised concentric circles at the floor, at mid-body, and below the rim; a spiral is sometimes engraved at the centre of the floor (fig. 3). These vessels are covered with either a pale yellow, colourless, green, or dark brown glaze. Pottery in this ware was popular among territories under Byzantine rule. Provenance studies combining archaeological and archaeometric investigations indicate that Zeuxippus Ware class I occurs in a large range of fabrics, with a compositional distinction between the most exquisite examples, labelled Zeuxippus Ware 'stricto sensu', and examples of the broader 'Zeuxippus Ware family'.[86] The former category is a very homogeneous production in terms of style and fabric. It was first thought to have been produced in the area of Constantinople, but this view has since been abandoned (see below).[87] The latter category gathers various examples which replicate more or less accurately the engraved decoration and the aspect, colour, and shine of the glaze of the Zeuxippus Ware 'stricto sensu'.

81　Rautman, Metropolitan Succession of Thessaloniki, 147.
82　Papanikola-Bakirtzi and Waksman, Thessaloniki Ware Reconsidered. See also Waksman *et al.*, Ateliers de Sirkeci, 460–462, fig. 3–5.
83　Waksman, Medieval Western Turkey, 109–110, fig. 2 – BZY411.
84　Liard *et al.*, Lead-Glazed Pottery at Late Medieval Corinth.
85　Papanikola-Bakirtzi, *Art of Sgraffito*, 22; Waksman and François, Zeuxippus Ware.
86　Waksman and François, Zeuxippus Ware.
87　Papanikola-Bakirtzi, *Art of Sgraffito*, 22, n. 5.

Fig. 3: thirteenth- to early-fourteenth-century bowl derivative of the Zeuxippus Ware class I (cat. n. 3–2–5), found on Ismenion Hill at Thebes, during excavations by the Ephorate of Antiquities at Boeotia and Bucknell University, © Jeff Vanderpool.

Provenance analyses have shown that the most exquisite examples of Zeuxippus Wares class I did not exclusively originate from Byzantium, and that the more hastily-executed examples are not exclusively provincial products. For instance, several fragments of unfinished plates and bowls, which were discovered at the Sirkeci excavations in Istanbul and are therefore indicative of a local production, are attributable to derivatives of the Zeuxippus family due to the diverse quality of their incised decoration.[88] Conversely, some Sgraffito Wares that have been archaeometrically ascribed to the region of Pergamon were originally identified as 'regional derivatives of Zeuxippus Ware' by Hayes, despite the fact that they are stylistically and technically very similar, if not identical, to Zeuxippus Ware 'stricto sensu'.[89] Finally, some fragments of crude bowls found in Corinth, and exhibiting gouged concentric circles at the centre of the floor and a faint green glaze, are also attributed chemically and petrographically to the region of Pergamon, even though these sherds are less carefully executed than the previous examples. Quite interestingly for us, the elemental composition of these sherds matches those of the technically-superior Zeuxippus Ware 'stricto sensu.'[90] It thus seems that the pottery products exhibiting the highest level of quality are not necessarily connected with the centre of economic and political power. Instead, there is evidence for production of high-quality Zeuxippus Ware on the periphery of Byzantium.

---

88 Waksman and Girgin, Vestiges de Sirkeci, 460, fig. 26, Group S2.
89 Waksman and François, Zeuxippus Ware, 670–671, with references.
90 Waksman and François, Zeuxippus Ware, 692.

Moreover, common findings of fine-quality Zeuxippus Wares were reported at Pergamon by Megaw – but they were not treated as local products – and this tradition of consumption was related with the prosperity of the city at the end of the twelfth century, when Pergamon enjoyed some recovery and became the new frontier thema of Neokastra after the Seljuks had been pushed back.[91] Megaw also suggested that the decline in the quality of the wares should be regarded as a later trend, although he admits that 'the Pergamon finds do not come from informative contexts'.[92] According to him, the historical context provided 'some circumstantial evidence of the date when Zeuxippus Ware was current there.'[93] The lower-quality Zeuxippus Wares are, according to Megaw, attributable to the decline of the city that followed the Fourth Crusade, when Neokastra passed – nominally at least – to the Empire of Nicaea.[94] Instead, one might want to consider that there was a diversified production of Zeuxippus Wares by the workshops operating at and around Pergamon during the twelfth century, maybe for different clienteles. This interpretation leaves more room for processes of flexibility, experimentation, and changes that inevitably regulate local craft activity, and for the social diversity that characterises a local group of pottery producers and consumers.

Conclusion

Provenance and technological approaches to pottery carry an enormous potential for examining patterns of social behaviour and cohesion in Byzantium. When empirical observations are pieced together and considered against a wider historical background, they foster new realms of interpretation of social structures and human agency in Byzantium. They emphasise the existence of improbable, shifting, but nonetheless significant interactions between people. Such studies help us re-draw ties and boundaries that were negotiated on a daily basis, between individuals with various cultural and social backgrounds that were located both within and outside the limits of the Byzantine Empire. Integrative approaches to pottery traditions can bring to light the existence of 'underground' channels of exchange through which Byzantine heritage was diffused and perpetuated (among the provinces of the Empire at its maximal extension) and perceived, used, and appropriated (by Latin groups developing trade and diplomatic activities in the East). Through these few case studies, I hope to have shed

---

91 Megaw, Zeuxippus Ware, 82–83.
92 Megaw, Zeuxippus Ware, 82.
93 Megaw, Zeuxippus Ware, 82.
94 Megaw, Zeuxippus Ware, 82–83.

light on the multifaceted ways these interactions are revealed through pottery traditions and on the type of new questions that they can offer to Byzantine studies.

Acknowledgements

This work was supported by the Williams Fellowship in Ceramic Petrology at the Fitch Laboratory, British School at Athens (2017) and by the 'Initiative d'Excellence' postdoctoral international program at the Université Bordeaux Montaigne (2018–2019). The Buckner W. Clay Dean of Arts & Sciences and the Vice President for Research at the University of Virginia facilitated the production of petrographic thin sections from pottery sampled on Ismenion Hill. Permission for petrographic study of pottery samples from excavations at Thebes and Corinth and archaeological prospection in the Mazi Plain was given by the Ephorate of Antiquities at Boeotia and the Greek Ministry of Culture. Special thanks are due to the First Ephorate of Byzantine Antiquities and to Profs. S. Larson and K. Daly (Bucknell University) for allowing access to and study of the pottery assemblages found during archaeological excavations on Ismenion Hill at Thebes; to Dr. Guy Sanders and the American School of Classical Studies at Athens for the lead-glazed medieval pottery assemblages from the Frankish Area at Corinth; and to Dr. Sylvian Fachard (ASCSA), Prof. Alex Knodell (Carlton College) and Dr. Eleni Banou (3rd Ephorate of Antiquities) and the Swiss School of Archaeology at Athens for the medieval pottery assemblages from archaeological prospection in the Mazi Plain. I would like to thank Prof. Fotini Kondyli (University of Virginia) and Dr. Guy Sanders for our fruitful discussions on the topic of this article. I am grateful to the staff of the Fitch Laboratory, British School at Athens, Archéosciences Bordeaux and the IRAMAT laboratories in France for facilitating the provenance and technological analyses of the pottery samples. As indicated in the article, the detailed analytical results pertaining to the pottery samples are published separately.

Bibliography

Antonaras, Anastasios, Early Christian and Byzantine Glass Vessels: Forms and Uses, in: Falko Daim and Jörg Drauschke (eds.), *Byzanz – das Römerreich im Mittelalter Teil 1 Welt der Ideen, Welt der Dinge* (Regensburg, 2010) 383–430.
Antonaras, Anastasios, Artisanal Production in Byzantine Thessaloniki (4th-15th Century), in: Falko Daim and Jörg Drauschke (eds.), *Hinter den Mauern und auf dem*

offenen Land. Leben im Byzantinischen Reich, Byzanz zwischen Orient und Okzident 3 (Mainz, 2016) 113–239.

Armstrong, Pamela, Some Byzantine and Later Settlements in Eastern Phocis, *Annual of the British School at Athens* 84 (1989) 1–47.

Armstrong, Pamela, Byzantine Thebes: Excavations on the Kadmeia, 1980, *Annual of the British School at Athens* 88 (1993) 295–335.

Armstrong, Pamela and Nergis Günsenin, Glazed Pottery Production at Ganos, *Anatolia Antiqua* 3 (1995) 179–201.

Armstrong, Pamela, Helen Hatcher, and Mike Tite, Changes in Byzantine Glazing Technology from the Ninth to Thirteenth Centuries, in: Gabrielle Démians d'Archimbaud (ed.), *La Céramique médiévale en Méditerranée. Actes du VIe congrès de l'AIECM2* (Aix-en-Provence, 1997) 225–229.

Balard, Michel, *Les Latins en Orient. XIe–XVe siècle*, Nouvelle Clio, L'histoire et ses problèmes (Paris, 2006).

Barton, Tom, Susan McDonough, Sara McDougall, and Matthew Wranovix (eds.), *Boundaries in the Medieval and Wider World. Essays in Honour of Paul Freedman*, Europa Sacra 22 (Turnhout, 2017).

Bouquillon, Anne, Analyses chimiques de quelques productions céramiques Byzantines des collections du Louvre, in: Véronique François, *La vaisselle de terre à Byzance. Catalogue des collections du Musée du Louvre* (Paris, 2017) 310–327.

Capelli, Claudio, Il contributo delle analisi petrografiche negli studi della ceramica mediterranea medievale e postmedievale. Tiziano Mannoni tra passato e futuro, in: *Atti L Convegno Internazionale della Ceramica 2017. Cinquant'anni di Studi sulla Ceramiche; Il Contributo del Centro Ligure per la Storia della Ceramica, Savona, 6–7 Ottobre 2017* (Padova, 2018) 35–42.

Capelli, Claudio and R. Cabella, The Archaeometric Study of White Slips: A Contribution to the Characterisation of the Medieval Mediterranean Productions, in: S. Y. Waksman (ed.), *Archaeometric and Archaeological Approaches to Ceramics: Papers presented at EMAC '05, 8th European Meeting on Ancient Ceramics*. BAR International Series 1691 (Oxford, 2007).

Charalambous, A.C., A.J. Salakis, N.A.Kantiranis, L.C. Papadopoulou, N.C. Tsirliganis, and J.A. Stratis, Cypriot Byzantine Glazed Pottery: A Study of the Paphos Workshops, *Archaeometry* 52 (2010) 628–643.

Davis, Jack and Sharon Stocker, The Medieval Deposit from the Northeast Gateway at the Palace of Nestor', *Hesperia* 82/4 (2013) 673–731.

Dik, Joris, E. Hermens, R. Peschar, and H. Schenk, Early Production Recipes for Lead Antimonate Yellow in Italian Art, *Archaeometry* 47 (2005) 593–607.

Dourou-Eliopoulou, Maria, The Catalan Duchy of Athens and the Other Latin Powers in Greece Especially the Principality of Achaea (1311–1388), *ΕΩΑ ΚΑΙ ΕΣΠΕΡΙΑ* 4 (1999–2000) 87–93.

Fachard, Sylvian, Alex Knodell, and Eleni Banou, The 2014 Season of the Mazi Archaeological Project, Northwest Attica, Greece, *Antike Kunst* 58 (2015) 178–186.

Flexner, James L., Historical Archaeology, Contact, and Colonialism in Oceania, *Journal of Archaeological Research* 22/1 (2014) 43–87.

François, Véronique, Les ateliers de céramique Byzantine de Nicée/Iznik et leur production (Xe-début XIVe siècle), *Bulletin de Correspondance Hellénique* 121/1 (1997) 411–442.

François, Véronique, *La vaisselle de terre à Byzance: Catalogue des Musées du Louvre* (Paris, 2017).

François, Véronique and Jean-Michel Spieser, Pottery and Glass in Byzantium, in: Angeliki Laiou (ed.), *The Economic History of Byzantium: From the Seventh through the Fifteenth Century*, Dumbarton Oaks Studies 39 (Washington, D.C., 2002) 593–609.

Georgopoulou, Maria, Late Medieval Crete and Venice: An Appropriation of Byzantine Heritage, *The Art Bulletin* 77.3 (1995) 479–96.

Gerstel, Sharon, Mark Munn, Heather Grossman, Ethne Barnes, Arthur Rohn, and Machiel Kiel, A Late Medieval Settlement at Panakton, *Hesperia* 72/2 (2003) 147–234.

Girgin, Ç., Sirkeci'de sürdürülen kazı çalışmalarından elde edilen sonuçlar, in: *Gün Isiginda: Istanbul'un 8000 yili: Marmaray, Metro, Sultanahmet kazıları* (Istanbul, 2007) 98–105.

Gosselain, Olivier, *Poteries du Cameroun méridional. Styles techniques et rapports à l'identité* (Paris, 2002).

Gosselain, Olivier, D'une histoire à l'autre: Retour sur une théorie des liens entre langues et techniques en Afrique, in: Nathan Schlanger and Anne-Christine Taylor (eds.), *La préhistoire des autres: Perspectives archéologiques et anthropologiques* (Paris, 2012), 83–98.

Gounaris, Vassilis and Yannis Frangopoulos, La quête de la nation grecque moderne et le "cas grec" comme un cas paradoxal de la construction du fait national contemporain, *Socio-Anthropologie*, 23–24 (2009) 115–153.

Hayes, John, *Excavations at Saraçhane in Istanbul. Vol. 2, The Pottery* (Princeton, 1992).

Jacoby, David, The Catalan Company in the East: The Evolution of an Itinerant Army (1303–1311), in: Gregory Halfond (ed.), *The Medieval Way of War: Studies in Medieval Military History in Honor of Bernard S. Bachrach* (Farnham, 2015) 153–182.

Kırmızı, Burcu, Material Characteristics and Production Technology of Zeuxippus Ware Type Ceramics from Kusadasi Kadikalesi/Anaia, in: Zeynep Mercangöz (ed.), *Byzantine Craftsmen – Latin Patrons. Reflections from the Anaian Commercial Production in the Light of the Excavations at Kadikalesi near Kusadasi* (Istanbul, 2013) 77–90.

Kırmızı, Burcu, Emine H. Göktürk, and Philippe Colomban, Colouring Agents in the Pottery Glazes of Western Anatolia: New Evidence for the Use of Naples Yellow Pigment Variations During the Late Byzantine Period, *Archaeometry* 57 (2015) 476–496.

Kondyli, Fotini, Stephanie Larson, Julian Baker, Florence Liard, Kevin Daly, Alexandra Charami, and Vassilis L. Aravantinos, Thebes at the Time of the Catalans: A Deposit Between the Ismenion Hill and the Elektra Gate, *Hesperia* 89 (2020) 757–831.

Kontogiannis, Nikos, Euripos-Negroponte-Egriboz: Material Culture and Historical Topography of Chalkis from Byzantium to the End of the Ottoman Rule, *JÖB* 62 (2012) 29–56.

Kuleff, I., R. Djingova, and G. Djinkov, Provenance Studies of Sgraffito Ceramics (12th–14th c.): Shumen, Varna, Tcherven North-Eastern Bulgaria, in: Yannis Maniatis (ed.), *Archaeometry, Proceedings of the 25th International Symposium* (Amsterdam, 1989) 533–543.

Lazzarini, Lorenzo, Nuovi dati sulla nascita e sviluppo del graffito veneziano, in: G. Ericani (ed.), *Atti del convegno La ceramica graffita medievale e rinascimentale nel Veneto* (Padova, 1989) 19–28.

Liard, Florence and Fotini Kondyli, Between Tradition and Experimentation: Exploring Technical Skills Behind the Art of Sgraffito in Medieval Thebes, in: Nikos Kontogiannis, Beate Böhlendorf-Arslan, and Filiz Yenişehirlioğlu (eds.), *Glazed Wares as Cultural Agents in the Byzantine, Seljuk and Ottoman Lands* (Istanbul, 2021) 133–156.

Liard, Florence, Fotini Kondyli, and Evangelia Kiriatzi, Exploring Diversity in Household Pottery Traditions in Crusader Greece: A Case Study from the City of Thebes, Boeotia, *Archaeometry* 61.5 (2019) 1011–1038.

Liard, Florence, Guy Sanders, Ayed Ben Amara, and Noémi Müller, Lead-Glazed Pottery at Late Medieval Corinth: Assessing Craft Production and Trade at a Greek City under Western Influence, *Hesperia* 91.3 (2022) 485–569.

Lis, Bartłomiej, Štěpán Rückl, and Maria Choleva, Mobility in the Bronze Age Aegean: The Case of Aeginetan Potters, in: Walter Gauss, Gudrun Klebinder-Gauss, and Constance von Rüden (eds.), *The Transmission of Technical Knowledge in the Production of Ancient Mediterranean Pottery: Proceedings of the International Conference at the Austrian Archaeological Institute at Athens, 23rd – 25th November 2012* (Vienna, 2015) 63–76.

Louvi-Kizi, Aspasia, Thebes, in: Angeliki Laiou (ed.), *The Economic History of Byzantium: From the Seventh through the Fifteenth Century*, Dumbarton Oaks Studies 39 (Washington, D.C., 2002) 631–638.

MacKay, Theodora Stillwell, More Byzantine and Frankish Pottery from Corinth, *Hesperia* 36/3 (1967) 249–320.

MacKay, Theodora Stillwell, Pottery of the Frankish Period: 13th and early 14th Century, in: Charles Williams II and Nancy Bookidis (eds.), *Corinth XX. Corinth the Centenary 1896-1996* (Athens, 2003) 401–422.

Magdalino, Paul, *The Empire of Manuel I Komnenos, 1143-1180* (Cambridge, 2002).

Mango, Cyril, *The Oxford History of Byzantium* (Oxford, 2002).

Megaw, Arthur, Zeuxippus Ware, *Annual of the British School at Athens* 63 (1968) 67–88.

Megaw, Arthur and Richard Jones, Byzantine and Allied Pottery: A Contribution by Chemical Analysis to Problems of Origin and Distribution, *Annual of the British School at Athens* 78 (1983) 235–263.

Mignucci, A., The 13th-14th century Venetian Ceramic Production of 'Graffita a Spirale Cerchio', 'Graffita S. Bartolo', and Glazed Ceramic: A New Reference Group and Attribution, in: Vassilis Kilikoglou, Anno Hein, and Yannis Maniatis (eds.), *5th European Meeting in Ancient Ceramics, 1999, Athens: Modern Trends in Scientific Studies on Ancient Ceramics*, BAR International Series 111 (Oxford, 2002) 245–252.

Molina, Gloria, G.P. Odin, Trinitat Pradell, Andrew Shortland, and Michael Tite, Production Technology and Replication of Lead Antimonate Yellow Glass from New Kingdom Egypt and the Roman Empire, *Journal of Archaeological Science* 41 (2014) 171–184.

Oka, R., L. Dussubieux, C.M. Kusimba, and V.D. Gogte, The Impact of 'Imitation' Industries and Imperial Restrictions on Chinese Ceramic Commercial Exports in the Indian Ocean Maritime Exchange, ca. 1200-1700 CE, in: Blythe McCarthy, Ellen Salzman Chase, Louise Allison Cort, Janet G. Douglas, and Paul Jett (eds.) *Scientific Research on Historic Asian Ceramics: Proceedings of the Fourth Forbes Symposium at the Freer Gallery of Art,* (London, 2009) 175–185.

Palamara, E., N. Zacharias, M. Xanthopoulou, Z. Kasztovszky, I. Kovács, D. Palles, and E.I. Kamitsos, Technology Issues of Byzantine Glazed Pottery from Corinth, Greece, *Microchemical Journal* 129 (2016) 137–150.

Papanikola-Bakirtzi, Despina, *Byzantine Glazed Ceramics. The Art of Sgraffito* (Athens, 1999).

Papanikola-Bakirtzi, Despina and Sylvie Yona Waksman, Thessaloniki Ware Reconsidered, in: Joanita Vroom (ed.), *Medieval and Post-Medieval Ceramics in the Eastern Mediterranean: Fact and Fiction* (Turnhout, 2016) 227–248.

Raptis, Konstantinos, Firing Glazed Wares in Byzantine Kilns: Continuities and Changes in the Technology of Glazed Pottery Production (11th-15th c.), *Journal of Archaeological Science: Reports* 29 (2020) 102–131.

Raškovska, Aleksandra, B. Minčeva Šukarova, O. Grupče, and P. Colomban, Characterization of Pottery from Republic of Macedonia II. Raman and Infrared Analyses of Glazed Pottery Finds from Skopsko Kale, *Journal of Raman Spectroscopy* 41 (2010) 431–439.

Rautman, M.L, Notes on the Metropolitan Succession of Thessaloniki, c. 1300, *REB* 46 (1988) 147–159.

Ratti, Carlo, Zbigniew Smoreda, and Maarten Vanhoof, Drawing Boundaries of Social Interactions, *Uses and Value. A Newsletter about Research in Economic and Social Sciences* 52 (2015), 2–5.

Sanders, Guy, An Assemblage of Frankish Pottery at Corinth, *Hesperia* 56/2 (1987) 159–95.

Sanders, Guy, Recent Developments in the Chronology of Byzantine Corinth, in: Charles Williams II and Nancy Bookidis (eds.), *Corinth XX, The Centenary: 1896–1996* (Athens, 2003) 385–399.

Silliman, Stephen, Culture Contact or Colonialism? Challenges in the Archaeology of Native North America, *American Antiquity* 70/1 (2005) 55–74.

Thomas, N., Material Culture and Colonial Power: Ethnological Collecting and the Establishment of Colonial Rule in Fiji, *Man*, New Series 24/1 (1989) 41–56.

Ting, Carmen, Thilo Rehren, Athanasios Vionis, and Vasiliki Kassianidou, The Origins and Evolution of Cypriot Glazed Ware Productions During the Thirteenth to Seventeenth Centuries CE, *Archaeological and Anthropological Sciences* 13 (2021).

Tite, Michael, Trinitat Pradell, and Andrew Shortland, Discovery, Production and Use of Tin-Based Opacifiers in Glasses, Enamels and Glazes from the Late Iron Age Onwards: A Reassessment, *Archaeometry* 50 (2008) 67–84.

Tite, Michael, Oliver Watson, Trinitat Pradell, Moujan Matin, Gloria Molina, K. Domoney, and Anne Bouquillon, Revisiting the Beginnings of Tin-Opacified Islamic Glazes, *Journal of Archaeological Sciences* 57 (2015), 80–91.

Tsevas, G.D., Ἱστορία τῶν Θηβῶν καί τῆς Βοιωτίας ἀπό τῶν ἀρχαιοτάτων χρόνων μέχρι σήμερον, Vol. 1, Κάδμος (Athens, 1928).

Uboldi, Marina and Marco Verità, Scientific Analyses of Glasses from Late Antique and Early Medieval Archaeological Sites in Northern Italy, *Journal of Glass Studies* 45 (2003) 115–137.

Vionis, Athanasios, The Byzantine to Early Modern Pottery from Thespiai, in: John Bintliff, Emeri Farinetti, Božidar Slapšak, and Anthony Snodgrass, *Boeotia Project, Volume II: The City of Thespiai. Survey at a Complex Urban Site*, McDonald Institute for Archaeological Research, Boeotia Book Series 2 (Barnsley, 2017), 351–374.

Vogt, Christine and Anne Bouquillon, Technologie des plaques murales décorées de Pre-
    slav et de Constantinople, *Cahiers Archeologiques* 44 (1996) 105–16.
Vroom, Jonita, *After Antiquity: Ceramics and Society in the Aegean from the 7th to the 20th
    Century A.C. A Case Study from Boeotia, Central Greece* (Leiden, 2003).
Vroom, Jonita, Some Byzantine Pottery Finds from Kaman-Kalehöyük: A First Ob-
    servation, *Anatolian Archaeological Studies XV* (2006) 163–170.
Vroom, Jonita, From One Coast to Another: Early Medieval Ceramics in the Southern
    Adriatic Region, in: Sauro Gelichi and Richard Hodges (eds.), *From One Sea to Another:
    Trading Places in the European and Mediterranean Early Middle Ages*, Seminari del
    centro interuniversitario per la storia e l'archeologia dell'alto medioevo, 3 (Turnhout,
    2012) 353–292.
Waksman, Sylvie Yona, Long-Term Pottery Production and Chemical Reference Groups:
    Examples From Medieval Western Turkey, in: Meya, Henrika (ed.), *Late Hellenistic to
    Medieval Fine Wares of the Aegean Coast of Anatolia*, Travaux de l'Institut des cultures
    méditerranéennes et orientales de l'Académie polonaise des Sciences, Tome 1 (Warsaw,
    2014), 107–128.
Waksman, Sylvie Yona and Véronique François, Vers une redéfinition typologique et
    analytique des céramiques Byzantines du type Zeuxippus Ware, *Bulletin de Corre-
    spondance Hellénique* 128/2 (2004–2005) 629–724.
Waksman, Sylvie Yona, Anne Bouquillon, Nadia Cantin, and Ildiko Katona, The First
    Byzantine 'Glazed White Wares' in the Early Medieval Technological Context, in: Sylvie
    Yona Waksman (ed.), *Archaeometric and Archaeological Approaches to Ceramics*, BAR
    International Series 1691 (Oxford, 2007).
Waksman, Sylvie Yona, Anne Bouquillon, Nadia Cantin, and Ildiko Katona, Approche
    archéométrique des premières "Byzantine Glazed White Ware" et de productions
    glaçurées romaines et romaines tardives, *Rei Cretariae Romanae Acta* 40 (2008) 531–
    536.
Waksman, Sylvie Yona and C. Girgin, Les vestiges de production de céramiques des fouilles
    de Sirkeci (Istanbul): Premiers éléments de caractérisation, *Anatolia Antiqua* 16.1
    (2008) 443–469.
Waksman, Sylvie Yona, N. Erhan, and S. Eskalen, Les ateliers de céramiques de Sirkeci
    (Istanbul). Résultats de la campagne 2008, *Anatolia Antiqua* 17 (2009) 457–467.
Waksman, Sylvie Yona, Nikos Kontogiannis, S. Skartsis, and G. Vaxevanis, The Main
    'Middle Byzantine Production' and Pottery Manufacture in Thebes and Chalcis, *The
    Annual of the British School at Athens* 109 (2014) 379–422.
White, Harriett, *An Investigation of Production Technologies of Byzantine Glazed Pottery
    from Corinth, Greece in the 11th to 13th Centuries* (PhD, University of Sheffield, 2009).
Williams, Charles and Orestis Zervos, Frankish Corinth: 1991, *Hesperia* 61.2 (1992) 133–
    191.
Wolff, Larry, Venice and the Slavs of Dalmatia: The Drama of the Adriatic Empire in the
    Venetian Enlightenment, *Slavic Review* 56.3 (1997) 428–55.
Yangaki, Anastasia, Pottery of the Byzantine Period, Trade Networks, Mapping, Network
    Analysis: A Case Study, *Journal of Archaeological Science: Reports* 21 (2018) 1103–1110.

Bruno De Nicola

The Trip of a Medieval Physician: A Rare Description of Mobility in Mongol Anatolia

Following the consolidation of the Seljuq Sultanate of Rum in the second half of the twelfth century, Anatolia became a borderland in which certain religious freedoms, economic opportunities, and cultural diversity made the region a pole of attraction to religious leaders, intellectuals, and professionals from the wider Islamic world.[1] This context faciliated and stimulated mobility of goods, people, and ideas in and around the peninsula. Hence, seen from the central lands of the medieval Muslim world, this remote territory became a refuge and a land of opportunity for people escaping conflict or seeking new economic and professional prospects. The reasons behind Anatolia becoming such an attractive location are multiple. Traditionally, historiography has argued that Anatolia was the region where the last remaining Seljuq rulers offered refuge to people escaping the Mongol invasions of Central Asia, eastern Iran, and Russia in the 1220s. However, more recently, it has been suggested that the impact of the Mongol advance does not explain the migration of literati and the sudden increase in court patronage existing in the region from the late twelfth century.[2] It seems, therefore, that the Seljuq rulers created favourable conditions in Anatolia prior to the Mongol advance, which might have increased the number of people arriving, but is not the cause of the favourable conditions for mobility in thirteenth-century Anatolia.

In fact, scholars and intellectuals did not only arrive in the peninsula from the east, like the famous cases of the families of Jalāl al-Dīn Rūmī (d. 1273) or Quṭb al-Dīn Shīrāzī (d. 1311), but a number of influential Muslim thinkers and per-

---

1 Madelung, Migration of Hanafi Scholars, 41–5; Khanbaghi, Champions, 179–98. For a case study of an Iranian family migrating to Anatolia and becoming important players on the Anatolian cultural scene, see Özergin, Selçuklu sanatçisi, 218–19.
2 Especially, but not only, during the reign of ʿIzz ad-Dīn Kılıç Arslān II (r. 1156–92); see Peacock, Saljuqs III. For an overview of the migration of intellectuals from the Persianate world into Anatolia and other parts of the Islamic world such as Damascus or Baghdad in this period, see Bulliet, Islam.

sonalities also came from the west.[3] For example, the Andalusian mystic Ibn ʿArabī (d. 1240) and the *maghrebi* traveller Ibn Baṭṭūṭa (d. 1377) were among those personalities who visited the region, attracted by economic prosperity and the intellectual atmosphere of medieval Anatolia.[4] Further, from the late twelfth century the increasing mobility of scientists, intellectuals, and professionals into Anatolia provided the conditions for literary production in the peninsula, first in Arabic and Persian, and then in Turkish, to grow exponentially.[5] This means that as the thirteenth century advanced, we find a growing volume of literature on a variety of subjects, including scientific, historical, religious, and legal texts, produced by both migrants and local Anatolian literati. Other texts, more difficult to categorise, have also been surfacing in recent years, mainly thanks to the increasing research carried out focusing on the analysis of unpublished manuscripts surviving from the period.

This chapter looks at one of these works, a collection of letters that has the particularity of documenting a rare trip of a physician around Anatolia in the second half of the thirteenth century. Not being a travel account, such as that of Ibn Baṭṭūṭa, this compendium offers an interesting alternative view of different aspects of Anatolian societies. After a short introduction to the production of the manuscript and the text in question, we aim to reconstruct the trip made by the physician and highlight some specific information provided in the account that offers a rather unique description of mobility in medieval Anatolia. The trip will be analysed in two different sections, one covering the stay of the author in the cities of Kastamonu and Sinop and the other looking at the information scattered in the letters regarding various cities in northern Anatolia. We aim to show how this little-known compendium of letters can serve as a testimony of the mobility of certain social classes in Islamic Anatolia while documenting some relevant and often unknown aspects of the social, cultural, and economic life of the region.

---

3 The most comprehensive study on the life and work of Jalāl al-Dīn Rūmī in English remains Lewis, *Rumi*. On Quṭb al-Dīn Shīrāzī, see Walbridge, *Philosophy of Quṭb al-Dīn Shīrāzī*.

4 There is abundant literature written on Ibn ʿArabi. As an introduction to his life and work, see Chittick, *Ibn ʿArabi*. For Ibn Baṭṭūṭa's trip in northern Anatolia, see Ibn Baṭṭūṭa, *Travels of Ibn Baṭṭūṭa*, 451–71.

5 The best way to visualise the large number of manuscripts produced in this period is to look at some of the available online databases of Islamic manuscripts. Especially relevant to medieval Anatolia are: https://www.islam-anatolia.ac.uk; https://www.fihrist.org.uk/ and http://www.yazmalar.gov.tr/.

The manuscript, the letters, and the author

The collection of letters from which we will reconstruct the journey has come to us compiled in a single surviving manuscript, presently available at the Suleymaniye Library in Istanbul.[6] Together, it consists of twenty-four letters forming a *munasha'āt* (compendium of letters) that include not only personal information about the author but also cover a variety of different topics. The manuscript is not unknown, but it has remained unpublished and only partially studied since Osman Turan brought it to attention back in the 1950s.[7] The dating of the manuscript can be clearly assessed by reference to the colophon to the date AH 709 (1309 CE), left by the anonymous copyist of the text.[8] The composition of the letters, however, is less precise because none of the letters is individually dated. Hence, the dating needs to be reconstructed from references included in the letters to a variety of specific mentions of historical personalities and events. Based on the analysis of these references, I have previously suggested that the majority of the letters were most likely composed in the mid-thirteenth century and only copied and compiled some fifty years after that period.[9]

The authorship of the letters is mentioned at the beginning of the work in a note apparently written by the anonymous compiler of the *munasha'āt*. The name of the author is Saʿd al-Dīn al-Ḥaqq, a name so far not found in any other source of the period but who appears to have been a medical doctor who composed these letters sometime after being appointed to a new post in the region of Kastamonu and Zalifre (modern Safranbolu) in north-western Anatolia. His professional status is elevated by the compiler of the work in the description provided by the compiler/copyist of the manuscript. The text presents him as a physician of kings (lit. healer of kings and sultans – *mudāwā-yi al-mulūk wa al-salāṭīn*), a master (*mawlānā*) and considered a teacher, knowledgeable of the world (*ustāẓnā ʿallām al-ʿālam*).[10] In addition, the letters are written mainly in the Persian language with a strong component of Arabic, and include several references to passages of the Qur'an, classical Persian literature, and original poems composed by the author of the letters. Consequently, both his professional activity and the highly elaborated literary skill shown in the letters suggest that Saʿd al-Dīn belonged to a social class of well-educated Persianised elite that we know

---

6 The manuscript is number 5604 of the Fatih Collection, Süleymaniye Yasma Eseler Kutuphanesi, Istanbul.
7 For a more detailed account of these letters see Turan, *Türkiye Selçuklulari*, 156–71; De Nicola, Letters, 77–90.
8 Fatih 5604, f. 130r.
9 De Nicola, Letters, 79–80.
10 Fatih 5604, f. 99v.

was present in thirteenth-century Anatolia.[11] The origin of the author is never specifically mentioned in the text, but it is plausible to suggest that he was not originally from Anatolia but possibly moved to the peninsula during the mid-thirteenth century.[12] If that is the case, then he would be yet another case demonstrating the mobility of individuals in medieval Anatolia, despite not being as famous as some other contemporary personalities, such as the above-mentioned Quṭb al-Dīn Shīrāzī and Jalāl al-Dīn Rūmī.

Despite the author's training as a medical doctor, his letters lack any reference to medical sciences and do not discuss any scientific knowledge.[13] Instead, the content of the letters is rather heterogeneous, and the collection includes personal letters written to friends who appear to belong to a circle of local literati culturally active in thirteenth-century Anatolia. A number of original literary compositions, both in rhyme and prose, are included in the letters. Among them, the majority are commentaries written by the author of the letters and his addressees of contemporary and classical literature. Further, the letters reflect a close interaction between the author of the letters and different personalities closely connected to the Seljuq court at the time of Sultan Rukn al-Dīn Kılıç Arslan (d. 1266). Among the court personalities mentioned in the letters are Akmal al-Dīn Nakhjavānī, Sharaf al-Dīn Yaʿqūb, and local Turkmen rulers from areas of Anatolia such as Kastamonu and Denizli.[14] At the same time, the compendium as a whole is suffused impregnated with Sufi terminology, which offers new evidence of the existence of loosely-organised Sufi activity and the formation of a relational fraternity that can be read as indicating a Sufi order (possibly Mevlevi) in embryonic from.[15]

Scattered across different letters in the compendium, the author includes references to different cities located in northern Anatolia. The aim of the author is simly not to offer a travel account, such as that of Ibn Baṭṭūṭa a century later, but from reading the letters he sent to his companions, we can pinpoint different stages in the journey that the physician Saʿd al-Dīn al-Ḥaqq took to visit northern Anatolian. There is no clear reason why the physician moves around the area and each new destination in the journey seems to be added based on a specific

---

11 De Nicola, Letters, 83–4.
12 De Nicola, Letters, 84.
13 Only briefly, the author mentions how he treated smallpox on himself. See below.
14 Akmal al-Dīn Nakhjavānī was an influential medical doctor who is mentioned in various contemporary sources of the period connected to members of the Mevlevi Sufi order founded by Jalāl al-Dīn Rūmī. See, for example, Rumi, *Mirror of the Unseen*, 345–7; Aflākī, *Manāqib al-ʿārifin*, vol. 1, 122–4 / *Feats of the Knowers*, 87–8. Sharaf al-Dīn Yaʿqūb was a doctor at the court of the Seljuq Sultan Rukn al-Dīn Kılıç Arslan and apparently also at the court of the Mongol Ilkhan Abaqa (r. 1265–82); see Turan, *Türkiye Selçuklulari*, 157.
15 De Nicola, Letters, 88. For a general view of Jalāl al-Dīn Rūmī's teachings, see Chittick, *Sufi Path of Love*.

motivation. What seems clear, however, is that offering a description of the geography of the region or its cultural set-up is not in itself the main motivation of the author or of the compiler of the work. Therefore, it is not surprising that references to places are somewhat incomplete, highlighting some aspects of his visit to a particular place but neglecting many others. Nonetheless, it is this lack of interest in solely describing the landscape or the populations, as happens in general medieval travel literature, which makes especially interesting and peculiar the descriptions he decided to include in his account.

Between desolation and paradise on earth: contrasting views on Kastamonu and Sinop

The point of departure for the trip was the region of Kastamonu and Zalifre, two remote areas of north-western Anatolia located in the borderland between Byzantium and an advancing Turco-Islamic frontier.[16]

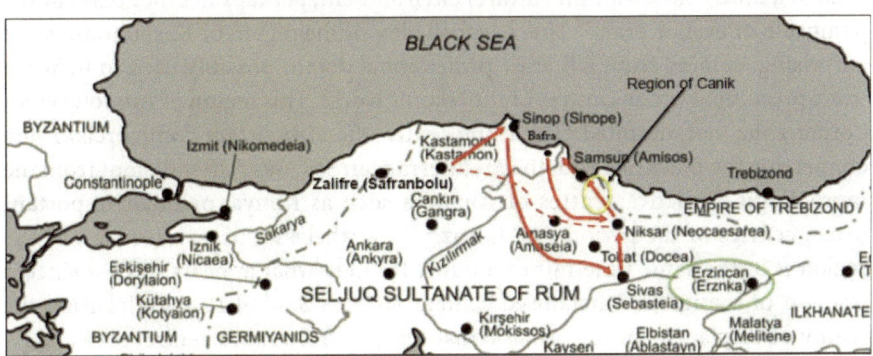

Map of Saʿd al-Dīn's travels in north western Anatolia

As we will see below, the chronology of the journey is imprecise and difficult to reconstruct, due to the unclear organisation of the letters. However, the initial letters of the compendium mention that it was to this area of the peninsula that, we are told by Saʿd al-Dīn al-Ḥaqq, he was sent to practise medicine. He may have arrived in these regions in the mid-thirteenth century, an era in the history of the region that is largely omitted by both the major Byzantine and Islamic narratives of the period. However, we know that since the beginning of the thirteenth century, a local Turkmen dynasty known as the Chobanids (Çobanoğulları, r.

---

16 For a general overview of medieval Kastamonu, see Heywood, Ḳasṭamūnī.

c.1211–1308) had established itself as rulers of the Kastamonu–Sinop area.[17] The Chobanids would reach their zenith of political and cultural development in the 1280s. At this time, Muzzafar al-Dīn Çobanoğlu (r. 1280–93), taking advantage of the Mongol recognission of his political control of north-western Anatolia, developed a policy of promoting and financing the composition of several texts in a variety of literary genres.[18]

The city of Kastamonu was not a place of vibrant cultural activity thirty years before the reign of Muzzafar al-Dīn, when these letters were composed. At least that is what we can infer from the description of the place given by Sa'd al-Dīn. No geographical information is provided about Kastamonu, but the author conveys his frustration at living in a place that is unpopulated (*'adīm al-rijāl*); a desolate place (*mauṭin-i nuzul*), lacking all types of professional guild (*aṣnāf*) and charitable foundation (*khayrāt*) or skilful (*majāl*) men within the general milieu of the place.[19] Further, he regrets the fact that he is deprived of the company of his friends and companions. His disappointment with his place of residence and professional destination seems also to indicate that Sa'd al-Dīn may have been used to a much more vibrant cultural environment, perhaps in other parts of the peninsula or even in Iran.[20] This negative view of the region of Kastamonu is not surprising, coming from a literate professional doctor possibly used to living in more prominent urban centres of the Islamic world. This region of Anatolia was a border zone that, despite being at the centre of an important commercial route connecting the Black Sea with the Mediterranean Sea, was rather distant from the more culturally-active centres of Anatolia such as Konya, or other important urban centres of the period like Tabriz.[21] Nevertheless, this adverse view of the region is at the same time rather unique. It offers what appears to be a sincere opinion of a migrant Persianised scholar such as Sa'd al-Dīn confronting the reality of displacement for professional reasons from more central areas of Islamic lands into peripheral western Anatolia.

Apart from this impression, no further information on Kastamonu as a town is given, but a reading of the letters that follow these initial missives offers a more comprehensive description of the city of Sinop, the first destination of the

---

17 Yücel, *Anadolu Beylikleri*, vol. 1; Korobeinikov, Revolt in Kastamonu, 87–118; De Nicola, On The Outskirts; De Nicola, *The Chobanids of Kastamonu*.

18 De Nicola, On The Outskirts. Some of these works have been edited and studied recently; see Khū'ī, *Majmū'ah-'i āṣār-i Ḥisām al-Dīn Khūyī*; De Nicola, Fusṭāṭ al-'adāla, 49–72; Yakupoğlu and Musali, *Selçuklu İnşa Sanatı*.

19 Fatih 5406, ff. 101b–102a.

20 I have suggested that he may have lived in Baghdad for a while; see De Nicola, Letters, 84.

21 On the commercial relevance of Kastamonu in the thirteenth and fourteenth centuries, see Cahen, *Pre-Ottoman Turkey*, 155–6. For an overview of trade in the Black Sea during the Medieval period, see Peacock, Black Sea Trade, 65–72.

physician's journey.[22] It is unclear at which point Saʿd al-Dīn decided to begin his travels to the north (see map on p. 187); we only have three letters in this compendium sent from Sinop, which are addressed to a companion of his, named ʿImād al-Dīn. We know that Saʿd al-Dīn is in the city on the shore of the Black Sea, because he laments in these letters the fact that his companion was unable to join him in the city.[23] This group of letters are all addressed to the same person, written in a personal tone, expressing the longing that the author feels for not being able to find his companion in the city. The letters refer to ʿImād al-Dīn as a beloved friend (*yār-i mushfiq*) and master, and references to mystical love between the friends suggest a personal relationship most likely built upon a shared connection with Sufi circles in northern Anatolia.[24] In between the expressions of fraternal love expressed by the author to his companion, Saʿd al-Dīn decided to send two versified descriptions of the city to ʿImād al-Dīn. In these two poems, apparently the original work of the author of the letters, a much more complete and favourable account of the city of Sinop is expressed, if compared to that of Kastamonu.[25]

The first poem comprises sixteen couplets in Persian, describing the city and its people.[26] The initial three couplets focus on the landscape in and around the city, describing precisely that the city is green and rich. He notices the abundance of palaces and gardens in the city while highlighting the fact that Sinop is located between two seas (*dar miyān-i dū daryā*), as a reference to the fact that the city was built in the middle of a small peninsula inside the Black Sea. The remaining couplets are more concerned with the people who inhabit the city and the different pleasures that the multicultural environment of this commercial city has to offer.

---

22 In the mid-thirteenth century Sinop was one of the most important ports in northern Anatolia, connecting trade between Islamic Anatolian territories with Byzantium and Crimea. See Redford, Sinop in the Summer, 125–49; Peacock, Sinop: A Frontier City, 103–24.
23 It is possible that this character is the historical ʿImād al-Dīn Zanjānī (d. 1281–2), an important figure in the Seljuq administration until his death. See De Nicola, Letters, 87.
24 De Nicola, Letters, 88.
25 The poems were published with Turkish translation by Osman Turan, *Türkiye Selçuklulari*, 159–60.
26 The translation of this poem is my own, and it is intentionally not literal. Whenever I considered it appropriate, I adapted the translation to reflect the meaning of the verses in the wider context of the *munasha'āt*. I would like to express my gratitude to Mohsen Husseini and Shervin Farridnejad for suggestions and corrections on specific parts of the poem. Any mistake or misinterpretation remains my own responsibility.

What can I say about Sinop?	[It] is a green and pleasant territory
The city is between two seas,	its soil is of amber and [its] air has a fragrant smell of musk.
It's full of gardens next to one another	and there are many palaces.
Its people are ingenious and amiable;	they are gracious and hospitable.
And that [entire city] is like paradise (*khuld-i barīn*)	and there, [people are like] the inhabitants of heaven.
There are lots of children here like pomegranate seeds	that are very beautiful to hug and kiss.
Their lips are sweet as sugar and their faces are [as shining and elegant] as silver	that the Pleiades feel embarrassed [when compared] to their beauty.
There are girls [as beautiful as] the full moon	that will please every desire of yours.
Each of [the girls] is [beautiful] like a Tatar gazelle	with pitch-black hair and red lips like pomegranate.
And their garden is like a precious ivory vase,	and above it, there is a musky-smelling crown.[27]
There are Rūs, Alānī, Rūmī, and Qipchaq [girls],	all of them with thousands of lovers.
[The look of] the beloved [girls is as elegant as] Khallukhī[28] and Kashmīrī,[29]	well known for their beauty and elegance.
They are as svelte/elegant as elm trees;	all are beautiful with silvery bodies (i.e. immaculate).

---

27 This couplet seems to be an allegory of female genitalia.

28 *Khallukh* (also *Khalaj*) is the generic name used in classical Persian to refer to ancient Turkish people. However, in classical Persian poetry the term refers to a city located in historical Khatāy (China), possibly located in eastern Turkestan, on the border between Tibet and the province of Xinjian. Persian poets generally associate people coming from this city as extremely beautiful and elegant. See Barthold, Ḳarluḳ. For references to the city of Khallukh among classical Persian poets, such as Firdawsi or Sa'dī, see the entry 'خلخ' in the Dehkhoda dictionary, see Anonymous, Khallukh. Dehkhoda Dictionary, available online: https://vajje. com/en/search?query=%D8%AE%D9%84%D8%AE%20.

29 Here it might be referring to women coming from Kashmir (northern India), but perhaps not as much as to the origin of these women as to the famous clothes made of cashmere wool that implies elegance and sophistication among the women of Sinop. I would like to thank Shervin Farridnejad for suggesting this reading of the poem and for different valuable suggestions made on my translation of the poem.

They are harmonious, good-looking and attractive,	[and] they are generous in their charm.
I hope you can have one of them;	then, destiny will favour you!
There are lots of beautiful cities,	but a city like this? Nowhere![30]

The poem makes use of the description of the human geography of thirteenth-century Sinop using different Sufi allegories and poetic strategies. The inclusion of such a long and literarily-elaborate poem poem in the middle of a letter sent to his Sufi master has not merely an informative purpose. The author makes an effort to convey the idea of Sinop as a place populated by beautiful and elegant people (both men and women), but adding subtle metaphors loaded with sexual meaning. The explicit reference to the desire to kiss and hug the children and the allegorical reference to women's genitalia are poetical attempts to describe to his friend, 'Imād al-Dīn, the pleasures he is missing in not joining him on his trip to Sinop. These constant references to beauty, elegance, and sophistication in the poem are also common throughout the letters. They should be seen through the prism of a literary genre based on mythical love and the fulfilment of sexual desires as a means for the elevation of the soul present in medieval Sufism.[31] Aspects of sexuality in medieval Anatolia have remained largely unstudied until recently.[32] However, the explicit references to sexual desires and practices with

---

30 چه توان گفت خطّه سینوپ   هست جایی لطیف خرّم و خوب
شهر که در میان دو دریا   خاک او عنبرست و مشک هوا
باغ بر باغ و شاخ بر شاخست   صفّه در صفّه کاخ در کاخست
مردم او ظریف و خوش خوند   دلنوازند و آشنا رویند
وآن بساطش بسان خلد برین   اندرو شاهدان حور العین
کودکانی بسان دانۀ نار   سخت زیبا و برای بوس و کنار
لب چون قند و عارض سیمین   خجل از گوشوارشان پروین
لدختران در او چو بدر تمام   حاصل آید ز هر چه داری کام
هر یکی همچو آهوان تتار   زلف ماند مشک و لب گلنار
هست بستانشان چو حقه عاج   بر نهاده بفرق مشکین تاج
روس و آلان و رومی و قفجاق   هر یکی را هزار جان مشتاق
خلخی دلیران و کشمیرند   همه در حسن خویشتن میرند
قد و بالاشان چو نارونست   هر یکی گل عذار و سیم تنست
همه موزون و خوب دیدارند   در کرشمه چه لطفها دارند
گر از ایشان یکی بدست آری   ای که بخت آن دمت کند یاری
شهرها نیک هست بسیاری   مثل این شهر کی بود باری

31 For a general overview of the scholarly debate on medieval Anatolian Sufism, see Kara-mustafa, Origins of *Anatolian Sufism*.

32 The study of sexual practices and prostitution in medieval Anatolia is still at an embryonic stage, but it appears that the topic has begun to attract the interest of scholars. See the recent publication by Leiser, *Prostitution in the Eastern Mediterranean World*. Scholars working on medieval Europe or on the Ottoman period have made advances in this field (including some references to Muslim Spain). See Otis, *Prostitution in Medieval Society*, 166, fn. 9; Sariyannis, Prostitution in Ottoman Istanbul, 37–65; Baldwin, Prostitution, 117–52.

both girls and boys mentioned in this poem and throughout the text offer an interesting window into the little-known sexual life of the Sufi-Persianate elite of medieval Anatolia, encouraging further investigation.

The poem also provides a unique description of the ethnic origin of a multicultural medieval city such as Sinop, and its strategic location in the middle of trade routes that connected the Russian Steppes with Anatolia and the Mediterranean Sea through the Black Sea. The author describes women in the city as being of Rūs,[33] Alānī,[34] and Rūmī[35] origins, which is in keeping with the geographical location of a city located on the northern shores of the Black Sea.[36] Further, the references to the city of Khallukh and the region of Kashmir are indications firstly of a poet (and an audience) with such an awareness of classical Persian literature as to be able to use these terms in an allegorical way to reflect elegance and sophistication. Secondly, it is possible that the reference also reflects the position of Sinop within a larger commercial network that went beyond the Black Sea. The Mongol conquest of Central Asia and Iran in 1220 and their conquest of Anatolia in the 1240s, while weakening the Seljuqs of Rum, at the same time created the possibility for goods and people of Central Asia, India, and Mongolia to migrate to this far western corner of the Islamic world.[37] Hence, it is plausible to suggest that the choice of Saʿd al-Dīn to use references to the Far East as allegories for the elegance of Sinop's inhabitants was made on the basis of the reality of this city as part of a larger commercial network known as the Silk Road. For example, in the following letter sent to his friend, a new shorter poem is included, reinforcing the idea of a Sinop as a home to a multi-ethnic population to the point that the author wonders if there is a direct route to China.[38]

What a pleasant place! This city is like paradise.	Its soil is like amber and its water is as sweet as honey.
Boys and servants are prowling around.	It is a conjunction of angels and dark-eyed *houris*.
There are lots of Rūmī, Qipchāq,[39] and Uyghurs.	Perhaps this is a temple of idols on the road to China.

---

33 Referring to people originally from the Black and the Caspian Seas, and from further north along the lower Volga and the Don rivers.
34 Possibly modern Ossetians or nomads from the Volga River.
35 The term may refer to Byzantine Christians or Muslims of Anatolia, depending on the context.
36 Peacock, Islamisation, 153.
37 On the Mongol conquest of Anatolia, see Melville, Anatolia, 51–101.
38 On the role of China in classical Persian literature, see an approximation by Ṭāʾifī et al., Chīn dar manshūr shʿir–i fārsī, 137–60.
39 Spelled as *qifjāq* in the original manuscript.

They'll become like Leylī and Majnūn	and acclaim Khusraw and Shīrīn.
Certainly the city is paradise on earth	[and] not the world, [so,] there is no place for [practising] religion.[40]

Like the previous one, this shorter poem adds to its description of Sinop's multicultural population, poetical constructions that mix references to religious mysticism and classical Persian literature. Nowhere in these letters dedicated to Sinop does the author explain the reason why he travelled to this city, only that they are written to express the longing (*firāq*) for his beloved companion, ʿImād al-Dīn, and the disappointment at them not being able to be in the city together. The Sufi idea of being able to draw closer to God by fully embracing the presence of the divine on earth appears to be reflected in Saʿd al-Dīn's analogy between Sinop and paradise in this short poem. To this image of a beautiful town populated by immaculate boys and girls, the author adds references to two famous love stories of classical Islamic literature – *Khusraw and Shīrīn* and *Leylī and Majnūn*. Together, they form a perfect combination for the Sufi imagery of a city where beauty, passionate romantic love, and harmony with the surroundings can be found. Hence, the final couplet concludes that, with such characteristics, when someone arrives in Sinop it is as if they have arrived in paradise, where, according to some Sufi traditions, the need for religious practice is made redundant and the *murid* (Sufi follower/disciple) is united with the divine.

Both poems are intertwined with short texts in prose across the letters that reinforce these ideas of *firāq* and the unbearable feeling of being distant from his beloved companion. Further analysis remains to be done on the meaning of these poems and a proper identification of one of the multiple Sufi traditions present in thirteenth-century Anatolia. However, for the purpose of this paper, after this second poem the author suddenly expresses a change in the narrative. He mentions that despite being in the company of some beautiful young boys and girls in Sinop, he cannot bear being away from ʿImād al-Dīn any longer and, without hesitation, decides to leave the city and continue his journey in the direction of Sivas, having found out that his companion was residing there at that time (see map on p. 187).[41]

---

40 كه خاكش عنبر آبش انگبين است   نه شهرست اين مگر خلد برينست
ملايک را قران با حور عين است   در غلمان و ولدان در تکاپوی
مگر بتخانه در راه چين است   چه رومی و چه قفچاق و چه ایغر
زهی خسرو زهی شيرين که اينست   شود ليلی و گويد همچو مجنون
که دنيا نيست و خود چه جای دينست   همانا دين و دنيا اندرين شهر

41 Sivas is located around 400 km east of Sinop.

A land of opportunities: mobility in medieval northern Anatolia

While in its description of Sinop the *munasha'āt* offers some unique information about the city's physical and human geography, the letters are not specific in their description of the landscape and population of Sivas in this period. It is unclear when Saʿd al-Dīn left Sinop for Sivas, but he does mention that he arrived at his destination in winter. He underlines the fact that it was a particularly cold winter, so harsh that even he was 'afraid of the cold' (*az tars-i sarmā*).[42] Instead, the missive describing the remaining parts of the trip show the author being more concerned with finding a way to get back to his friend ʿImād al-Dīn and searching for professional opportunities in the area. The multiplicity of local rulers and officials of the rather decentralised Seljuq Sultanate of Rum encouraged, among the literate and professional social group to which Saʿd al-Dīn belonged, a constant search for patronage and financial support from members of the political elite.[43] One of the letters explains that, after arriving in Sivas, he met with (or was contacted by) Amir Majd al-Dīn, the Seljuq governor of the nearby city of Erzincan.[44] Saʿd al-Dīn suggests that the governor offered him an opportunity to work with him, but we are not told if this was in his capacity as a medical doctor or as an official in the administration of Erzincan. However, the narrative of the letters tries to convey the message that, despite the tempting offer put forward by the governor, the author of the letters ultimately declined.[45] The reason for the refusal of this apparently appealing opportunity was that just when he was about to leave for Erzincan, he received a letter from his master and companion ʿImād al-Dīn from the city of Amasya, asking to join him in the city of Niksar, which was also nearby. I believe that the intention behind this short story is to highlight the higher regard that Saʿd al-Dīn had for his companion and master over the economic opportunities offered by a powerful secular ruler.

Because the compendium only includes the letters written by Saʿd al-Dīn but not those received by him, we do not have the original letter sent by ʿImād al-Dīn from Amasya. However, in one of his letters, Saʿd al-Dīn tells us that he eventually travelled to Niksar to finally reunite with his master (*makhdūm*).[46] He did not stay long in that city since, in the next letter, he explains that only five or six days

---

42 Fatih 5406, f. 119r.
43 Peacock, *Sufis*, 206–26. On patronage in northern Anatolia, see Yücel, *Anadolu Beylikleri*, vol. 1, 152–3.
44 Fatih 5406, f. 119v. This is not the only reference made to Erzincan in the text. A previous letter also mentions a certain Amīr Sharaf al-Dīn Maḥmūd, which, according to Turan, might be a reference to the governor of that city during the early reign of Sultan Kaykāvus II (r. 1246–57, d. 1280). I am not fully convinced of this identification. See Turan, *Türkiye Selçuklulari*, 158; De Nicola, *Letters*, 82.
45 Fatih 5406, f. 119v.
46 Fatih 5406, f. 119v.

after arriving in Niksar, he was sent by his master to visit family (*farzandān*) (lit. children). It is strange that after writing the long letters lamenting not being able to meet his master in Sinop, and after rejecting a good professional opportunity in Erzincan in favour of being with ʿImād al-Dīn, the physician stayed in the company of his companion for only a few days before he was on the road again. This reference to his family/children is the only mention in the letters of an aspect of the author's personal life.[47] However, we receive no further information regarding where his family lived, who the members of his family were, or why he was sent to visit them by ʿImād al-Dīn. We are told that he left Niksar on foot, but could not make swift progress in his journey because of the abundant rain and snow that fell that year.[48] It was the weather that forced him to stop in Samsun, a city located 150 km to the north-west of Niksar on the shores of the Black Sea.[49] From the letters it appears that he never made it to his family during this journey, but the direction of his journey (going north-west from Niksar) suggests that he might have been going back to either Sinop or Kastamonu when he was forced to stop in Samsun. This remains in the realms of speculation, but even if his origins might have been Iranian, it seems plausible that Saʿd al-Dīn's family (or community) was already settled in Anatolia by the time he left Kastamonu in pursuit of his itinerant master, ʿImād al-Dīn.

In addition to his quest to be in the company of his master, the reconstruction of this journey offers some new perspectives into the mobility of people across territories supposedly divided by religion. During his forced layover in Samsun, new professional opportunities appeared for the physician. In a further example of the close relationship between this professional elite and local rulers, the Amīr of Samsun,[50] when he knew that a medical doctor was in town, ordered him to go to practise medicine in the nearby region of Canik.[51] In the thirteenth century this region was a borderland between two rival polities, the Sultanate of Rum and the

---

47 The fact that the text refers to his children might also be interpreted as the children of the master. In other words, Saʿd al-Dīn would not be going back to his family but to his original community of brothers. This essay is not the place to theorise further about the meaning of this fragment, but I have tried to convey the idea of the text, which implies that Saʿd al-Dīn was being sent back home (be that family home or Sufi community).

48 The text literally says that he could not continue because 'heavenly grace did not help' (*faẓl-i āsmānī kumak nakard*), which should be interpreted as a poetic way of implying difficult weather conditions.

49 Fatih 5406, f. 119v.

50 The name of the amir is not given. The text only refers to him as the *Bayklarbikī* (Beylerbey or Bey of Beys), a Turkish title meaning 'commander of commanders' that was common among Turkmen local rulers in Seljuq Anatolia. See Ménage, Beglerbegi.

51 In the text, the name of the region appears as *jāyint* but certainly referring to Canik, a mountainous region to the east of Samsun. See Taeschner, Djānīk.

Christian Empire of Trabzon.[52] However, the letters seem to suggest that the border was more permeable than previously assumed. Saʿd al-Dīn makes specific mention of the fact that he was working in the Christian side of Canik when, during that winter, he decided to leave the *Dār al-Kufr* (land ruled by infidels) and return to Samsun. No further details about his stay in those lands is provided, nor is the visit narrated as something out of the ordinary. This clear reference to his stay in the territory under the control of the Christian Empire of Trabzon points in the direction of Saʿd al-Dīn acting as a doctor on the Christian side of the border. Hence, it is clear that either the Christian patients were used to receiving care from Muslim doctors, or a significant Muslim population already lived in the Christian lands of Trebizond to require the medical assistance of Muslim doctors brought from across the border (see map on p. 187). It is also possible that both things happened at the same time. His stay among 'infidels', even if short and poorly described, is an interesting testimony to a frontier between the Muslim principalities loyal to the Seljuqs and the Christian enemies of Trabzon that was not closed but rather remained permeable, at least for skilled professionals.

The following stages of the journey reveal some solidarity networks that were already in place among the Sufis of the thirteenth century. On his return to Samsun from the Trabzon countryside, Saʿd al-Dīn found that all his friends and companions who apparently had travelled with him previously, had left. The direction taken by the physician after visiting Canik seems to confirm the idea, suggested above, that he was going towards Sinop or Kastamonu to visit his family/community. He left Samsun, following the coast of the Black Sea, until he arrived at the small town of Bafra, located some 50 km to the north-west (see map on p. 187). On his arrival, he found accommodation with a Sufi master named Sirāj al-Dīn, who hosted him and gave him shelter until he was able to join another group of fellow travellers to continue his journey.[53] However, an unforeseen event happened at this point when, while waiting for some fellow travellers (*hamrāhān*), he observed that he had large blisters on his body; his hands and feet were covered in blisters like rubies that looked like shackles. The blisters were as big as pearls (*shāhwār*), swollen and waterlogged.[54] These symptoms of smallpox, described in the letter, had an impression on the doctor who, unable to suppress his literary talent, adds a short quatrain describing the symptoms caused by the illness:

---

52 For an overview of the relationship between the Seljuqs of Rum and the Empire of Trebizond in the thirteenth century, see Shukurov, Trebizond, 71–136.
53 Fatih 5406, f. 119v.
54 Fatih 5406, f. 120r.

My forearms have become [a string of] jewels and my hand has a thousand pearls,	My shank is [full of] gems, [red] rubies and pure [like] spinel.
I am unable to sit or keep moving,	I have no desire to rest, nor to eat or sleep.[55]

He rested for twenty days, constantly scratching (*kharāsh*) his skin (*pust*) until the symptoms of itching and burning diminished. He performed some treatment on himself by rubbing a plaster (*marham*) over his skin to relieve the itching, irritation, and pain caused by the smallpox blisters.[56]

After this period, he was able to walk again and ride a horse to continue his journey. He writes another letter to 'Imād al-Dīn, in which the author offers new information on the work possibilities open to literate professionals such as Sa'd al-Dīn in Seljuq Anatolia. According to the letter, he received an offer to be the *fiqahat* (expert in jurisprudence) at the office of the Head of Religious Endowments (*Daftar-i dīvān-i awqāf*). At the same time as receiving this new job offer, the physician mentions to his friend that he came to know of his arrival in Niksar. When weighing up the opportunity of a good salary in the office of endowments against reuniting with his friend, Sa'd al-Dīn opts for the latter. In accordance with the general theme of fraternal love contained in the letters, he rejects the post because of his love for his friend and how much he would suffer by being taken away from him by this new job. However, in addition to this more expected argumentation, Sa'd al-Dīn gives us an unusual insight into the 'job market' of professionals in medieval Anatolia by adding that it would be economically more beneficial to him to work 'freelance' than to enter the service of the court. Sa'd al Din claims that had he accepted the job (which paid him twenty or thirty *'ard*),[57] people would think that he could not make money for himself and argues that '… freely and without being under the supervision of the officials (*'āmilān*), I can make more than 300 *'ard*, horses and clothing in a month or two'.[58]

After leaving Bafra, the doctor rejoined his friend 'Imād al-Dīn back in Niksar (see map on p. 187), where he spent the rest of the winter. At the end of the letter, he revisits the idea of returning to see his family, having been frustrated previously by the inclemency of the weather and his illness. He expresses his wish of restarting the journey to his homeland in the spring, with the intention of staying there permanently, only 'if they make him happy' (*khūsh dārand*), or otherwise returning after a short visit to Niksar if he feels unwelcome.[59] Unfortunately, the

---

55 ساعد شده مرصع و در کف هزار دُر   ساقی پر از جواهر و یاقوت و لعل ناب
    نه چارهٔ نشست و نه یارای رفتنم   نه آرزوی تکیه و نه شوق خورد و خواب

56 Fatih 5406, f. 120r.

57 *'ard* is a term that literally means mule, but in the context of the text is used as an alternative for income.

58 Fatih 5406, f. 120v.

59 Fatih 5406, f. 120v.

letter finishes here, leaving us without a clear indication of whether he did make the trip back to his family or providing any clear reference to the place to which he was travelling.

Despite this uncertainty, based on the remaining letters, which follow the three letters describing his travels, some possibilities about Saʿd al-Dīn's return journey can be suggested. Saʿd al-Dīn's travels are only described in any kind of detail up to this point, and the detailed description is confined to just three letters out of the twenty-four which make up the full compendium. Some of these remaining letters make specific reference to different personalities, including close friends of the author and government officials; others simply appear without addressee; but all of them share the characteristic of being undated and having no place of origin. Therefore, it is difficult to offer a clear schedule of Saʿd al-Dīn's travels after he returned to Niksar and, consequently, these letters could have been written before or after the other three letters. A clear chronology of the writings is difficult to establish with precision, but it is worth highlighting the fact that the references to northern Anatolian cities is recurrent among other letters of the compendium. The city of Sinop is mentioned again as an important place in the narrative of the author. In these new references to the city he previously described as 'paradise on earth', we see new examples of the existing solidarity networks among these individuals across northern Anatolia.

A passing reference in a letter entitled 'on desire' (*dar shauq*), but with an unspecified addressee, claims that Saʿd al-Dīn was willing to travel to Sinop to meet the addressee.[60] He has to excuse himself because a companion of his (possibly the head of his Sufi community), an unidentified person called Mawlana Zayn al-Dīn, prevented him from travelling and forced him to stay in the city from where he was writing the letter.[61] Unfortunately, we are not told which city this is, nor when the letter was written. However, if we assume that the arrangement of the letters followed some sort of chronological sequence, it is possible, albeit based on a certain speculation, that this is referring to a return journey from Niksar back to Kastamonu. A few letters further on in the compendium another short poem is included that has separation (*firāq*) and sorrow as the main topics but adds some further information about the mobility of the author. He mentions that 'Since I have left Niksar, I am wretched because of sorrow / and I am distressed because of separation', and a few lines below in the same letter he mentions that 'I arrived in Kastamonu and my issues are settled down as I wish, and I have no misery except for being separated from you'.[62]

---

60 Fatih 5406, f. 122r.
61 Turan, *Türkiye Selçuklulari*, 163.
62 Fatih 5406, f. 123v.

It should be pointed out that there is a clear contrast here between the author's more positive view on Kastamonu and the negative impression given at the beginning of the journey. This differences in his perception of the city where this trip began can be interpreted in two different ways from the available material. On the one hand, it might be argued that his arrival in Kastamonu, mentioned in this last poem, occurred sometime before the author became disappointed with the city and decided to begin his journey through northern Anatolia. On the other hand, this passage could be seen as an indication of a trip that was made from Niksar back to Kastamonu as a return trip from the one described above. If it is the latter, it is possible that Kastamonu could have been the place where his family lived, and his more optimistic view of the city was connected to the feeling of returning to this borderland between Byzantium and Mongol Anatolia that has become his homeland.

Conclusion

The compendium of letters written by Sa'd al-Dīn al-Ḥaqq offers an unconventional account of mobility in medieval northern Anatolia. The letters show how the need for government officials by both the Sultanate of Rum and local leaders contributed to the mobility of literate officials with a Persio-Iranian background into border areas of the Islamic world, such as Anatolia. The journey of this thirteenth-century Sufi physician offers an alternative view about how the mobility of people operated at a regional level when compared to the very different perspective given by the more general historical narratives of the period. The letters reveal individuals travelling across the territory motivated by professional ambition, but also by their own personal and spiritual interests. The text unravels a sophisticated literary style in the composition of these letters, which appear to have been important vehicles in the transmission of original literary production, personal feelings, and religious (mainly Sufi) ideas.

Further, the reconstruction of this journey offers some remarkable information on aspects even less commonly available in other sources. The letters evidence the multicultural environment of a vibrant commercial city, such as Sinop, and a network of interconnected areas of northern Anatolia in the thirteenth century. Cities such as Kastamonu, Sinop, Sivas, Niksar, Samsun, and even the Christian-dominated lands close to Trabzon, were part of a common space with – it would seem – soft borders. The frontier between the Sultanate of Rum and the Empire of Trabzon was, at least temporarily, permeable enough to allow the transit of this physician on both sides, allowing Sa'd al-Dīn to visit patients presumably of different religious confessions in the border area. Overall, the letters contained in this manuscript offer a unique description of individual mobility in a culturally-diverse and interconnected borderland between Byzantium and Mongol-dominated Anatolia in the thirteenth century.

Acknowledgements

This work was supported by the Project ISLAMANATOLIA under the ERC Grant 284076, the Institute of Iranian Studies, Austrian Academy of Sciences (Vienna, Austria), and the Austrian Science Fund (fwf-start, Nomads' Manuscripts Landscape project, Y-1232 G30).

Bibliography

Aflākī, Shams al-Dīn Aḥmad, *Manāqib al-'ārifīn, 2 vols*, ed. T. Yazıcı (Ankara, 1959–61).
Aflākī, Shams al-Dīn Aḥmad, *The Feats of the Knowers of God: Manāqeb al-'Ārefīn*, trans. John O'Kane (Leiden, 2002).
Anonymous, Khallukh, *Dehkhoda Dictionary*, available online: https://vajje.com/en/search ?query=%D8%AE%D9%84%D8%AE%20.
Baldwin, James E, Prostitution, Islamic Law and Ottoman Societies, *Journal of the Economic and Social History of the Orient* 55 (2012) 117–52.
Barthold, W., Ḳarluḳ, *Encyclopaedia of Islam*, First Edition. Retrieved on 19 December 2018 from: http://dx.doi.org/10.1163/2214-871X_ei1_SIM_3946.
Bulliet, Richard, *Islam: The View from the Edge* (New York, 1994).
Cahen, Claude, *Pre-Ottoman Turkey: A General Survey of the Material and Spiritual Culture and History c. 1071–1330* (New York, 2010).
Chittick, William C., *The Sufi Path of Love: The Spiritual Teachings of Rumi* (New York, 1983).
Chittick, William C., *Ibn 'Arabi: Heir to the Prophets* (Oxford, 2012).
De Nicola, Bruno, The Fusṭāṭ al-'adāla: A Unique Manuscript on the Religious Landscape of Medieval Anatolia, in: Andrew Peacock and Sara Nur Yildiz (eds.), *Literature and Intellectual Life in Islamic Anatolia in the 14th-15th Centuries: Historical, Social and Political Perspectives* (Würzburg, 2016) 49–72.
De Nicola, Bruno, Letters from Mongol Anatolia, *Iran: Journal of the British Institute of Persian Studies* 56/1 (2018) 77–90.
De Nicola, Bruno, On the Outskirts of the Ilkhanate: The Mongols' Relationship with the Province of Kastamonu in the Second Half of the 13th Century, in: Suzan Yalman and Filiz Yenisehirlioglu (eds.), *The Ilkhanids in Anatolia – Cultural Encounters in Anatolia in the Medieval Period* (Istanbul, 2021), 117–135.
De Nicola, Bruno, *The Chobanids of Kastamonu: Politics, Patronage and Religion* (London, 2024).
Encyclopaedia of Islam, Second Edition. Retrieved on 18 December 2018 from: http://dx.doi.org/10.1163/1573-3912_islam_SIM_1355.
Fatih Collection, Manuscript 5604, Süleymaniye Yasma Eseler Kutuphanesi, Istanbul.

Heywood, C. J., Ḳasṭamūnī, *Encyclopaedia of Islam*, Second Edition. Retrieved on 18 December 2018 from: http://dx.doi.org/10.1163/1573-3912_islam_SIM_4008.

Ibn Baṭṭūṭa, *The Travels of Ibn Baṭṭūṭa, AD 1325–1354*, trans. H. A. R. Gibb, vol. 2 (London, 2004).

Karamustafa, Ahmet T., Origins of *Anatolian Sufism*, in: Ahmet Yaşar Ocak (ed.), *Sufism and Sufis in Ottoman Society: Sources, Doctrine, Rituals, Turuq, Architecture, Literature and Fine Arts, Modernism* (Ankara, 2005) 67–95.

Khanbaghi, Aptin, Champions of the Persian language: the Mongols or the Turks? in: Bruno De Nicola and Charles Melville (eds.), *The Mongols' Middle East: Continuity and Transformation in Ilkhanid Iran* (Leiden, 2016) 179–98.

Khū'ī, Ḥusām al-Dīn, *Majmū'ah-'i āṣār-i Ḥisām al-Dīn Khūyī*, ed. S. 'Abbas'zadah (Tehran, 2000).

Korobeinikov, Dimitri, The Revolt in Kastamonu, c. 1291–1293, *ByzF* 28 (2004) 87–118.

Leiser, Gary, *Prostitution in the Eastern Mediterranean World: The Economies of Sex in the Late Antique and Medieval Middle East* (London, 2017).

Lewis, Franklin D., *Rumi: Past and Present, East and West – The Life, Teachings and Poetry* (Oxford, 2000).

Madelung, Wilferd, The Migration of Hanafi Scholars Westward from Central Asia in the 11th to 13th Centuries, *Ankara Üniversitesi İlahiyat Fakültesi Dergisi* 43 (2002) 41–5.

Melville, Charles, Anatolia under the Mongols, in: Kate Fleet (ed.), *The Cambridge History of Turkey*, vol. 1 (Cambridge, 2009) 51–101.

Otis, Leah Lydia, *Prostitution in Medieval Society: The History of an Urban Institution in Languedoc* (Chicago, 1985).

Özergin, Kemal, Selçuklu sanatçisi nakkas Abdülmü'min el-Hoyî hakkinda, *Belleten* (turk Tarih Kurumu) 34/134 (1970) 219–29.

Peacock, Andrew, Saljuqs III: Saljuqs of Rum, in: Encyclopaedia Iranica Online. Retrieved on 18 December 2018 from: http://www.iranicaonline.org/articles/saljuqs-iii.

Peacock, Andrew, Black Sea Trade and the Islamic World down to the Mongol Period, in: Gülden Erkut and Stephen Mitchell (eds.), *The Black Sea: Past, Present and Future* (London, 2007) 65–72.

Peacock, Andrew, Sinop: A Frontier City in Seljuq and Mongol Anatolia, *Ancient Civilizations from Scythia to Siberia* 16:1 (2010) 103–24.

Peacock, Andrew, Sufis and the Seljuk Court in Mongol Anatolia: Politics and Patronage in the Works of Jalāl al-Dīn Rūmī and Sulṭān Walad, in: Andrew Peacock and Sara Nur Yildiz (eds.), *The Seljuks of Anatolia: Court and Society in the Medieval Middle East* (London, 2015) 206–26.

Peacock, Andrew, Islamisation in the Golden Horde and Anatolia: Some Remarks on Travelling Scholars and Texts, *Revue des mondes musulmanes et de la Méditerranée* 143 (2018) 67–180.

Redford, Scott, Sinop in the Summer of 1215: The Beginning of Anatolian Seljuk Architecture, *Ancient Civilizations from Scythia to Siberia* 16/1–2 (2010) 125–49.

Rūmī, Jalāl al-Dīn, *Mirror of the Unseen: The Complete Discourses of Jalal al-Din Rumi*, trans. Louis Rogers (San Jose, CA, 2002).

Sariyannis, Marinos, Prostitution in Ottoman Istanbul, Late Sixteenth–Early Eighteenth Century, *Turcica* 40 (2008) 37–65.

Shukurov, Rustam, Trebizond and the Seljuks (1204–1299), *Mésogeios* 25–26 (2005), 71–136.

Taeschner, F., Djānīk, in *Encyclopaedia of Islam*, Second Edition. Retrieved on 18 December 2018 from: http://dx.doi.org/10.1163/1573-3912_islam_SIM_1993.

Ṭāīfī, Shirzād, Kūy, Būbīn and ʿAlīreẓā Pūrshabānān, Chīn dar manshūr shʿir-i fārsī, *Pizhūhishnāmah-ʾi Zabān va Adab-i Fārsī (Gawhar-i gūyā)* 4/3 (1389/2010), 137–60.

Turan, Osman, *Türkiye Selçuklulari hakkında resmî vesikalar: metin, tercüme ve araştırmalar* (Ankara, 1958).

Yakupoğlu, Cevdet and Namiq Musali, *Selçuklu İnşa Sanatı* (Ankara, 2018).

Yücel, Yaşar, *Anadolu Beylikleri Hakkında Araştırmalar*, 2 vols. (Ankara, 1991).

Walbridge, John, The Philosophy of Quṭb al-Dīn Shīrāzī: A Study in the Integration of Islamic Philosophy. PhD thesis (Harvard University, 1993).

John Haldon

Mobility and Microstructures: Concluding Remarks

Looking at questions of social mobility, of the various social-institutional structures that people inhabited and at the role of individual agency, throws up a wide range of methodological and some theoretical issues for the study of any society, and that of the medieval east Roman or Byzantine world is no different. Issues of physical mobility, of the movement of individuals or groups, the logistics of transport, throw up similarly a range of questions shared with other societies, including issues of transport technology, livestock, communications networks, and all the many aspects of movement and social life that these entailed. Most of the papers in this volume are concerned with upward social mobility: to what extent, under what circumstances, and when was it possible for individuals to move from the social and cultural context into which they were born into areas of society where access to wealth, resources, status, and privilege was greater? How far did social stratification impact people at different levels of society, in different socio-economic and cultural sectors, in different geographical regions and locations (provincial/metropolitan, urban/rural, etc.), and in what ways? Was the state dominated by the imperial court and the church to the degree that our sources seem to suggest, and if it was, what strategies did people employ, adapt, or develop in order to improve their lives (and, indeed, what did 'improve' mean for them in the first place), and how did individuals as well as groups act in such a process? If society was more pluralistic in terms of centres of power, sources of authority and of social control, how was this manifested and through what social institutions? And finally, how did those in power respond, whether these were 'the authorities' inhering in the operations of church and state, or local persons (or groups) of influence?

But physical mobility also plays a role, both in respect of the relationship between individuals and the state – the location of a crime, for example, the place in which legal proceedings were enacted, the impact on the individuals concerned with respect to their work and their habitation, as highlighted in the contribution by Ekaterini Mitsiou (chapter 5). The movement of goods likewise entails movement of people, whether as merchants or those concerned with the business of transporting things over longer or shorter distances. And individuals move for many other reasons – pilgrimage, 'professional' reasons (such as doctors, architects, people with specialist knowledge in general), flight from oppression or insecurity, for example.[1] Unlike the analysis of social microstructures, however, the study of medieval communications and transport, the topographical and physical geographical constraints on movement in space, in short the physical dimensions of mobility, have received a great deal of attention in the last two decades, so that an emphasis on the social is perhaps to be expected in this collection.[2] But the essays in this volume present a series of approaches to all these topics and accompanying questions, exploiting the available archaeological, documentary, and archival material and covering the whole span of Byzantine history.

One of the most important aspects of this collection is its implicit emphasis on the relationship between agency and structure, between the way in which individuals were constrained or not by the social and cultural framework within which they lived their daily lives. Looking at the way the institutions of the church or the state inflected and dominated society as a whole provides us with important information about one aspect of the Byzantine social, economic, and cultural world. But we need also to examine the other side of this coin and ask to what extent questions of belief and perception affected these institutions and social structures. How did ideas and assumptions, the personal and group narratives through which people made sense of their world, reinforce, challenge, nuance, or even reconfigure the framework within which people lived? How did the specific interests of different and sometimes competing social groups, whether identified by rank and status or by socio-economic and cultural situation, impact social and cultural options at any given time? To what extent did location – urban or rural, metropolitan or provincial – determine the outcomes for individuals? All of these aspects are affected by the degree to which certain key ideas are held across a society as a whole, and the extent to which the beliefs and ideology of the dominant political elite are relevant or not for the day-to-day interests and identities of other sectors of society. They represent key elements both in understanding why people act in particular ways in particular circumstances, as well as how the society – and with it, the political order, the state – responded to various pressures and stresses. Thus they also have a significant

---

1 See, among many studies on pilgrimage, for example, the essays in Daim *et al.*, *Pilgrimage to Jerusalem*; also Allen, *Eastward Bound*.
2 For example, Daim, *History and Culture of Byzantium*, ch. 9; Kislinger *et al.*, *Handelsgüter und Verkehrswege*; Macrides, *Travel in the Byzantine World*; Allen, *Eastward Bound*; also monographs such as Dimitroukas, *Reisen und Verkehr*; Galatariotou, Travel and Perception. For a broader survey of geographical knowledge and travel in the Byzantine world see also Haldon, *De thematibus*, 34–51.

impact on social cohesion. The extent to which, and the forms through which, a particular set of religious beliefs or a political ideology penetrates through a society as a whole, as well as notions of the law, of rights, responsibilities, and the sources of judicial, moral, and spiritual authority; all these affect the ways in which people perceive and respond to the world around them, as well as being the means through which a cultural system hangs together under stress.[3]

Appreciating the role of the individual and of groups of people as agents in their social and cultural context helps us to understand the role played by individual choice as well as by collective action. It also helps us to understand how people exploited the range of options at their disposal or were constrained and inhibited in their social lives by economic or cultural situation, social convention, and so forth. The seven main chapters above address, for different periods and for different socio-cultural groups, the ambiguities of daily life and the multiple roles and contested situations or moments in which both individuals and groups of people found themselves. Social 'structures' – relational and institutional – determine the access people have to resources, both material as well as cultural and spiritual; such structures thus also determine the range of possibilities – the structural capacities – open to people to act in particular ways. But at the same time they permit the generation of microstructures, intersecting and overlapping pools of relationships through which people carry on their day-to-day lives. These aspects are nicely illustrated, but in very different contexts, in the contributions from Christos Malatras and Bruno De Nicola (chapters 6 and 8).[4] And it is in the play between the microstructures into which individuals are born, on the one hand, and on the other, the broader sets of social, economic, and cultural relationships within which these particular structures are themselves inscribed, that we can observe the dynamics of a socio-cultural system.

One of the great advantages of thinking about past societies in these terms is that it enables the historian to appreciate the obvious, but often ignored, fact that Byzantine society shares many fundamental characteristics with its neighbours, but that these features are configured and articulated differently, reflecting local, regional, and supra-regional cultural 'ways of doing'. Understanding how the 'symbolic universe' of the culture (the shared world of knowledge and concepts, tacit and voiced, implicit and explicit, that inform people's lives and understanding of their universe) determines and informs social action, and how such action reacts back upon that ideational space, is a key aspect of this. Without it we cannot fully appreciate why people in the Byzantine world acted (and could act) as they did, but more importantly we cannot hope to understand the processes of historical change that, often imperceptibly over time, alter the outward appear-

---

3 See discussion in Goldstone and Haldon, Ancient States, Empires and Exploitation, 11–15.
4 See Callinicos, *Making History*, xxii–xxxii, 85–102.

ance, the texture, and the inner workings of society. The contributions in this volume thus also help us to avoid a mechanistic view of medieval society and to gain some insight into the conjunctural, emotional, and 'lived' experience of the individuals and groups who populated the historical landscape.[5]

It is worth underlining the point that what people believe, as the expression of human perceptions of their world and their effectiveness in it, also has a material impact – social action in pursuit of a particular aim conceptualised within one set of structural relationships can promote practices which transcend or transform those relationships. This is obvious as soon as we think about our own times, but it is surprising how often studies of past societies seem to ignore this. In very different ways, and at different scales, this point is explored in chapter 2 by Christos Makrypoulias, in a penetrating discussion of social mobility within the Byzantine military, and chapter 3 by Efi Ragia, addressing the question of social connections, interrelationships, and identities in provincial society.

Along the same lines, Yannis Stouraitis (chapter 4) explores the problems surrounding the ways in which such associations and identities were constructed in medieval texts and why. It is easy to assume that the individuals and groups referred to in narrative histories of the period were somehow reflections of actual social identity and motivations. Yet as Hans-Georg Beck and others showed very clearly, while this may be the case, it is just as often not, and that a careful interrogation of the sources in question is an essential.[6]

Asserting the relevance of intentions as a fundamental element in human consciousness and practice is not to assume thereby either that intentions can ever be identified or located, or – more importantly – that the intentions ascribed to actions by the actors, or by other commentators (such as chroniclers and historians), are necessarily true. It is simply to underline the point that we cannot take structures as objects for analysis without also taking the agents who both constitute and are in turn constituted by them as part of the same equation. Beliefs respond to perceptions of the world as much as they represent a narrative about the world and imply therefore 'conjuncture' and 'contingency'.

Yet at the same time, how people responded to changes they saw or events that concerned them does permit us to limit the range of motives underlying those actions and responses. Even if we cannot know much about the particular beliefs of most of the individuals who peopled the history of the Byzantine world, we may still deduce something of their views and of the issues that concerned them from their reactions to events as described in chronicles, histories, letters, and the whole range of written testimony to which we have access. This can work at many

---

5 For discussion of this and related concepts, see Haldon, *Byzantium in the Seventh Century*, 324–326; Haldon, Towards a Social History, 9–13.
6 Beck, Byzantinische Gefolgschaftswesen; Kazhdan, Microstructures; Weiß, *Oströmische Beamte*.

different levels – from the application of an 'acceptance-theory' approach to governance and the way the imperial court and rulership functioned, to discussion of the reasons why people might have challenged the imperial government or the rule of a particular emperor at a given moment.[7]

One of the important concepts that the essays in the volume repeatedly invoke, either implicitly or explicitly, is that of 'identity'.[8] It is important however it is used – of people who share particular sets of skills, lifestyle, or economic or political status (such as military commanders or other types of soldier, members of the clergy, the inhabitants of a village community or an urban artisanate, and so forth), of individuals in one of their many roles in their domestic and private lives as defined both by the law as well as by societal convention and habit (such as parent, god-parent, sibling, or whatever), or of much broader groups of people who might be classed, and class themselves, by 'ethnic' linguistic or other marks of distinction, perceived or ascribed. Identities make up a key element in both the practical day-to-day aspect of social life as well as in the 'thought-world' of a culture. Identities are multi-dimensional, a product of the need to define oneself and others in contrast to those around one. Social-institutional roles and self-perceptions generally overlap or even contradict one another at different levels of social experience and practice – a point which immediately raises the question of whether individuals possess an 'essential' identity, a consciousness of themselves that exists beneath all other forms of context-determined identity and praxis.[9] This is a problem I will avoid addressing here, but it has been a significant aspect of much of the discussion around the value of the term.

Everyone in society belongs to more than one group of mutually-recognised 'identity-sets'. Each 'identity' carries with it a reservoir of culturally-determined and -inflected ways of behaving in both public and private, framed and configured by the specific context in which other people are encountered. People's behaviour tends to conform to the need to fulfil key criteria of their social and

---

7 See, for example, Pfeilschifter, *Der Kaiser und Konstantinopel.*

8 For the hermeneutic and heuristic issues associated with the term: Pohl, Strategies of Identification; on approaches to identity from a sociological/social-anthropological standpoint: Brubaker and Cooper, Beyond 'Identity'; and the older discussion in Berger and Luckmann, *Social Construction of Reality*, esp. 194–204.

9 Since the 1960s there has been a series of debates around the concept of identity as used in respect of the subject/self, focusing in particular on structuralist and post-structuralist challenges to traditional psychoanalysis, and represented especially in the work of Lacan and his later adherents. For useful older surveys and discussion, see Hall, Theories of Language and Ideology, 157–62; *idem*, Ideology/Subject Couplet, 113–21; Ellis, Ideology and Subjectivity, 186–94. For Rome, Byzantium and the western medieval world more particularly see Stouraitis, Roman Identity in Byzantium; Haldon and Stouraitis, The Ideologies of Identities and the Identities of Ideologies; and the essays in: Crostini and La Porta, *Negotiating Co-Existence*; Corradini *et al.*, *Texts and Identities*; Papaconstantinou and Talbot, *Becoming Byzantine*; and Page, *Being Byzantine*, 7–21.

institutional roles, such as 'parent' or 'sibling' or 'relative', 'soldier' or 'priest' or 'farmer', for example.[10] Perceptions and assumptions about one's own and others' social and economic status likewise directly affect patterns of behaviour and the ways in which identity is given expression – the poor behave differently in the presence of the rich or powerful than before their peers, and vice versa.[11] At the same time, social and cultural values are modified according to the context in order that the individual can give expression to their understanding of 'self' and present the version felt to be most appropriate (or necessary) to the social context. Not all of these different roles are necessarily compatible, and can sometimes, when juxtaposed too closely, cause embarrassment, for example, or social anxiety of some sort. Identity is processual and performative as well as functional. Social interaction embodies sets of power relations, so that not all individuals or groups are able to present the identity they would (or think they would) prefer in every situation. Feelings of inferiority or superiority, for example, affect such situations very markedly. Different sets of identities, based on appropriate patterns of socially-determined and culturally-normative behaviour have different values according to the context in which they function: a hierarchy of interests informs most human social interaction. As a consequence, observable social praxis is often the result of clashes and contradictions generated by a specific context in which an individual or a group has to adopt a particular pattern of behaviour in order to preserve their identity for that particular context.

What Byzantines – or indeed any medieval people – believed and how those beliefs affected how they acted is therefore an essential aspect of how their society worked. The ways in which what people thought about their world impacted on the way they acted on a day-to-day basis as well as in respect of their response to perceived problems or worries is an important consideration in the chapters above. I do not mean to suggest that belief determines action in any absolute or mechanistic sense – on the contrary, what and how individuals believe represents their contingent reaction to the world they see around them as well as a means of representing themselves to themselves and to others, depending upon social/cultural context. But although sets of ideas or beliefs should not be characterised as fixed or essential, it is also the case that the group and cultural narratives generated to explain the world do provide the framework within which social

---

10 The best introduction to this approach to the question of social roles, identities, and the institutionalisation of social practices according to context and self-image, is still, in my view – and in spite of flaws pointed out by later critics – Berger and Luckmann, *Social Construction of Reality*, and Schütz, *Der sinnhafte Aufbau*. There is a vast social-psychological and social-anthropological literature on these topics, to which I cannot begin to do justice here, although some of this material will be found in the notes to most of the works cited.

11 Indeed, such degrees of differentness are also embodied in law: see, for example, Patlagean, *Pauvreté économique*, 25–27.

action can be thought, and thus offer a way into the cultural logic of a specific historical moment. How did people in the eastern Roman empire construct their world in their own minds, and what did that set of ideas entail in terms of the way they understood what was happening to that world? And how did all this affect how they understood themselves as members of a community, when they saw themselves in this light at all?[12] Issues of leadership are just as important here; that is to say, the role of emperors and their advisers as well as of the cultural and political elite, in the life of the eastern Roman state.

Actions speak, if not louder than words, then at least as forcefully. Whether people invest in church-building or the endowment of religious foundations, artwork and decoration, or charity; whether they invest in court offices, tax-farms, or commercial ventures, or a combination of all of these, such activities obviously reflect prevailing values and assumptions about what is important in their world. What people believe directly affects patterns of wealth investment and, in consequence, the ways in which elites, for example, appropriate and consume wealth, as well as the ways in which political regimes are able to maintain themselves, or not. Whatever aspect of Byzantine society we want to look at, we need to build beliefs and their contingent social effects into our model of causal relationships. Indeed, the effect of what people believed about a situation upon their reactions or responses is a key element of social action. Social practice is predetermined by a range of limiting and qualifying conditions into which people are born and that circumscribe both their field of action and the possibilities open to them intellectually. But the cumulative effects of social praxis have unforeseen outcomes, so that intentions are rarely matched by results. Marx's famous comment at the beginning of his *The Eighteenth Brumaire of Louis Bonaparte* is a useful reminder of all this: 'Men make their own history, but they do not make it just as they please; they do not make it under circumstances chosen by themselves, but under circumstances directly encountered, given and transmitted from the past'.[13] Politics and cultural practice are not secondary but are rather the expression of sets of relationships between people, and between people and their cultural environment, in a multitude of different contexts.[14]

One of the merits of the essays in this volume is the emphasis on social inequalities, horizontal divisions, and vertical solidarities, and the way these need

---

12 Recent perspectives in Stouraitis, Roman Identity in Byzantium; *idem*, Reinventing Roman Ethnicity; *idem*, What did it mean to be Roman in Byzantium?; contrasting perspectives: Kaldellis, *Hellenism in Byzantium*; *idem*, From Rome to New Rome; idem, *Byzantine Republic*.
13 Marx, Eighteenth Brumaire, 96.
14 I have sketched out some approaches to understanding and analysing Byzantine society in Haldon, Towards a Social History of Byzantium.

to be picked apart in order to get at the dynamics of society as it worked on a day-to-day basis. Boundaries, whether soft or hard, need to be probed to find out how they affect people in day-to-day relationships. It is usually taken for granted, but just as often glossed over in historical scholarship, that eastern Roman society was stratified, highly exploitative, and in some respects deeply divided. It is easy to see the imperial court and those who made up the social elite of the empire in our written sources, and it is not so hard to see the middling and upper levels of urban populations also. But the vast mass of the subjects of the eastern Roman emperors are less obvious, present but silent in legislation and histories and other types of text, objects of the views, prejudices and often hostility (although occasionally also the sympathy) of those who were literate. These were the working populace of the cities, great and small, and the rural populations of the provinces, the great majority of farmers and herdsmen, along with the craftsmen, artisans, and others of similar status and occupations in small rural towns or in villages. Most farmers and herdsmen were peasant tenants of varying legal status, some semi-free, some free, but all subject to the coercive power of the state fiscal apparatus, a landlord, or both. The differences in wealth between the ordinary rural population of the empire and the social elite were massive, and such dramatic disparities could only be overcome through a constantly fluctuating combination – varying by region and situation – of physical force, ideological constraint (secular law as well as ecclesiastical; custom and tradition; inherited and timeless 'ways of doing'), and patronage. Yet at the same time the boundaries between these various groups were by no means impermeable, indeed in many cases quite the contrary. There existed many connections between people that created vertical as well as horizontal bonds and affinities, whether through daily work, village life, through confraternities and similar structures, monastic communities, military service, even landlord-tenant relationships, all of which might overlap and intersect in a multitude of different ways. Such tensions and the possibility for conflict can easily be written out of the modern history of the Byzantine empire, and while it is the case that we learn far less than we should like about them, because our sources are either silent or non-existent, they lie beneath the surface of the historical events that we can see and they informed people's beliefs and actions. The essays in this volume offer some important insight into how such processes worked 'on the ground'.

There are two significant challenges facing historians of Byzantine society. First, there is the fact that most, although certainly not all, of our written sources come from educated and literate individuals. These may not necessarily be members of the social elite, but for the most part they are not representative of the great mass of the population, so that our knowledge of ordinary people's lives is relatively constrained. Secondly, there is a well-recognised Constantinopolitan bias in our written sources. Of course, there are documents and sources of various sorts from provincial contexts, and these help to adjust the balance. But it does mean that our knowledge of what life was like away from Constantinople is less secure than it might otherwise be.

The strategy followed in this volume goes a long way to re-establishing a balance between centre and periphery in medieval East Roman society, as well as to re-assesssing what we know about metropolitan life and politics. Through analyses of sets of institutions that transcended this division – such as particular categories of middle-ranking military officer, or village society, indications for social and geographical mobility – and of archaeological evidence, in particular ceramics (illustrative of networks of movement, knowledge, and resources), we obtain a clearer picture of the complex networks of personal and institutional interrelationships that characterised people's lives on a daily basis. But such analyses also show how such networks created social and cultural spaces that permitted individuals greater 'Spielraum' within their personal lives and relationships than we might otherwise suspect, especially during times when the established political and cultural order was challenged by events such as warfare or changes in the political geography – as we have seen in the case of thirteenth-century Anatolia presented in the final chapter.

Together, these chapters offer an excellent example of how this sort of research can and should be done, and provide a series of finely-detailed case studies that further our understanding of Byzantine society and its inner workings. It is a collection that sees the historical process, as it is revealed in the different types of documents, archaeological data, and other sources, as effects of the multi-layered, multi-compartmental yet integrated pools of overlapping socio-cultural and economic activity that make up social and economic relationships. It also presents the historical process as an archaeology: history, like anthropology, should be concerned with revealing foundations, digging up and unmasking, explaining, and reconstructing. The essays in this volume make a significant and highly constructive contribution to this effort.

Bibliography

Allen, Rosamund (ed.), *Eastward Bound. Travel and Travellers, 1050–1550* (Manchester/ New York, 2004).

Beck, Hans-Georg, Byzantinische Gefolgschaftswesen, *Bayerische Akademie der Wissenschaften, Philologisch-Historische Klasse, Sitzungsberichte* (1965) 3–32.

Berger, Peter and Thomas Luckmann, *The Social Construction of Reality* (Harmondsworth, 1967).

Brubaker, Rogers and Fred Cooper, Beyond 'Identity', *Theory and Society* 29 (2000) 1–47.

Callinicos, Alex, *Making History. Agency, Structure and Change in Social Theory* (Leiden/ Boston, 2004).

Corradini, Richard, R. Meens, C. Pössel, and P. Shaw (eds.), *Texts and Identities in the Early Middle Ages* (Vienna, 2006).

Crostini, Barbara and Sergio La Porta (eds.), *Negotiating Co-Existence: Communities, Cultures and Convivencia in Byzantine Society*, Bochumer Altertumwissenschaftliches Colloquium, Bd. 96 (Trier, 2013).

Daim, Falko (ed.), *History and Culture of Byzantium. Brill's New Pauly Supplements* II: vol. 10, English edn. J.N. Dillon (Stuttgart, 2019).

Daim, Falko, Johannes Pahlitzsch, J. Patrich, Claudia Rapp, and J. Seligmann (eds.), *Pilgrimage to Jerusalem. Journeys, Destinations, Experiences across Times and Cultures* (Mainz, 2020).

Dimitroukas, Ioannis, *Reisen und Verkehr im byzantinischen Reich vom Anfang des 6. Jhr. bis zur Mitte des 11. Jhr.* (Athens, 1997).

Ellis, John, Ideology and Subjectivity, in: Stuart Hall (ed.), *Culture, Media, Language* (London, 1980) 186–194.

Galatariotou, Catia, Travel and Perception in Byzantium, *DOP* 47 (1993) 221–241.

Goldstone, Jack and John F. Haldon, Ancient States, Empires and Exploitation: Problems and Perspectives, in: Ian Morris and Walter Scheidel (eds.), *The Dynamics of Ancient Empires. State Power from Assyria to Byzantium* (Oxford, 2009) 3–29.

Haldon, John F., *Byzantium in the Seventh Century: The Transformation of a Culture* (Cambridge, 1997).

Haldon, John F., Towards a Social History of Byzantium, in: John F. Haldon (ed.), *A Social History of Byzantium* (Oxford, 2009) 1–30.

Haldon, John F., *The De Thematibus ('on the themes') of Constantine VII Porphyrogenitus*, trans. with Introductory Chapters and Notes (Liverpool, 2021).

Haldon, John, and Yannis Stouraitis, The Ideology of Identities and the Identity of Ideologies, in: Yannis Stouraitis (ed.), *Identities and Ideologies in the Medieval East Roman World* (Edinburgh, 2022) 1–19.

Hall, Stephen, Some Problems with the Ideology/Subject Couplet, *Ideology and Consciousness* 3 (Spring 1978) 113–121.

Hall, Stephen, Recent Developments in Theories of Language and Ideology: A Critical Note, in: Stuart Hall (ed.), *Culture, Media, Language* (London, 1980) 157–162.

Kaldellis, Anthony, *Hellenism in Byzantium: The Transformations of Greek Identity and the Reception of the Classical Tradition* (Cambridge, 2009).

Kaldellis, Anthony, From Rome to New Rome, from Empire to Nation-State: Reopening the Question of Byzantium's Roman Identity, in: Lucy Grig and Gavin Kelly (eds.), *Two Romes. Rome and Constantinople in Late Antiquity* (Oxford/New York, 2012) 387–44.

Kaldellis, Anthony, *The Byzantine Republic. People and Power in New Rome* (Cambridge, MA., 2015).

Kazhdan, Alexander, Small Social Groupings (Microstructures) in Byzantine Society, in: *XVI Internationaler Byzantinistenkongress. Akten II.2, JÖB* 32.2 (1982) 3–11.

Kislinger, Ewald, Johannes Koder, and Andreas Külzer (eds.), *Handelsgüter und Verkehrswege. Aspekte der warenversorgung im östlichen Mittelmeerraum (4. Bis 15. Jahrhundert)* (Vienna, 2010).

Macrides, Ruth (ed.), *Travel in the Byzantine World* (Aldershot, 2002).

Marx, Karl, The Eighteenth Brumaire of Louis Bonaparte, in: Karl Marx and Friedrich Engels, *Selected Works* (London/Moscow, 1968) 96–179.

Page, Gill, *Being Byzantine. Greek Identity before the Ottomans* (Cambridge, 2008).

Papaconstantinou, Arietta and Alice-Marie Talbot (eds.), *Becoming Byzantine. Children and Childhood in Byzantium* (Washington, D.C., 2009).

Patlagean, Évelyne, *Pauvreté économique et pauvreté sociale à Byzance, 4e–7e siècles,* Civilisations et Sociétés 48 (Paris, 1977).

Pfeilschifter, Rene, *Der Kaiser und Konstantinopel: Kommunikation und Konfliktaustrag in einer spätantike Metropole* (Berlin, 2013).

Pohl, Walter, Strategies of Identification. A Methodological Profile, in: Walter Pohl and Gerda Herdemann (eds.), *Strategies of Identification. Ethnicity and Religion in Early Medieval Europe* (Turnhout, 2013) 1–64.

Schütz, Alfred, *Der sinnhafte Aufbau der sozialen Welt* (Vienna, 1960).

Stouraitis, Yannis, Roman Identity in Byzantium: A Critical Approach, *BZ* 107 (2014) 175–220.

Stouraitis, Yannis, Reinventing Roman Ethnicity in High and Late Medieval Byzantium, *Medieval Worlds* 5 (2017) 70–94.

Stouraitis, Yannis, What did it mean to be 'Roman' in Byzantium?, in: Jonathan Shepard, Peter Frankopan, and Averil Cameron (eds.), *Byzantine Spheres: The Byzantine Commonwealth Re-evaluated* (Oxford, 2022), forthcoming.

Weiß, Günter, *Oströmische Beamte im Spiegel der Schriften des Michael Psellos* Miscellanea Byzantina Monacensia (Munich, 1973).

List of Figures

Ekaterini Mitsiou: Mobile Criminals: Crime and Punishment in Thirteenth-Century Byzantine Epirus

Map Murder cases in Epirus (© Ekaterini Mitsiou) (created with Google Maps and QGIS)

Florence Liard: Pottery Traditions as Indicators of Interactions, Connectivity, and Microstructures in Byzantium

Fig. 1 Map of Greece and the eastern Mediterranean, with indication of the sites mentioned in the text: 1. Thebes; 2. Mazi Plain; 3. Corinth; 4. Constantinople; 5. Chalkida; 6. Caffa; 7. Genoa; 8. Pergamon; 9. Venice; 10. Anaia; 11. Thessaloniki.

Fig. 2 Fragment of bowl in Glazed White Ware V found in the Frankish Area at Corinth, during excavations by the American School of Classical Studies at Athens; photo courtesy of the ASCSA excavation team on Ismenion hill at Thebes.

Fig. 3 Thirteenth- to early fourteenth-century bowl derivative of the Zeuxippus Ware class I (cat. n. 3-2-5), found on Ismenion Hill at Thebes, during excavations by the Ephorate of Antiquities at Boeotia and Bucknell University; photo courtesy of the ASCSA excavation team on Ismenion hill at Thebes.

Bruno De Nicola: The Trip of a Medieval Physician: A Rare Description of Mobility in Mongol Anatolia

Map Map of Saʿd al-Dīn's travels in north-western Anatolia

Notes on Contributors

Bruno de Nicola is Research Associate at the Institute of Iranian Studies of the Austrian Academy of Sciences (Vienna, Austria). He specialises in the cultural history of medieval and early modern Eurasia, the Mongol Empire, and the study of Islamic manuscripts. In 2019, he was awarded the STAR-Prize (FWF-Research Fund), making him the Principal Investigator of the international research project Nomads' Manuscripts Landscape (NoMansLand). His most recent major publications include *Women in Mongol Iran: The Khatuns, 1206–1335* (Edinburgh, 2017), and *The Chobanids of Kastamonu: Politics, Patronage and Religion in 13th century Anatolia* (London, expected in 2023).

John Haldon is Director of the Climate Change and History Research Initiative at Princeton University. His research focuses on the history of the medieval eastern Roman (Byzantine) empire; on power and resources in pre-modern state systems; and on the impact of environmental stress on pre-modern social systems. His most recent publications include: *The De Thematibus ('on the themes') of Constantine VII Porphyrogenitus. Translated with Introductory Chapters and Notes* (Liverpool, 2021); SDG 13: Climate Action. How Societies Succeeded or Failed to Respond to Environmental Disruption, in: M. Gutmann and D. Gorman (eds.), *Before the SDGs: A Historical Companion to the UN Sustainable Development Goals* (Oxford, 2022) 385–424 (with Adam Izdebski, Luke Kemp, Lee Mordechai, and Benjamin Trump); New Palaeoenvironmental Evidence on the Possible Impact on Agriculture of Early Arab-Islamic Raiding Activity on Crete, in: M. Van Berkel and L. Osti (eds.), *The Historian of Islam at Work. Essays in Honor of Hugh N. Kennedy* (Leiden, 2022), 614–633.

Florence Liard is Assistant Professor of Ancient History at the Université Saint-Louis in Brussels and an Associate Researcher at the Fitch Laboratory of the British School at Athens. She specialises in the technology and trade of Greek pottery from the Late Hellenistic to the Early Modern periods, with a focus on lead-glazed ceramics. She has participated in fieldwork research on Crete and Naxos, as well as in Attica, Corinth, and Thebes. Her recently-published research includes multidisciplinary analyses of medieval pottery from Thebes in *Hesperia* (2020) and (2022).

Christos Makrypoulias holds a PhD in Byzantine History from the University of Ioannina, Greece. He specialises in the military and administrative history of the Byzantine Empire, focusing on aspects of war such as military and nautical technology, siege warfare, and the interplay between military organisation and society. His most recent publications include Boots on the Ground. Byzantine Infantry in the Eleventh Century, in: Georgios Theotokis and Marek Meško (eds.), *War in Eleventh-Century Byzantium* (London/New York, 2020), and An Overview of Armed Conflicts in Late Byzantium: Theoretical Foundations and Current Research, *Byzantina Symmeikta* 31 (2021) 177–191 (with Taxiarchis G. Kolias and Georgios Kardaras).

Christos Malatras is Research Associate at the University of Cologne. He has held postdoctoral fellowships in Greece (Academy of Athens), Turkey (Koç and Boğaziçi Universities), the USA (Dumbarton Oaks), and Germany (University of Cologne and Eberhard Karl University of Tübingen), and has taught Byzantine history at the Democritus University of Thrace, the University of Thessaly, and the University of Ioannina. He is author of the monograph *Social Stratification in Late Byzantium* (Edinburgh, 2023), and co-edited the volume *TAKTIKON: Studies on the Prosopography and Administration of the Byzantine themata* (Athens, 2021), as well as having written several articles on the social, cultural, and administrative history of Byzantium and on sigillography.

Ekaterini Mitsiou is postdoctoral researcher at the ENCHANT-Project (Entangled Charters of Anatolia (Austrian Academy of Sciences and University of Vienna). Her research focuses on the economic, social, and ecclesiastical history of Byzantium, (female) monasticism, Gender Studies, and Digital Humanities. Her most recent publications include the co-edited volumes *Women and Monasticism in the Medieval Eastern Mediterranean: Decoding a Cultural Map* (Athens, 2019) and *A Companion to the Patriarchate of Constantinople* (Leiden/New York/Cologne, 2021).

Efi Ragia is Assistant Professor of Byzantine History at the University of Thessaly. Her research interests focus on the institutions of the Byzantine Empire as well as the social history of Byzantium and the history of Asia Minor. Her most recent publications include a chapter in *Travaux et Mémoires* on the agrarian policy of the first Palaiologoi and an article in *Revue des Études Byzantines* on the social position of soldiers in Middle Byzantine times.

Claudia Rapp is Professor of Byzantine Studies at the University of Vienna and Director of the Institute for Medieval Research of the Austrian Academy of Sciences. Her research deals with the social and cultural history of Late Antiquity and Byzantium. The award of the 2015 Wittgenstein Prize of the Austrian Science Fund enabled her to work with a team on the project 'Moving Byzantium: Mobility, Microstructures and Personal Agency'. Her recent publications include the co-edited volumes *Euchologia* (Studia Patristica 108, 2021), *New Light on Old Manuscripts: The Sinai Palimpsests and Other Advances in Palimpsest Studies* (2023), *Armenia and Byzantium without Borders. Mobility, Interaction, Responses* (2023), and *Mobility and Migration in Byzantium. A Sourcebook* (2023).

Yannis Stouraitis is Senior Lecturer in Byzantine History at the University of Edinburgh. He specialises in the social and cultural history of the Byzantine Empire, focusing on the socio-ideological aspects of war, collective identifications and ideological attachments, and the construction of historical memory. His most recent major publications include the edited volumes *Identities and Ideologies in the Medieval East Roman World* (Edinburgh, 2022) and *War and Collective Identities in the Middle Ages: East, West, and Beyond* (Leeds, 2023).

Index of Names

Index of Places

Index of Terms